Sohar

FREDRIK BARTH

THE JOHNS HOPKINS UNIVERSITY PRESS
Baltimore and London

Sohar

Culture and Society in an Omani Town

The Johns Hopkins University Press, Baltimore, Maryland 21218
The Johns Hopkins Press Ltd., London

Library of Congress Cataloging in Publication Data
Barth, Fredrik, 1928—
  Sohar, culture and society in an Omani town.

  Bibliography: pp. 255–57
  Includes index.
  1. Ṣuḥár (Oman) I. Title.
DS248.S93B37   1982   306'.095353   82–9925
ISBN 0–8018–2840–6   AACR2

Contents

Preface

This monograph attempts two tasks: to give a portrait of life and society in the town of Sohar in Oman, and to give an analysis of cultural pluralism in the town and how it is maintained. Sohar is an old trading town on the Eastern coast of the Arabian peninsula; and it is at one and the same time a traditional Islamic city, a living and changing community, and a meeting place of a number of different cultures, peoples, and modes of life. There is thus much diversity within the town, and many ways in which its population is linked with the larger world. A number of its central institutions are distinctive and require considerable description and explanation for someone unfamiliar with them to form an adequate picture of their character. To try to encompass much of this within the format of one monograph is an ambitious endeavor; the task of trying to ascertain all these relevant facts by direct empirical observation is far more ambitious. Yet there is very little previously published data on which to build (see References), and so I was challenged to make the attempt during my wife Unni Wikan's and my own field work residences in Sohar in the periods March–August 1974 and December–January 1975–76.

As a result, many of the main lineaments of the description and analysis that follows are intuitive, though consistent with the body of observations and facts which we obtained. Properly, the whole set of statements made in this text should have been treated as a provisional working hypothesis, to be checked and tested through more rigorous and comprehensive data collection. A larger team of workers, over an extended period, would have been required to accumulate the desired data. Yet the picture of the community of Sohar that would then have emerged in the end, it is hoped, might not have been so different from that presented here, though it would have been subsantiated and documented. So, given the lack of comparable available materials—as well as my own personal bent—it seemed more useful to put together the results of my wife's and my own two brief periods of field work, rather than wait, secure the resources and time to train and field a larger team, and then at some distant future time attempt to produce a different, and more definitive, type of study of Sohar.

With respect to my second objective, I feel less need to apologize. To increase our understanding of the processes and conditions of cultural pluralism is an urgent task in the world today, and I have trust in a methodology that develops theoretical and analytical perspectives in an immediate confrontation with the reality which one meets in the raw data of participant field observation.

The present monograph is in a sense a companion piece to Unni Wikan's *Behind the Veil in Arabia: Women in Oman.* As different in scope, focus, and style as they are, they nevertheless supplement each other quite closely. Hers succeeds, where mine fails, through a close interactional analysis, to depict living people in real-life situations, made accessible and understandable to all those who have not had the good fortune to reside among them. Mine may be a help in locating these individuals in a larger social system and in generalizing about certain features of that system. I deeply appreciate the help she has given me in reading and commenting on several versions of this manuscript, and the benefit I have had from writing most of my manuscript after hers was completed, and thus being able to lean on her analysis. We have both drawn freely on our joint field materials. I should like to acknowledge, however, my disproportionate debt to her, due to her exceptional command of Arabic and her capacity to combine spontaneous intimacy and analytic perceptiveness in her friendships and acquaintances in the field. To facilitate cross-use of the materials, the pseudonyms employed for persons are the same in the two books.

Beyond acknowledging my debt to my wife, my thanks go first and foremost to some very close friends and a great number of valued acquaintances in Sohar. Living among them was a privilege and an experience I shall cherish always. I also wish to acknowledge my debt to the Omani authorities who have supported our work in their country in a number of essential and gracious ways, and among them especially H. E. the Wali of Sohar, Hamud bin Nasr; H. E. Shaikh Amor Ali Ameir; H. E. Najib El Zubeidi; and H. E. Nassir Seif El Buali. In Sohar we received friendly help from the staff of ILACO and Prospection, Mr. and Mrs. Spiker, and most particularly Jack and Ottley Sims. Friends in Muscat also gave much encouragement, advice, and help; I wish particularly to mention Leila Ingrams, William and Diana Peyton, and Martha Holst.

The field work was financed by grants from the Norwegian Research Council for Science and the Humanities and the Wenner-Gren Foundation for Anthropological Research. I gratefully acknowledge their support.

Part 1
The Community Described— First Approximations

I Major Features of Sohar, and the Methodological Problems These Raise

Sohar town is the largest trading and administrative center on the Batineh coast of the Sultanate of Oman and the third largest settlement in the state. Its anthropological description and analysis confront us with all the difficulties characteristic of complex societies: with an urban population of about 12,000, plus some 10,000 in the close surroundings, the primary community is so large that the investigator cannot even begin to know all its members. Systematic data must therefore be gathered by means of some kind of sample or segregate that can be meaningfully related to the whole. However, the members of the community are differentiated and dissimilar with respect to a great number of features which in fact constitute this particular organization of society: they differ in occupations, skills, and orientation; they are divided in class, wealth, and rank; and they identify themselves and one another as members of different ethnic groups. Moreover, Sohar participates in complex historical civilization: since the inception of Islam it has been part of that world religion and the literate Arabic great tradition. Consequently, there is more than a thousand years of (fragmentary) historical documentation for the town, providing a perspective both difficult to ignore and difficult to handle. Finally, today, as in the past, members of the local community of Sohar participate in various larger, in part global, macrosystems, though in a relatively modest place within them. Once "the emporium of the whole world" (Williamson 1973:11), in the ethnographic present of 1974–75, it was an important provincial center in the Sultanate of Oman, an entrepôt of international trade and both a provider and a recipient of international labor migration, among other things.

The present study attempts to capture major empirical features of this complex society—in itself a complex operation that requires quite comprehensive presentation of both descriptive data and analytical argument. It does not seem possible to find a simple and tight logical succession in the presentation of these two faces of the study. On the one hand, I hold that surface data on the concrete events and overt patterns observable in daily life in Sohar are highly legitimate and

1

important in any description of its society and culture, and must provide the basis for the construction of theories and models that depict the more fundamental processes and determinants behind these events. On the other hand, any description of fact is already highly selective, and the most appropriate criteria by which to select are provided precisely by whatever insight in such underlying processes and determinants one has achieved. I shall attempt to perform both an exposition of data and an elaboration of analysis as I go along, and thus alternate between description and theoretical argument. But while the description may be essentially cumulative, I have sought to make my analytical steps consecutive—that is, to provide provisional conceptual frameworks in the earlier parts of the text which are reconstituted and recast in the subsequent text to accommodate the results of an unfolding description and argument. Those who would have the premises of a model clarified first and their implications specified thereafter would come closer to their taste by reading this book backward.

THE TOWN OF SOHAR

Sohar lies near latitude 25° N on the east coast of Arabia, solidly in the Afro-Asian desert belt. Its total precipitation is less than 40 mm per year, and temperatures range from a monthly average maximum of 25° C in January to 39° C in June. High humidity makes the climate even more trying for Sohari residents.

As one approaches Sohar today, on a modern highway from Muscat over a seemingly endless and featureless plain and then by unsurfaced road through a belt of dusty date orchards, the town seems most dull and unimpressive, no more than an overgrown village. Here is none of the beauty of traditional southern Arabian architecture, with its white buildings and narrow streets; on the contrary, the town sprawls randomly and is composed mainly of low huts built of date palm thatch. A few recent cement buildings—a bank, a gas station—stand out incongruously, while some parts of the town contain mainly older, tumbled-down brick houses and open areas (new construction is banned until a zoning plan has been developed). The imposing tower and walls of the fort provide the main landmark.

One sees a variety of cars and trucks; and the whisper of the wind in the palm trees and the murmur of the surf are mixed with the buzz of an occasional small private generator by night and of irrigation pumps and a couple of flour mills by day. Otherwise, there is little evidence of the twentieth century. In 1974–76 no part of Sohar was supplied by electricity. There was no piped water at any point; everyone depended on private or public shallow wells. There were no arrangements for

Sohar from the sea. The main tower of the fort is seen in the center of the photograph.

sewage disposal or nightsoil collection; a scheme for garbage collection had just been launched. No telephone facilities existed, even for the administration (the first lines from Muscat were due to be opened later in 1976). There was no postal distribution from the small post office in the decaying customs house. Despite the urban character of the settlement, there was no commercial supply of milk, and those who did not keep their own milk animals had to depend on powdered milk. Likewise, meat was essentially unavailable: a part-time butcher slaughtered one to three goats or sheep in the market three mornings a week, for immediate sale—and was immediately sold out, leaving all but the most fortunate to fall back on canned fish. Sand and dust are everywhere, and penetrate everything. The air is hot and sticky; a piercing sun envelopes all in light and heat.

The first impression of people is both picturesque and more attractive: men and boys in long white robes and embroidered caps, and occasionally in a side street a glimpse of a brightly dressed woman wearing a black face mask. Racially, the population is very mixed: soft white skinned Arab town boys; weatherbeaten, lean bedouin; black Africans; occasionally an Indian. People are generally slight of build, graceful, and meticulously clean. Perhaps the most striking feature is their style: their politeness and elegance of manner, their subdued speech and gentle expression, their control of movement and practice of mutual respect turn what would elsewhere in the Middle East be a jostling crowd into something more like a choreographed ballet.

The town faces the Indian Ocean, a largely calm and shallow sea running up 'to a straight and exposed shoreline along the Batineh coast. The sea has provided opportunities for two main activities: fishing and trade. On an average day, several score small fishing vessels will land their catch on the beach of Sohar, handing most of it over for sale to the auctioneers of the fish market. Within sight up or down the coast will also generally be one or a few larger, high-sterned sardine-fishing vessels and a team or two of men drawing land seines onto the beach.

Trade by sea has been very important till recently, and custom house records show figures of twenty to thirty ships *(dhows)* calling per day until about 1960. Today, there are maximally only a couple of *dhows* at anchor, loading or unloading by small boat through the mild surf on the beach. Most transport has been taken over by trucks going to Dubai harbor on the Gulf or to the modern port of Mattrah, 230 km to the south. While twenty years ago, twenty or twenty-five *dhows* used to be owned by residents of Sohar alone, today only two small vessels (locally known as *sambaks*) are run from the neighboring village of Zaffran. The *dhows* that call on Sohar are now largely Iranian owned, but frequent the traditional waters: the Omani coast, the Gulf, Baluchistan, Bombay, and southward and westward to the Yemens, Somalia, East Africa, and Zanzibar.

An almost continuous line of settlements faces and partly invades the 10- to 30-m-broad zone of gray, dirty sand of the beach. Sohar itself is strung out along the coast, and is nearly continuous with the smaller villages to the north and south. Inside the settlement again is a belt of cultivated land, extending 2–3 km inland. All crops are irrigated from wells and lift pumps; diesel has replaced animal power in all but a few, quaintly traditional cases over the last twenty years. The main crops are dates in terms of area and limes in terms of value, with mangoes and other fruits as subsidiary crops. The orchards are occasionally interspersed with fields of mixed vegetables or fodder, the latter also sometimes sown under the date trees.

Most of the cultivated land is owned as private property by the residents of Sohar and other coastal villages; in recent years there has been a tendency for owners also to build houses in these gardens and move there temporarily in the hot season, or even permanently. The inner part of the orchard belt is owned partly by settled bedouin of the tribes traditionally controlling or adjoining these areas. Their settlements form a more dispersed belt of palm-thatch compounds, conveniently located so as to be close to the gardens and also to have free access to the uncultivated plain for pasturing flocks, mostly sheep and goats. This plain stretches another 30 km inland, partly covered by open acacia forest, partly bare. With the sedentarization of the local bedouin along the orchard fringe, and the decrease in local camel keeping following the motorization of transport, other more mobile bedouin from the inner desert of Oman have invaded this belt. Finally, about 35 km in from the coast, the main line of Oman's mountains rises steeply, occupied by a scattering of mixed farmers, tribally organized.

Despite its unprepossessing appearance, Sohar constitutes a classical example of the traditional Islamic city. It is administratively divided into wards (as will be shown in map 1, chapter 8) and its residents consciously and confidently see themselves as *hadr* (urban), in contrast to the supposedly dirty and uncouth bedouin. Its central ward, Higra, surrounded by a crumbling fortified city wall, contains two essential pillars of urban society: the market (*suq*) for commerce and the fort (*hosn*) for law and order.

The market is the bustling center of life in Sohar. It includes (*a*) the subsidiary fish market, with sites for three simultaneous auctions (frequented mainly by retailers) and two rows of low bench stalls selling the fish to consumers; (*b*) the approximately twenty open stalls for vegetables and fruits (in large part Lebanese produce trucked in from the Gulf ports), with an adjoining site for a tiny livestock market and infrequent meat market; and (*c*) the largely covered main bazaar. This bazaar embraces about 150 open-fronted small shops distributed along a simple grid of longitudinal and transverse lanes. Through these narrow lanes pass a medley of customers from the town and the surrounding countryside, mixed with an occasional coolie staggering under his load. The shops offer canned and powdered foods, biscuits, Pepsi-Cola, cheap crockery, yard goods, etc.—all manufactured goods, today mostly from China but also from Western Europe, Eastern Europe, India, Japan, and the United States. Everything is imported and local products are not seen—even the native pharmacist imports most of his herbs and medicines from elsewhere in the Middle East. Indeed, very few goods are produced in the town at all: there are only two very inactive blacksmiths, four *halwa* (sweets) cookeries, two bakers, and a half dozen tailors. Yet as a center supplying the resident population, surrounding villages, and countryside, and as a wholesale and transport center for a larger region, the market nonetheless attains considerable size and volume.

Local traffic is almost completely motorized. A burned down area of the market and a section of beach provide the main parking areas for Land Rovers, trucks, and cars; a small area of collapsed houses in the other end of the bazaar serves as a fodder market and stables for donkeys and the occasional camel—the predominant form of land transport only ten years ago. Eight to ten garages and two gasoline pumps serve the needs of the new forms of transport.

While the market is very much the center of most crowds and most activity, the center of power lies unequivocally elsewhere, in the large and dominant fortress of Sohar. Here the Wali—the Sultan's appointed governor—holds court, and from here he directs and controls all public matters. Under his command is a small contingent of guards and soldiers, in part locally recruited, in part hill men from the mountains inland, of the dominant Beni Omar tribe there. A few other public buildings also play a subsidiary role: the customs house, the post office, two schools, a number of mosques, the club that has replaced a number of privately controlled and more factionally oriented meeting places, and a handful of restaurants and teashops.

The clientele of all the places mentioned so far is almost exclusively male. Segregation of the sexes is the most consistent and striking feature of organization in Sohar society. Women live a life separated from all public arenas and comprehensively shielded from contact with unrelated males. Their world is made up of the compounds and neighborhoods of the residential quarters of town; even within these confines they keep their face covered with a mask (*burqa*) in the company of all but the most closely related persons, and their figure shrouded in a cloak (*abba*) when moving by back streets farther than to the closest neighbors.

However, the social differentiation of Sohar has many dimensions beyond those of division of labor and sex. The most important are wealth and property; descent; the stigma of slavery; religious faith, sect, and school; language; and ethnic group. Thus, there is a drastic range of wealth from the (till recently, abject) poor coolies and laborers to the rich traders and landowners, and an active circulation of property reflecting swift changes, both rising and declining, in the position of many persons through their life variously affected by speculation, trade, political instability, and labor migration.

Patrilineal descent ascribes membership to one or another of perhaps fifty different tribes, ranging from large to small and from insignificant to the dynastic Al Bu Said. Slavery was till some twenty years ago an important institution, and families today are variously tainted by slave descent or the intermixture of slave blood. Hindus as well as Moslems reside in Sohar, and of the latter both Shiahs and Sunnis are present; the Sunnis are represented by all four orthodox schools. There is also a significant congregation of Ibadhis, the dominant faith in the interior and of the Al Bu Said family. Besides Arabic, the languages Persian, Baluchi, Zidgali, and Kutchi are spoken as mother tongues, and distinctive traits of culture characterize each ethnic group in question. There is no one-to-one correspondence between these different statuses. A Baluchi may be rich or poor, fisherman or farmer. While the Hindus specialize as merchants, they have no monopoly or even predominance in the market, and adjoining shops selling identical wares may be owned by a Hindu, an Arab, and a Baluchi. Some neighborhoods show a predominance of either Arabic, Persian, or Baluchi-speaking households, but all are mixed to some extent, and many seem indiscriminately so.

In daily intercourse, persons from the different categories also meet and mix—not just in the market, where one would traditionally expect the colorful diversity of the East to mingle. The friendships established between young men cross ethnic groups, sects, and occupations. The guests at a wedding include different categories—indeed, bride and groom may themselves belong to different language communities, different classes, different tribes. Business partnerships unite persons of contrasting faith and ethnic group. The informal gatherings of women visiting for coffee and socializing bring together poor and wealthy, Shiah and Sunni, Arab and Zidgali, purebred and slave. This is not because people lack intensity in their embracement of identity, faith, and honor, or because the real differences in values and customs are slight; quite to the contrary, but common ideals of poise, grace, and politeness do play a part in muting the divisions and sustaining relationships. Nor is this intermixing a recent and temporary phenomenon: while both assimilation and accommodation can be demonstrated to be taking place, the main ethnic and religious components all have a local history stretching back hundreds of years.

SOME THEORETICAL PERSPECTIVES

In a complex society like this, a wide variety of activities and events takes place. Since persons differ in skills and resources, roles, values, and purposes, we cannot expect their behavior to conform to a single pattern or to be conditioned by the same constraints. Yet their acts affect each other, though to varying degrees, some very directly and profoundly, others less so or hardly at all. How closely persons are affected by each other's acts does not correlate very directly with how similar they are in culture and life situation. The intrigues of matchmaking in a Sunni Arab family will be important to some others of their group, but will neither interest nor affect a Hindu merchant, as long as marriages somehow eventuate and the consequent trousseau cloth, etc., are purchased. On the other hand, division of labor and relations of employment connect persons of *dis*similar groups and cultures more often and more closely than persons of similar life situations. For most purposes, neighbors of different class and ethnic groups are more interdependent than kinsmen and affines at opposite ends of town, and the acts of the Wali and his retainers may be more fateful than those of a person's cotribesmen or associates in the local community or congregation. In the description of behavior and social relations, and in the analysis of their interconnection in systems, one thus cannot order events according to the concepts of custom or culture, though each actor is constrained by customs and rules, some of which are common to many or to all. Nor can the anthropologist be guided, to the extent that one may be in the study of many other societies, by the knowledge, understandings, and conceptualizations of particular in-formants on their own society: besides being, of course, unaware of some of the fundamental forces and processes that shape societies and cultures, they are in part fundamentally unsympathetic to each other's values and in part ignorant of them and of each other's life situations and premises.

An understanding of Sohar is therefore best built up through a synthesis. I shall attempt to do this cumulatively from the events and diverse circumstances revealed in daily life. I shall not impose, even for heuristic purposes, an image of "the social structure" or even assume that we shall arrive at such a structure in the end, but shall seek to characterize partial patterns and to aggregate, where possible, by identifying the microevents that reveal or are constituents of the major and significant processes of this society. Such a procedure also gives me an opportunity to depict what appear as essential realities of life for the people of Sohar: what is taken for granted among them, what the rules and institutions are that divide them and that are subject to disagreement, and what the various objects of striving and struggle are.

In the opening paragraph of this chapter, however, certain difficul-ties of description and analysis were mentioned which need further discussion at this introductory stage. The first difficulty concerned size. Sohar has a large population; how are the samples or segregates on which we have information to be related to the whole? For the kinds of data we need, it is obvious that sample surveying techniques provide no answer. As so frequently in social anthropological description, our task is to find out what kind of things there are to know about this society, rather than to attempt a rigorous recording of answers to questions that are already in principle known to the investigator. We need to follow a discovery procedure whereby significant institutions and life circumstances are revealed, arenas are located, and the con-siderations affecting people's decisions are learned. In the field, this was achieved by wide-ranging visiting and association, and especially by participant exposure to the flow of events and activities that arose from or impinged upon a range of friends and acquaintances. Though these actual individuals were in many respects fortuitously selected, the events and acts were in a more genuine sense a random sample of what constitutes the society of Sohar, selected not by us from our pre-conceptions or inadequate provisional understanding of what this life was about but by the probabilities inherent in the spontaneous flow of that life itself.

The second difficulty concerned social differentiation. The members of Sohar are so diverse; how could the range of persons and cultural and subcultural items be covered? Unni and I entered on our separate sides of the basic segregating line of gender, and we tried to spread our contacts in terms of ethnic group, occupation and wealth, location, and faith. Equally important, we pursued the networks in which our contact persons were enmeshed, and we exposed ourselves to interaction in the open and public arenas that were available and in those to which our friendships introduced us. Whereas no claims to completeness can be made on such a basis, considerable breadth and variety can be claimed. But for intimate and private interaction, our data are biased toward urban Arab Sunnis, and are weakest on Persian-speaking Shiahs (*Ajams*) and on Bedouin. However, by exposing ourselves to the scenes, arenas, and individual events of the lives of some persons, we were also led to appreciate something of the life situation of their diverse alters, and could pursue a variety of issues and topics in conversations and interviews with these others. A complex society cannot be exhaustively described from the points of view of all its participants unless such a description were to run into scores of highly repetitive volumes, but neither can it be captured through a traditional anthropological monograph centered on the life and practices of one of its component categories or groups. It is in the relations between *different* persons that complex society is constituted, and in the contexts of organization and meaning that envelop them severally or together. While no gazetteer of these relations can be exhaustive, their forms and contexts begin, after a period of participation, to take on familiarity and exhibit recurrent patterns. If this description can show how interactions arise (in terms of the persons and resources involved) and can describe the range of contexts that is found or constructed for their performance, then it depicts the structure of this complex society as I understand it.

One might argue that not only is a more literally complete descrip-tion of a complex society impossible in practice, but it is not even achieved by real life, in the sense that a great deal of social, interactional potential of Sohar's personnel and organizations remains at any one time unrealized. If all the world is a stage, then in the world of complex societies it is one that lacks the unity of a single script, and this generates a surfeit of partly simultaneous sketches that are rarely carried through to their conclusion undisturbed by alien plots: there are more

ideas for scripts even than there are actors to perform them. And all
the while, the scene itself is being constructed and dismantled in
accordance with partial and conflicting designs. People live with this
complexity, and create for themselves a life in it by making it partially
predictable through their attempts to understand (or ignore!) it and
partially manageable through their attempts to control its impact on
their own life. At any one place and time, the result has a recognizable
character and uniqueness. The character and uniqueness, and how
they come about, are what the anthropologist describing a complex
society must try to depict and analyze.

The third difficulty noted was that of handling the historical context
of the world religion and civilization of which Sohar is but a relatively
inconspicuous part. Indeed, the kind of internal constitution which I
discussed in the preceeding paragraph might already be felt to invite a
historical treatment and to require an account of how Islam and other
aspects of the Arabic and other great traditions have influenced Sohar.
Such an account of Sohar would conform to one contemporary fashion
in anthropology. In a banal sense, the condition of society in Sohar
today is a product of its particular history in the past. But a claim to
explanatory power for such an account is spurious. Telling how it *was* is
no more insightful than telling how it *is*; a sequence of events, whereby
the later are revealed to follow from the earlier, surely "explains"
nothing, but only transfers our puzzles to those *earlier* events, now
established as primary and initial in the description. Furthermore, a
moment's thought will show that this procedure is encumbered by an
inherent additional weakness. Through an analysis of anthropological
field data we should be in a position to know more about the present
than we can hope to know about the past; there is hardly any piece of
information about the present which we are precluded from ascertain-
ing if we judge it to be useful for our analysis. Surely, it must be poor
method to design one's argument so that the present, which one knows
more about,is sought to be explained by a past about which one knows
less.

On the other hand, in Sohar as in other societies, various features of
the past are made relevant to life in the present, and this contemporary
store of knowledge and justification—or complication—of life is very
much part of the contemporary scene. It is difficult for the anthropologist to handle these references to the past in Sohar, however,
because knowledge of the past is so extensive (partly written, partly
verbal tradition, partly personal recollection), much of it so irregularly
and infrequently activated, and all of it so unequally known to different
persons, often in contradictory versions. Moreover, it might *also* be of
interest to be able to judge the authenticity of the contemporary store
of historical knowledge in terms of its truth and adequacy, and this

entails an amount of historical scholarship which adds great burdens as well as potential insights to anthropological analyses. Other interesting potentials of critical historical information concern the antiquity or duration of institutional features uncovered by the analysis of contemporary society: for example, the present mode of operation of the Wali's court, or the nearly free market for real property. Finally, certain conditions and circumstances may be observed which do not seem capable of being generated from presently observable processes, and this invites a search for other or additional processes in the past, to identify the sources of such features wherever possible: for example, the present situation of ex-slaves in a society that no longer acknowledges slavery. The following text will occasionally attempt all these things where the need arises and some data are available to me, but it does so only incidentally to an investigation focusing on contemporary Sohar and the diversity it sustains.

Finally, I mentioned a fourth difficulty: that elements of life in Sohar are contained within numerous, much larger systems, and so "Sohar" as an object of sociological description is very unclearly demarcated and separated from these larger contexts. More correctly, one might say that of the events that take place in Sohar, some are better understood in the contexts of systems of regional or even global scale than in a peculiarly Sohari context. This formulation in fact contains the key to how I shall try to handle the issue. Residents of Sohar participate, both conceptually and actually, in a number of primary social fields of very different scale, from predominantly endogamous clusters of agnatically related households to the world market. For a numer of purposes they are significantly affected by events that take place outside the local scene, under circumstances and constraints very different from those observed in Sohar. This is true for everyone, even members of the simplest and most isolated society, whose fate is suddenly one day decided in an office in some distant metropolis. But in the case of complex societies, *in casu* Sohar, a great number of these physically exogenous events are already built into the design of local persons and society in recognizable ways. They have their effect and become apparent on the local scene through the agency of pre-established persons or institutions: the macrosystem in question already has a precipitate in persons within Sohar which makes them susceptible to—in a real sense *parties* to—the event.

In this perspective, one can discover the organized way in which Sohari residents are part of larger systems by observing certain, however modest, acts and events of such macrosystems that arise locally. The purchase of ten pounds of sugar in the marketplace in Sohar is an event of the world sugar market, as can be shown by the way such trade is organized in Sohar, however minuscule the effects of that event on that market. The response of a boy in Sohar to information about a speech by the Egyptian President is an event of Pan-Arab politics, however insignificant within the larger picture. But, by virtue of their localization in Sohar, these microevents of large-scale systems also have a series of local implications for the balance of a merchant's accounts, for the alignment and rivalries of some boys in a youthful network, for the possible acceptance or rejection of claims to legitimacy by local political authorities, etc. Given this situation, we should seek not to insulate and abstract Sohar as "a system" but to trace the events of life in Sohar to those contexts which shed the greatest possible light upon how they arise and upon their implications (see Barth 1978*b*).

2

Sohar and the Larger World

Sohar in 1974 gave a first impression of having a very traditional, or perhaps even archaic, Middle Eastern condition of life, something that was even more characteristic of most other towns of Oman, and a fair reflection of the country's recent extreme isolation. Oman was in fact a closed country, like a Tibet of the Middle East, until Sultan Qaboos succeeded his father, Said bin Taimur, through a sudden coup on 23 July 1970, and opened the doors to rapid change and progress. Partly from shrewdness and financial poverty, partly from eccentric conservatism, Sultan Said had neglected the development of communications and education, imposed exile on any Omani who acquired more than an elementary-school education abroad, banned radios, sunglasses, and cement houses, and resisted foreign development iniatives other than a limited amount of oil prospecting. Yet Oman has always been very much part of a larger world, and to understand the character of local life in Sohar it is important to understand in what ways it has been separate and in what ways it is connected with the rest of the world. Many of these premises are being rapidly negated by contemporary development, yet they, and even more their effects, are still very much in evidence. In this chapter, changes occurring over the three years preceeding my field work will be noted incidentally among the many other facts and conditions of far greater duration and antiquity which shape or have shaped the life of the present residents of Sohar.

Oman is geographically like an island surrounded on three sides by the sea and on the fourth by the empty sands of Arabia. Only a very small population of highly specialized bedouin regard these sands as anything but a nearly impassable barrier. The core of the "island" is made up of a chain of mountains centering on the Green Mountains, which reach a height of about 3,000 m. Though they receive most of the rain that makes Oman habitable, their color comes from the rock of

13

which they are composed, and not from any notable excess of vegetation.*

The main regions of Oman for my purposes are three: inner Oman, the twin ports of Muscat and Mattrah, and the Batineh coast with Sohar.† Of these, inner Oman or Oman proper is composed mainly of a string of oasis towns facing the inner desert, much as the Batineh towns face the sea. Inner Oman and the Batineh coast thus represent two very different faces of Oman. Though historically interconnected and often united, they are both ecologically and socially very distinct and there is very little communication between them: only a handful of the persons we knew in Sohar—widely traveled elsewhere in the world —had ever been to inner Oman.

Muscat, on the other hand, is an integral premise and part of the society of Sohar. Almost inaccessible by land until 1972, Muscat has functioned as a kind of independent "port of trade," which dominated the sea and so controlled the Batineh coast throughout most of the recent centuries, as well as controlling, or having influence over, inner Oman. For two centuries Muscat has served as the capital of the state of which Sohar has been a part. In the framework of a highly absolute and personal political structure it is the seat of government and the source of legitimacy for the provincial authorities. A succession of Walis (governors) were sent to Sohar to govern on behalf of the Sultan of Muscat in accordance with a state-wide design of transfers and promotions; apart from the last years of Sultan Said's rule there were also

---

*Indeed, the name Jebel Akhtar would perhaps be better translated as "Dark" than "Green" Mountain; the Arabic term *Akhtar* is used both for greeness and to describe dark skin as opposed to white. The eagerness with which lush vegetation is reported from these barren mountains reflects perhaps as much a longing inspired in a singularly harsh country by so romantic a name as the modest terraces and scrub found there.

†The immense and sparsely inhabited southern province of Dhofar, which has been part of the Sultante since 1879/1829, is ecologically and culturally distinct and essentially without significance for people in Sohar except that its main town, Salalah, served as the residence of Sultan Said for a number of years until he was overthrown. The population of Dhofar includes some tribes of aboriginal south-Semitic-speaking Qara (Thomas 1929, 1931, 1932) as well as a majority of Arabs. Since 1963 the province has been the scene of local insurgency, supported by Communist interests (cf. Smiley 1975, Fiennes 1977), now essentially terminated.

The Sultanate of Oman also includes the small and demographically and economically insignificant northern province of Mussandam, comprising the mountainous cape at the entry to the Arabian Gulf. The population here is likewise predominantly Arab, but includes an aboriginal population of Shihuh, which reportedly forms a separate language community.

recurrent visits to Sohar by the reigning Sultan. But it is only recently with the development of modern administration and communication that the ordinary resident of Sohar would have any business in Muscat or other reason to travel there. Even today, despite the highway constructed in 1972, which reduces travel time to less than three hours, Muscat remains a very differently constituted society from that of Sohar, with rather different families, groups, and ways.

But the provincial isolation of Sohar is reduced by the participation of its population in a number of larger systems, both conceptual and real, other than that of the Sultanate. For a number of purposes, Sohar has been more a part of these other, larger worlds than a part of Oman. First, people of Sohar identify themselves very clearly as members of the larger Arab world. Though many other peoples have come from the coasts of Asia and Africa and settled in Sohar, many of the inhabitants today regard themselves as the descendants of pure Arabs of one or another of perhaps fifty different tribes, grouped in the southern (Yamani) and northern (Nizari) main branches of common Arab origin. These branches mean little to the average man today, and in-depth genealogical knowledge is almost nonexistent—among women, many are unable even to give their own tribal name. But the fact of Arab identity, implying the knowledge by someone or other of these genealogies, is clearly asserted by some and highly valued by all.

Much of this pride and identity centers on the Arabic language itself. As the language of the Holy Koran and of most of the great nations of the Middle East, it epitomizes a cosmopolitan tradition and identity. By virtue of it, men who have any interest in such matters can associate themselves with what they regard as the greatest civilization in history—a view of Arabic civilization that in Sohar is embraced by all, even the resident Hindus. Also from the more parochial viewpoint of the women, a similar value is attached to Arabic as the speech of the highest-ranking group in the region. This self-evaluation on the part of Omanis may appear somewhat exaggerated when seen from the outside, in view of the multiplicity of local and unsophisticated dialects and in part even debased patois reflecting East African and Indian contacts in some coastal towns. Nonetheless, it serves most people unquestionably as a source of identity and finds formal expression, for example, in the great emphasis placed on rather elaborate poetry and song pantomime at calendrical festivals and weddings.

Second, most residents of Sohar are associated as Moslems with a great tradition of cosmopolitan culture. This has several aspects. In practicing Islam, one partakes of an international field of theology and scholarship. Islam is a complex tradition of jurisprudence as well as a religion in the narrower, Christian sense; it also implies a view of world history and a special place for each subtradition in this history. All four orthodox schools of Islamic law, Hanafi, Shafi, Malaki, and Hanbali, are represented in Sohar, entailing an awareness of their various sources and precedents in the great centers and law courts of Islam. These four schools are seen as the four mutually supportive pillars of the house of Islam; adherence to one of them (generally determined by descent, but adjustable by conviction) is an act of orthodoxy without being a challenge to adherents of the other schools, and provides scope for more or less learned, but always polite discussion. In expounding these schools of law and their intricate but minor differences, literature and precedence from the core areas of the Moslem world are constantly reiterated and confirmed. Members of all four schools pray together as one congregation in joint, Sunni mosques, and thus provide each other with a vivid metaphor of the diversity and universality of Islam. Most people in Sohar partake of this Sunni tradition.

The main schism of Islam is represented within the local society in the form of the Jaffari school of the Shiah faith (after the Imam Ja'far; they are also known as Imamis). Shiism goes back to the early division of Islam over the rights of Ali, the Prophet's relative and son-in-law, to succeed to the leadership of the Moslems; and Shiahs emphasize the tragic figures of the martyred Ali and his sons as the legitimate line. The Shiah faith is prevalent, especially in Iran. It is represented in Sohar both by persons of Persian descent and by Arabs descended from Gulf communities. Shiahs maintain their own places of worship, overtly only slightly different from Sunni mosques, and refuse to pray together with Sunnis or admit them to their mosques.

Finally, Oman is particularly identified with the Ibadhi movement of Islam, which dominates inner Oman, counts the Sultan's dynasty among its members—and so most Walis of Sohar, including the present one—and is also represented as a minority in the population of Sohar. The origin of the Ibadhis also goes back to the early days of Islam, to a faction that totally dismissed descent as a criterion for leadership and so rejected Ali—though he was duly elected by the community of believers as their leader—because he did not explicitly repudiate those of his following who favored him for reasons of descent. From this sprang a separatist movement that established itself in the mountains of Oman under an elected leadership—often worldly and political as well as legal and spiritual, and sometimes identical with the ruling house in Muscat. The last elected Imam was driven from inner Oman by Sultan Said, assisted by British forces, in 1959; he died in exile in Cairo. Ibadhis have separate mosques, but can also pray together with Sunnis.

The congregations, groupings, and religious factions of daily life on the local scene are thus for residents of Sohar not parochial and petty alliances but directly identifiable as the perpetuation of parties to decisive events in world history. Though many people seem uninterested, or possibly even unaware of this, it must give those who care a feeling of participation in a cosmopolitan mainstream that one would otherwise not expect in an isolated periphery. This fact stands out most clearly if one tries to imagine its opposite: an Oman inhabited by a separate speech community, with a religion uniquely that community's own and a view of history focusing on only those events which have taken place in Oman. As things are, the subjective world of people of Sohar could remain open even when Oman was politically closed.

As far are religion goes, this depended far more on identifications and understandings than on physical practice. Islam has little formal centralized religious organization, and very few actual activities connect the religious life of Sohar with the outside. Mosques are locally financed by donations of land (*waqf*) and community-based alms (*zakat*), and are built by individual initiative. Only the larger mosques have an imam—an officer comparable to a priest or minister—and he is elected or confirmed by the local congregation. Though such posts require theological competence, no larger centers for religious study existed in Oman until very recently, nor have religious students been active in the wandering and studying tradition of some Islamic regions. Consequently, the imams of Sohar are largely locally recruited and trained.

Another aspect of Islam, the Haj pilgrimage, has rather more effect in causing individuals from Sohar to travel and communicate outside the local scene. The injunction to all believers who are physically and economically able to perform the pilgrimage to Mecca is acknowledged by both men and women, and has been realized up to four times by some old and prosperous persons. But compared to the attention and emphasis given to the Haj in many Moslem societies, the reaction in Sohar is very low key: no elaborate send-off or reception, no use of the honorific title of haji, no scenes of recounting what the pilgrim has seen and learned. The most I could obtain, even by explicit elicitation in suitable contexts, were very detailed itineraries of the route of travel. This is highly consistent with Omani ideals of grace and abhorrence of bragging and egocentricity, but it drastically reduces the community effect of such a relatively high frequency of individual long-distance pilgrimage.

If religion is important mainly in opening Sohar conceptually to the rest of the world, secular activities are more effective in physically tying Sohar to the outside. Most radical is the practice of labor migration. Though the experience gained from such travel is managed with as much reticence as the Haj, it occurs so frequently that it affects nearly everyone's world view directly. Indeed, we know only two adult men who have not been abroad on labor migration—one a transsexual, the other a sardine fishing boat owner who came into property at an early age and so had neither the cause nor the opportunity to absent himself.

The typical pattern has been for young men in Sohar—many as early as ages ten to eleven, others not till in their late teens or early twenties—to seek work and experience abroad, and to spend a period of five to ten, or even twenty years away before settling down to a life in Sohar. The reasons for this are several, often in combination but each singly sufficient to justify labor migration. For more than a century, the economy of the region has been depressed and opportunities for local employment few and poor. Boys have sought independence, and to prove themselves as males and adults, by fending for themselves. Particularly in the absence of local educational opportunities, foreign travel and work have been explicitly regarded as broadening, and have often in fact provided opportunities for gaining literacy, some episodes of formal training, and positions of responsibility. Even Sohari women, themselves stationary, recognize that seeing the world is the way to gain knowledge. Finally, until constrained by a law enacted in 1974, bride prices have been very high—of late in the neighborhood of 1000–1200 Rials, or more than $3,000, among average, respectable families—and such sums have to be earned by the prospective grooms themselves, an almost insuperable task within Sohar for most youths.

So the young men, and many older ones, go abroad. Today most go to the oil boom shaikhdoms of Abu Dhabi, Dubai, etc., in the Gulf, and since 1971–72 even to the recent Omani oil installations or the expanding center of Muscat-Mattrah. Before that, the main labor markets were Kuwait, Bahrain, and Saudi Arabia. Others have worked as sailors all over the Indian Ocean, the Gulf, and the Red Sea, or have signed on and then gone ashore in Bombay or Karachi, or East Africa, and worked as servant boys or dishwashers in restaurants all night while attending school in the daytime. In previous generations, pearl fisheries in the Gulf, seafaring, trading, and piracy served the same purposes. The result is a pattern of prolonged absences by some male members of most households, and remittances from wage-earning persons abroad, and on the other hand a local community in Sohar composed of men nearly all of whom have extensive individual experience of other and distant places, other cultures and styles of life, and often other languages.

With Oman's sudden wealth and modernization, Sohar has also over the last couple of years become the recipient of a considerable labor migration. The new hospital is stocked mainly with Pakistani and Indian doctors and almost entirely with Indian nurses, the new schools with Egyptian and Jordanian teachers. Two Indian contracting companies, bringing their own personnel, were in 1975 engaged in Sohar, and there is a considerable influx of individual and privately engaged

migrants, especially from Iran and Pakistan. A few Westerners working for the U.N., other development contracts, or humanitarian institutions have also arrived. Altogether, there were in 1976 about 1000
such non-Omanis present in Sohar.

But also before, there was much movement of people into Sohar.
The Hindu community, though centuries old, is composed mainly of
persons who were born in Bombay or elsewhere in India and the
present Pakistan, and who generally retire to Bombay before death.
(Cf. chapter 17.) A number of other resident Soharis are themselves
immigrants, especially from Iran and Baluchistan, or their parents or
grandparents were (cf. chapter 4). Major ethnic groups trace their
origins from these places, some Arab tribes are considered to have
arrived relatively recently from distant areas of origin, and persons of
slave descent hail from Zanzibar and East Africa. So also in this respect,
Sohar is thought of and experienced as open to the world.

The third major way in which Sohar has always been closely tied to,
and dependent on, the outside is through trade. Until Oman obtained
its first substantial oil revenues in 1969, the main national exports were
dried limes, sold mostly to Iraq and Iran. Sohar is a major producer
and the major port of shipment for this crop, which in 1971 totaled
1,500 tons, for a value of one-half million Rials. (See *Oman*, statistical

*A section of Higra, the central ward of Sohar, seen from the fort's tower. Hadirah ward
stretches northward under what appears as a solid cover of trees. The large building in the
right foreground is the custom house.*

appendix.) The prosperity of the town has thus been dependent on this export, and the imports financed by it. The trade has always been fully monetized, employing currencies largely minted abroad, especially the Indian Rupee, and the Maria Theresa dollar until the 1940s or '50s; and prices are still frequently cited by both traders and ordinary townsmen in Rupees, Dubai Dinars, Saudi Rials, etc. Wealth, though often created and lost within the bazaar of Sohar, involved the handling of wares that moved on a world market if one excepts speculation on the local sector of real estate. The result is a notable degree of openness in the whole economy, both in the sense of impermanence and rapid circulation of wealth and in the sense of sensitivity and vulnerability to external fluctuations.

A somewhat longer historical perspective adds a further dimension to this picture, since it shows Sohar as highly variably, but sometimes prominently, involved in an open, international society. We need not go back to the extensive second-millennium B.C. copper mines in the foothills inland from the town, or the district's status as a valued province in the classical Persian empire, but rather we should focus on the pattern of change and continuity of the Islamic town. Tenth-century Arab geographers depict Sohar already as a structurally perhaps similar but physically infinitely grander and more glorious trading center: ". . . it is not possible to find on the shore of the Persian Sea nor in all the land of Islam a city more rich in fine buildings and foreign wares than Sohar" (Istakhri, quoted by Miles 1919:455). Less authoritative tradition plausibly and suitably identifies it as the birthplace of that highly cosmopolitan and peripatetic figure Sinbad the Sailor. More recently, Oman experienced a period of political and commercial prominence between the Portuguese and British epochs, that is, around 1650 to 1790, when it was the key imperial power in the whole Indian Ocean. Though naval dominance passed, imperial possessions remained, Zanzibar being separated from Oman only in 1856 and the last overseas possession, Gwadar, on the Baluchistan coast, being sold to Pakistan in 1958. Only the last hundred years or so of these events are recalled by the people of Sohar with any historical accuracy, while earlier epochs are depicted in traditions of more fabulous character, such as stories of a far-sighted princess who could see the enemy fleets assembling on the distant Baluchistan coasts, and the submergence of an earlier and much grander Sohar under the seas, still sometimes visible below twelve fathoms of water.

Though we are not dealing with an imperial, or prosperous, phase of Sohar, this background can nonetheless add to our understanding in two ways. It suggests the historical genesis of patterns of interactional and participatory competance that characterize the male residents of Sohar—the concrete features of which are difficult to pin down, but

which it is one of my major purposes to specify and explain. It also gives
warning that the town of Sohar may confront us with organizational
and institutional patterns of an urban and large-scale potential that we
might not otherwise be prepared to recognize in the isolated, dusty,
and overgrown fishing village that meets the eye of the unsympathetic
outsider. But it should not tempt us to deny the parochial and closed
aspects of this local social milieu. Indeed, these are aspects that at least
the male residents of Sohar themselves experience clearly and I think
in some ways with frustration. Thus emerges a basic, constituting
characteristic of Sohar: it is composed of an aggregate of persons who
are individually and separately often sophisticated and cosmopolitan,
both in their codification of their own identity and in their personal life
experiences, yet enmeshed in the constraints of a highly traditional and
numerically small-scale town. This contradiction is perhaps the prime
basis for the remarkable readiness with which progress and social
change have been accepted since the accession of Sultan Qaboos in
1970, but it also produces a characteristic distance and lack of identification by the individual with the collectivity of Sohar. These complex
attitudes were perhaps most neatly expressed by one acquaintance:
commenting on his compatriots' heady response to the sudden modernization and change of Oman, he chose to cite an old proverb: " 'My,
how big the world is,' said the frog, as they lifted him out of the village
well."

3

The Formal Administrative and Political Constitution of Sohar

The formal administration of the province and town provides a framework for the daily life of all Soharis. This is not to say that it somehow precedes and is independent of other features of social organization: the shape of politics and administration in Sohar of course reflects the cultural and social facts of ideology, interests, loyalties, and divisions that form the stuff of its residents' daily lives. But in their activities and choices, Soharis see themselves as contained and affected in a number of ways by the state of which they are members. What is more, this is also a shared and common framework for all, regardless of the cultural differences that obtain between them. A sketch of the formal administration and how it functions therefore provides a convenient starting point for a description of other features of organization and life in the town. At later stages of the analysis I shall return to particular aspects of this administrative system and attempt to show how they provide important parameters for the forms of pluralism that are sustained within the community.

Sohar is composed of half a dozen clearly demarcated wards. These in turn form a municipality, which is part of the province, which is again part of the state. On the lowest level of formal administration, one or several shaikhs are recognized for each ward, but certain descent groups and minority groups also have recognized shaikhs, and so one person may well find himself subject to two or three different recognized authorities. The municipality, on the other hand, though it has certain specialized officers, has no separate central person of authority. Both these levels of organization are therefore markedly dependent on the next higher level, that of the province, with its central Wali, or governor. The analysis of the present and recent historical role of shaikhs and political processes on the local level is best given in a later chapter, after more of the complex and crossing identities and groupings of Sohar social organization have been explicated. In the present chapter, I shall concentrate, in harmony with both Sohari representations and practical realities, on that crucial representative and agent

22

of authority, the Wali. As I shall show, this offical holds the key to a number of aspects of the social system of Sohar.

The Middle East exhibits a variety of fundamentally differently constituted corporate groups and political systems. It is a world of absolute rulers, but also one of independent egalitarian tribes, religious brotherhoods, colleges of theologians and jurists, and guildlike common-interest groups of merchants and craftsmen. Oman shows examples and features of most of this variety, and people in Sohar are familiar with them as well as with Western ideas of democracy, but Sohar itself is entirely dominated by a model of the centralized, absolute state as a precondition of order and civilization. This state is centered on the Sultan in Muscat. However, in all daily activity of Sohar his sovereignty (*sultah*) is represented and exercised by his locally resident deputy, the Wali. As far as most townspeople are concerned, all matters concerning them fall within the Wali's competance and capability. No question is too private and no issue too fateful to be outside his legitimate province, and the option that exists to appeal beyond him to the supreme figure of the Sultan is for most purposes so theoretical as to be uninteresting. As it is constituted, the town of Sohar thus contains and realizes within itself the essence of the traditional centralized Islamic state.*

The task of the Wali is to govern, that is, to uphold state authority and law and order, settle disputes between people, maintain public facilities, and direct public policies and public works. The most conspicuous and public of these tasks is his settlement of cases in his nearly daily court, which epitomizes his role in the awareness of the townspeople. Before his court come all private cases (*huqaqiya*) that cannot be settled by the parties or (optionally) their shaikhs, as well as all criminal cases (*genahiya*) and also all conflicts over the enforcement of or appeals against the rulings of municipal or other public officers. The volume of this business indicates something of its importance: the Wali's deputy estimated this court to handle on an average more than 200 separate cases per month. Such a figure is no measure of criminality or other comparative legal statistics, but it does indicate how closely people depend on the Wali. Since these cases mainly involve men and are drawn primarily from a town population of 3,000 men, and each involves two or more persons, it suggests that most men may be directly involved in at least one case before the Wali every year. The diversity of conflicts treated suggests the same: the most common are land and property disputes, including matters of right of way, fences, etc., as well as title. Second are family disputes, mainly husband-wife cases

---

*Cf. von Grünebaum 1954: "There is nothing too slight, too personal, too intimate not to stand in need of being arranged by the divine will."

involving the wife's residence location and rights to visit, unfaithfulness or refusal of sexual access, mistreatment or failure of
support—but also choice or acceptance of partner, absence of virginity
at marriage, etc. Third come money matters and debts—conditions of
sale, failure of payment or repayment, etc. The cases are thus such as
touch on the lives of everyone, not just a specialized sector of the
population. The authority of the Wali is characteristically mobilized to
sustain the normal and proper working of social transactions in everyday affairs. The state thus underwrites and enforces the rules and
terms of interpersonal social relations and decentralized and diffuse
social processes, rather than initiating and directing collective social
endeavor.

To sustain him in this governing role, the Wali is supported by a
characteristic range of props. Most imposing is the fort itself: nearly
1,000 m² in area, containing structures including the main, high tower.
In the memory of older people, this fort was not just the seat of
government but was also the place of refuge for the whole town population in periods of insecurity, particularly during the irregularly
recurring attacks by marauding bedouin tribes from the interior. Until
1974 the main tower was also the private residence of the Wali. Today
the whole edifice of metal-studded gate, with armed guards in the
gatehouse, etc., serves to impress with his power and permanence
those seeking the Wali or being taken to his jail.

The administrative facilities are basically simple (as of 1974). The
court building contains two main rooms: a large waiting hall and an
inner room for the procedings. The inner room is flanked by an open
veranda, which catches the sea-breeze and also gives access through a
window to communications from women, who can thus plead while
remaining segregated and out of the men's sight. There are twenty-
four guards (askars) on duty who serve as doormen, as messengers, to
summon witnesses, etc., and as sentries. In the outer waiting hall are
two scribes, who also write summonses, notices, and such. The inner
room contains, besides the Wali himself, two qadhis, religious judges
who know Moslem law (Shariah). In matters clearly involving this law,
the Wali turns to them for judgment, but must agree to their verdict for
it to be valid; in matters involving compromise and negotiaion, he may
consult them at his own discretion. The qadhis in Oman are overwhelmingly of the Ibadhi sect, but in matters of personal law they judge by the
sect and school of the person(s) concerned; only in criminal cases is the
Ibadhi interpretation of the Shariah universally applied. Finally, the
Wali has a deputy, the Naïb Wali, who assists him and may substitute
for him.

Most decisions are within the Wali's competence, but not life sentence or death penalty: such cases are always sent to Muscat. The Wali

also has direct telegraphic connection with Muscat, and can consult the ministries or the Sultan's court when he might so wish. Formerly, his position was one of much greater isolation and consequent responsibility: a letter of consultation to Muscat, by ship or by camel, could take up to seven days, and the Wali could not leave his fort (for example, to inspect or intervene personally in his district) without the consent of the Sultan. The Wali himself characterizes his position today as one of much greater power than at that time, emphasizing the

The Wali of Sohar in his inner office.

resources at the government's, and thus his, command and the swiftness of action, rather than his own reduced autonomy vis-à-vis the
source of authority in Muscat. In 1976, a red telephone stood in
readiness on the Wali's desk, shortly to be connected to put him in
instantaneous contact with Muscat.

Looking downward in the hierarchy, an information and intelligence network connects the Wali with the town and province he is set to
govern. Traditionally very elaborate, according to the rumors and
stories I was told, it involved a triple set of informers spying on each
other as well as on the town. Today it seems to be a much simpler system
but includes both explicit investigators and confidential sources as well
as the Wali's own personal network of connections and confidants. The
information thus obtained is important both to enable the Wali to see
through deceptions and judge cases swiftly and surely, and to prevent
him from acting in the vacuum of feedback so easily created by a
position of high authority.

The present Wali of Sohar, Hamud bin Nasir, is of the dynastic
family Al Bu Said. He father served as Wali in various provinces for
the old Sultan, but chose to discontinue and is now councillor to the
Shaikh of Qatar; his father's brother is court minister to the Sultan. His
own career started with a number of years' service with the British
Trucial Oman Scouts in Sharja, on the Gulf. In 1961 he returned as
Wali in a succession of provinces for durations varying from seven
months to seven years; since January 1972 he has served in Sohar.
Where local people see the Wali as personifying authority and the state,
and grant him immoderate authority and respect, his own emphasis is
consistently on the delegated and temporary character of the authority
vested in him, his exchangeability with any other servant of the
government in acting as the Sultan's proxy, and the self-evidence of his
acquiescence with such postings, transfers, and other instructions as
the government might decide. He is, he says, a servant of the Sultan, and
it is not for him to question the intentions or instructions of his
government, or the terms they offer him. In 1976 there were rumors
that the Wali might be posted to the large and politically rather
complex interior town of Nizwa. People thought he was reluctant to be
transferred, and they assumed that he was in a position to refuse—
indeed, that he had threatened to resign if pressed. Whatever the facts
of the matter, townspeople see their Wali as the apex of central
authority for their purposes, and thus as the personification of legitimate power.

The scene of the Wali's court, and a review of the cases handled on a
random day, may serve to introduce the reader simultaneously to the
characteristic Omani style of self-presentation and to the character of
this kind of administration.

At 9 A.M. on 6 May 1974 the waiting hall is crowded with people; they sit in dignified silence or engage in soft-spoken, general, polite conversation. Batches of two to five persons are let into the courtroom at a time, so as always to keep the bench facing the Wali and his two *qadhis* stocked with pleaders of two to four consecutive cases. In some ways the Wali acts in a very imperious manner: he hears evidence when and from whomsoever he wishes; shifts his attention anytime he likes, perhaps in the middle of someone's explanation of his case; he starts speaking whenever he wishes, thereby interrupting others, he turns to joke with the head *qadhi* in the middle of business that may be transacting; he gives verdicts without softening the blow, or faltering or showing pity; he occasionally flashes high anger. He sometimes lectures and admonishes freely. But he also clearly shows the characteristic Omani respect for the sacredness of the other's person, and never takes advantage of or riducules a pleader's clumsiness in the unfamiliar setting. When necessary, he repeats his explanations or decisions with gentleness and patience. He lets himself be interrupted by new arrivals when they make the rounds and individually shake hands to greet everyone in the room—as some do routinely, others not at all—even when the newcomer is an insignificant person and the Wali is speaking with someone of importance. He also lets himself be interrupted by other speakers though he may also continue speaking, as others often do also when interrupted. But sometimes he demands attention by saying *"Sábr"* (patience, halt, wait), which is understood and obeyed by all.

Case 1. The first case is a municipality officer's complaint against a houseowner. The owner has been told to close a drain that runs into the street, but has not done so. The circumstances are largely confirmed by a witness and admitted by the houseowner. The Wali declares that he will arrest him unless the drain is now closed.

Case 2. A says B has cut down his live, good date trees; B says they were dead. Wali deputes an *askar* to inspect the logs to find out whether they are green and report by tomorrow.

Case 3. A group of nomad shepherds have been ordered by a tax inspector to settle permanently in their present camp. They appeal to the Wali, explain the need to wander to find pastures for their goats. The Wali allows them to continue as nomads.

Case 4. A garden owner wants to evict a family who has built a hutment on his boundary line. The matter is presented in a long written petition, which is read out loud by the head *qadhi* in a deep, sonorous voice. The *qadhi* rules that the family has the right to stay. The landowner objects. The *qadhi* gives his argument. The landowner rejects the decision strenuously; he is small and thin and very agitated. The Wali stops him, and asks severely if he thinks the *qadhi* is biased

against him. The man answers abusively, whereupon the Wali's anger
flames up and he calls an *askar* to throw the man in jail. The man
continues to argue angrily, even as he is hustled away by the *askar* .

Case 5. A houseowner appeals the market inspector's refusal of
permission to build an extension of his house into an open passage
area, as he claims it represents a repair and reconstruction of a previously existing building. The Wali sends an *askar* to collect evidence on
the spot.

Case 6. A has a written deed to a piece of land, yet B persists in
cultivating it. The head *qadhi* reads the deed document out loud. B
objects that his father owned it and used it before him. The *qadhi*
argues that the written deed must be decisive.

Case 5. The market inspector from this case huddles into a whis-
pered consultation with the Wali, then leaves.

Case 6. B argues against the validity of the deed, and says that all the
neighbors can substantiate his claim. The *qadhi* accepts in principle the
relevence of such evidence. Both parties argue eloquently. B there-
upon produces an elaborate and clearly old written document (though
not an official deed) in support of his claim. The Wali reads out this
long document with all its flowery language and ceremonial frills.
Everyone listens raptly. The *qadhi* collects the papers. Both parties to
the dispute lean forward and fling themselves into simultaneous
monologues arguing their case. The Wali turns to another man who
has been waiting on the bench, and proceeds to pay him 30 Rials on a
private debt. He then listens to the case for a while, then proceeds with
the next case.

Case 7. A man has a letter from the municipality of a neighboring
town and province (Shinaz), demanding a payment of 400 Rials. The
Wali refers him to the Wali of Shinaz. The man says no, they will not
listen to me because I live here. The Wali directs the assistant *qadhi* to
write a letter to the Wali of Shinaz concerning the matter. Then he
returns to the previous case.

Case 6. (which has been proceeding noisily with the head *qadhi*).
Together, they reach the decision that the head *qadhi* will go tomorrow
to the site. There the two parties will produce witnesses to interpret and
substantiate their conflicting documents and claims.

Case 8. Dismissed, as the letter introducing it is misaddressed to "the
Shaikh of Sohar," a nonexistent person who would have been of lower
rank than the Wali.

Case 9. Three persons own a garden jointly; a group of four others
lay claim to it. The first three are represented by only one of them, who
claims to speak for the others. As he has no proof of such authority, the
Wali postpones the case until proof is produced or all the owners meet.

Case 4. A *wasta* (mediator/spokesman/patron) appears on behalf of the arrested man. The Wali declares that the government will hold the land as security for his good behavior, and orders the man released.

Case 10. The head *qadhi* reads a letter of complaint in the case: A has closed B's right of way to B's garden. This is confirmed by witnesses. "And why have not you and your friends just opened the road again?" Because A resists and threatens, and, futhermore, the trees used to barricade the road were cut in B's garden. Verdict: A is sent off to jail with an *askar*.

Case 11. A very old and unsophisticated man wishes to have a passport for the Haj pilgrimage, but lacks papers to establish his identity. The Wali treats him gently yet impersonally and without condescension, directs him where to sit, then explains several times to be sure he understands that he must produce three witnesses and come back with them.

Case 12. A husband complains against his wife and father-in-law. The latter are summoned. Summonses are written by the clerks in the waiting hall, and sent off with *askars* to be served immediately.

Case 4. The arrested garden owner reappears with his patron. The Wali lectures him to show respect, and not build a fence than can inconvenience his neighbor, or plant new trees against the hut. The man is sullen and negative, and the Wali shows irritation, but the patron quickly intervenes and guarantees that the conditions will be respected.

Case 13. A garden owner complains that he wishes to build a thorn fence around his property, but his neighbor says he will pour gasoline on it and burn it down if he does. The Wali says: "Build your fence. If he burns it down, *then* complain to me."

Case 14. An old woman has been sitting outside the window on the veranda for a long time. She is a widow with no close relative to plead her case. Complaint: she has been living in a hut on a shaikh's land, but now he wants to plant trees there, and has evicted her. The Shaikh is summoned, and the case postponed till tomorrow.

Case 9. The representative of one group of owners comes back with a witnessed declaration that he speaks on behalf of the others. But meanwhile the other party has left. Case postponed.

Case 15. A prominent shaikh arrives, who has been called from the approximately 150-km-distant town of Kabura. He has been charged 50 Rials for damages to a Sohar resident in connection with an automobile accident, but refuses to pay. The Wali lectures him, does not let himself be interrupted when the shaikh starts defending himself, just continues his monologue: a shaikh should be an example to the people; his position gives him responsibility, not privilege; the claimant has been patient and waited eight months instead of two. The Wali threatens to arrest the shaikh. He says the shaikh was chosen by the Sultan because he would be straight, but now he cannot be trusted. How can there be a crooked shaikh? Money is finally paid in court before witnesses. All present rise in respect for the sheik as he leaves.

16. A woman complains about not receiving support money from her husband. He defends himself, claiming to have sent the money. He is instructed to bring his father-in-law, but complains that he has already spent three days waiting here and cannot stay longer without losing his job in road construction, 100 km away. The second *qadhi* is instructed to write a letter for the company excusing him, and the parties are summoned for a later date.

Case 17. A tenant cultivator appeals his landowner's demands. The eighteen Rials rent for the garden has always been paid regularly before. Now the crop has been poor, the tenant is unable to pay, and

The gatehouse of the fort.

would rather relinquish his tenancy. The owner refuses to release him from his contract, and demands payment. The head *qadhi* admonishes each side to show understanding: God will reward the owner for letting the tenant free; the tenant should honor the agreement to pay, then discontinue the tenancy by not renewing the contract. Final decision: nine Rials to be paid now, nine Rials deferred until the crop has been sold.

At about noon, the Wali breaks off proceedings and calls for his meal—dates, followed by coffee. Shortly thereafter, the court is closed for the day because of the arrival of the Sultan himself on a surprise visit from Muscat.

It is above all by the succession of such cases that the Wali affects the community he governs. Only rarely do more complex and comprehensive matters arise that involve a greater number of persons, and thus potentially a challenge to authority. Such cases were more common before (see Chapter 17), but still occasionally do occur. For instance, disputes about land and grazing between the tribally organized bedouin are political matters of importance still, in which the Wali consults with the Ministry of Interior. Likewise recently, a ruling was made by several Walis on the Batineh coast that fishermen should divide sardine-fishing rights along the beach so that each had rights only in his province, to avoid cross-province conflicts. All the sardine fishermen were much against this ruling, and a move was afoot to present a collective petition to the Sultan. In earlier epochs, on the other hand, direct challenges to authority and the state itself also took place, as in the long confrontation with the independent forces of the Imam in interior Oman until 1959, and a Baluch soldiers' mutiny a few years previously. Occasional public works may also be of signal importance: the construction of a new lane of shops in the market, in former times the construction of defensive walls and towers and of irrigation canals, and today (authorized and financed through the central ministries) the construction of roads and other development.

But first and foremost it is, and has been, the cumulative effect of the settlement of a myriad of small cases that has served to increase or erode a Wali's authority, and thereby the degree of order and security in the town. Numerous historical cases can be found to illustrate the effects of the quality of administration on such trade-based towns in the Middle East: how security and justice encourage trade, enterprise, and prosperity and how their absence leads to failure of trade, exodus of traders, and swift decline. Obviously, changing economic and commercial factors provide the preconditions for prosperity or decline, but given the same basic situation, one town may grow as another falls apart.

A key factor in this tradition of government, besides political skill, is *style*. Even where political compromise is necessary, the fiction of absolute authority should be maintained, and the Wali should be at once Solomonic and sovereign. There can be no horsetrading over sovereignity, no political participation, no giving heed to factions or interest groups. Pleaders meet as private, separate individuals before the controller of justice and power; they should prove their right, not their following or support. The *wasta* who may appear should be there at most as a reliable character witness or one prepared to take responsibility for the pleader's good behavior, not as a patron defending his clients. When the sardine fishermen sought to abrogate the Walis' decision, it was essential (and very complicated) for them to avoid the appearance of insubordination and political pressure, or the emergence of any leaders of the collectivity; great effort was made to emphasize the petition as a humble request for favor in a matter of welfare for "us poor folk." Whatever political realities of interest groups and factions do exist cannot be allowed to be exhibited and flaunted before the Wali, and his style should demonstrate their absence, and the powerlessness of the person before the state.

In this context, one can understand better the tremendous emphasis on information and confidential intelligence in these traditional political systems: the understanding of attitudes, public support, and crossing factions which is required for political realism must be acquired by the Wali elsewhere, by covert channels, and must be at his command in advance of the public occasions for imperious decisions. These ideals of style are reflected in folk descriptions of the much-admired Wali Sultan bin·Hamud of some years back: "No one dared to complain to him, unless they were in the right and had been wronged by someone. He was very severe with unnecessary and unfounded complaints. And you must never talk back to him. With Sultan bin Hamud, you gave your evidence when you were asked, in brief words, and that was all." The slave Wali Mudaffar of about forty years ago is likewise greatly admired for his severity and forcefulness. But such severity should be for a purpose, and not in conflict with justice. Mudaffar's elder brother and predecessor as Wali, Salem, was so repressive that, according to the popular account, the population of Sohar petitioned Sultan Feisal bin Turki to transfer him. But the Sultan answered, "No. Since you have spoken against him, you shall have him for as long as he lives." So they all had to try to settle their cases between themselves with the aid of the shaikhs, and avoided going to the Wali altogether, for as long as Salem lived.

In a formal interview, the Wali, in characteristic Omani fashion, emphasized the diversity of role solutions and the individual character of each Wali. In harmony with Omani ideals, he was quite unwilling to give an account of his personal ideals or of critical experiences and notable successes in his career. It would be *seb* (wrong and shameful) to applaud one's own acts, he explained; "And perhaps what a person thinks he has done well, some others may think he has done badly. Also, it is for the government to judge what is good and right. But the Wali should make his province function as well as possible." What are the qualities required to make a good Wali? "By each according to his own character. But he must not be accessible to favors and bribes. He should be honest *(amana)*, and he should be compassionate *(ikhlas)*. A Wali should know (that is, be true to) his God; he should know his Sultan; he should know his government; he should know justice."

It is the same from the point of view of most of the townspeople of Sohar. Their model of the state is one not of participation from below but of imposition of (necessary and desired) constraints from above defining the area of choice and free activity for the individual. In the imagery of one informant: "If you try planting a garden without fences, animals come and go, they spoil the crop, they eat; if there are fruits, thieves steal them—nothing will grow properly. But if you put control over it, have a strong wall and a gate and a lock, then everything will prosper and your garden will be green." As we may see through both a comparison with inner Oman and a discussion of local political history and change in Sohar, this is not the only form of administration that is familiar to Sohar and not the only one that could persist there; but it is entirely dominant in the present constitution of Sohar, and, to my understanding, supplies the premises for the kinds of ethnic plurality and subcultural complexity characteristic of this community. Starting out with the image of these regulating and protecting walls, we may now focus on the variety of private gardens that have sprung up between them.

Part 2

The Categories of Cultural Diversity Within Sohar

The cultural multiplicity found within Sohar does not show any single, overarching pattern. Thus, one cannot know from a person's ethnic group membership what will be his/her occupation, or from a person's religious congregation what will be that person's class, or neighborhood of residence, or mother tongue. To understand the constitution of persons and society, and the conditions of reproduction of cultural diversity, we first need to sort out all the main identities that among Soharis entail participation in a distinctive cultural tradition—a significant body of knowledge, beliefs, skills, and standards that is shared by members of that particular social category and embraced by them as distinctively their own.

Identities or social categories may be ordered in two ways. They may be grouped in sets of alternatives, where a person can normally occupy only one position, that is, either Arab or Baluchi or some other ethnic group but not simultaneously several, and either Sunni or Shiah or Hindu but not simultaneously a member of several religious communities. We thereby sort out the dimensions—ethnicity, religious community, etc.—along which participation in cultural traditions is divided and ordered. Second, we may search for patterns in which some identities are regularly associated in persons, that is, observe that Baluchis are regularly Sunnis, though they vary in class and occupation, while an Arab ethnic identity does not predicate religious affiliation. Only after mapping the whole inventory of such social categories, and their patterns of order, can we specify the circumstances under which any particular cultural tradition is maintained and affected by the coexistence of other cultural traditions in this complex plural situation. The following six chapters seek to document briefly each major set of alternative culture-bearing identities, leading to a general discussion of the patterns they exhibit in chapter 10.

Ethnic Groups

The population of Sohar sees itself as composed of a number of distinctive ethnic groups, each with its characteristic cultural heritage. A person's membership in one or another of these groups entails, as far as Soharis are concerned, a distinctive historical and geographical origin (though there is disagreement about the specifics), an unalterable ascribed identity (though processes of assimilation are acknowledged sometimes to take place), a distinctive mother tongue (though this may also be "lost"), and embeddedness in a distinctive kinship network (though individual exceptions are recognized to exist). The primary groups that constitute the present Sohar are Arab, Baluch, Ajam (that is, Persian), Zidgali, and Banyan (that is, Kutchi-speaking Hindu). Other groups are very recent and not yet entrenched in the social system of Sohar, or they have disappeared and will be noted only in passing.

Men do not signal ethnic identity in style of dress, but wear a common range of colors and cuts, except for the Banyans. The most common male dress is an ankle-long tunic *(dishdasha)* in white material without belt, and a small, soft embroidered cap *(kumma)*, also white, with light-colored embroidery. But various tan and khaki-colored cloth, or even pastel or strong blue, purple, etc., may also be used, and some men wear belts, with or without the traditional curved silver dagger. White or checkered blue or red, small turbans are also fairly common (especially among persons working in the sun); and the flowing robes and headdress with black double-hoop support characteristic of the Gulf, are also worn, by persons who have migrated there to work. Women's clothes are in part ethnically distinctive as I shall mention below, but in public they are largely hidden beneath identical black cloaks *(abba)*. Despite lack of explicit signs, however, Soharis claim to be able to spot a man's ethnic identity in public by his "face"—presumably, his physiognomy, build, posture, and perhaps particularly facial expressions reflecting mother tongue. Though I can believe that this is largely true, the signals are so submerged in more marked variations of color, racial type, class, and wealth that I myself

37

*An Arab, head of a small tribe. For a portrait of a male Ajam, see
the illustration on p. 51; for a Banyan, see the illustration on
p. 55; for a Baluch, see the illustration on p. 205.*

was never able to achieve any degree of reliability in my attempts at
identification, and people were not able to point out or describe
precisely the features by which they could tell.

The predominant ethnic group, both numerically and culturally, is
the Arab. People who regard themselves as Arabs make up from
one-half to two-thirds of the population of Sohar, and the Arabic
language is spoken by all. Although for some purposes migrations
from the Yemen and the Syrian desert are referred to, Arabs ideally
regard themselves as "local" stock, and pride themselves on being the
original and real Omanis, despite a state-sponsored ideology that
frowns on such statements and makes citizenship the "real" criterion of
Omani status. All the cultural features described in this book, unless
otherwise specified, are regarded as the culture of this group; and it

provides a common reference and set of premises for the whole population.

A clearly contrasting ethnic identity is that of the Baluch. All Baluchis in Sohar are regarded as descended from ancestors in Baluchistan, the country on the north coast of the Gulf of Oman, in Iran and Pakistan. Many families know their own history of migration, and the village or region of Baluchistan from which they (that is, their agnatic ancestors) hailed: different Baluchis with whom I discussed this reported to be from first-generation to seventh-generation immigrants. Two modes of migration have been common. First, the Sultans of Oman have for centuries systematically recruited soldiers from Baluchistan for the army, and such recruits have often brought their families and settled in Oman.* Second, groups of Baluchi families have fled their homeland for political or purely economic reasons, and come by ship to the Oman coast, asking the local Wali's permission to settle. Where land was available and other circumstances congenial, such permission has been granted, creating usually a Baluchi settlement that in due course has grown, through further immigration and internal growth, into a mixed but predominantly Baluchi village. The two villages of Sallan and Zaffran, adjoining Sohar to the north, have such a history. These Baluchi settlers characteristically brought their own language and customs and continued to practice them in their new locality. They were in contact with Baluchistan through visits and new migrants and to some extent kept up with the changing customs and style of their places of origin.

The Baluch female dress has very wide, flowing sleeves and a very loose bodice, in contrast to the Arabs' more close-fitting and swung-waisted dress. The pantaloons are wide at the top and very narrow at the calf, whereas those of the Arabs are more straight. Both dress and pantaloons have elaborate embroidery and appliqué, while those of Arabs are much simpler. These featues of dress they reportedly share with Baluchistan, and also certain items of jewelry, the cut of their *burqa* (facemask), and their (now largely abandoned) special wedding burqas. But they also modify their styles, and in part adopt those of their Arab neighbors. In a certain number of customs, the explicit contrast to Arab customs is emphasized. Thus, Baluchis marry in the summer season, whereas Arabs avoid the summer; the Baluchi groom buys gold

---

*Kelly (1968) traces this policy of recruitment of Baluch mercenaries to Ahmad ibn Sa'id, who was elected Sultan in 1749, and claims it was not practiced by the preceeding Ya'ariba dynasty (Kelly 1968:10). However, the Portuguese report both confronting and employing Baluch soldiers in Oman in the sixteenth and seventeenth centuries (see Miles 1919:196), so there is every reason to assume the pattern to have considerably greater antiquity.

(particularly at least one gold sovereign of British Indian mint), which he himself presents to his bride, whereas Arab grooms give a bride price to the father-in-law, for him to buy gold for the bride at his discretion; for Baluchis the fact of virginity remains private, whereas Arabs give public proof; the Baluchi nuptial hut is constructed in the bride's home, whereas Arabs place it in the groom's home. This last feature is also connected with a Baluch preference for initial uxorilocality, often extending over a number of years and effecting a pattern of matrilocal joint households, rather than the Arab pattern of patrilocality (see table 1, chapter 12). Finally, Baluchis also normally use the Baluchi language, an Indo-European language of the Iranian branch, both as a domestic language and among themselves in public. In settlements with a considerable Baluchi population, the resident Arabs (at least the men), normally have considerable bilingual fluency.

Local people estimate Baluchis in Sohar and adjoining coastal villages to constitute about one-quarter of the local population. The extent and intensity to which Baluchi custom and language are cultivated vary considerably (as I shall discuss in chapter 18), but many Baluchi homes, especially where they cluster in neighborhoods, show a cultural vitality that is striking, and in many ways more colorful and assertive than that of Arabs.

Ajams, that is, Persians, form the third major group in Sohar, as on the Batineh coast generally. The name is the traditional Omani name for Persians; thus, all pre-Islamic structures are referred to as having been built by the Ajams, the Sassanian government of that time. But the Ajams of Sohar are more recent immigrants from Iran, varying from first generation to eighth generation in different families. By Soharis they are so strongly associated with the Shiah sect that townspeople often refer to that religious community as Ajam rather than Jaffari, and may even call Arabs of the Shiah persuasion "Ajam," whereas Sunni Persian speakers are sometimes differentiated as "Irani." Their own view is that the term properly refers to an ethnic group. There are 2,000–3,000 Ajams in Sohar; in their domestic customs they are very similar to Arabs and can be distinguished from them only by the more transient, changing markers of local style. There are variations in the dialect of Persian spoken by different blocks of Ajams hailing from different parts of Iran (see chapter 18) and a tendency to loss of full command of the Persian language in many families.

Zidgalis form a small minority group. I do not know their true ethnological position, but the agreement in Sohar is that they are a people found only on the Oman coast, especially in the Batineh. Though they claim originally to be descended from Arabs, they accept the folk etymology of their name as being Sindh-gali, that is, a man from Sindh, the lower Indus valley. Their language is clearly Indo-Aryan, and closely related to Kutchi, modern Sindhi, and the language of the Khoja minority group in Mattrah-Muscat. The total population of Zidgalis in Oman probably does not reach 10,000; in Sohar today there are only eight households of Zidgalis, with a population of perhaps fifty persons. In the particulars of their customs—for example, with respect to marriage practice—they resemble Baluchis closely. Competence in the Zidgalis language is transmitted to children only when both parents are Zidgalis.

Finally, the Banyans form a distinctive, traditional community in Sohar and other major towns on the Batineh coast. Kutchi speakers from Sindh and Kutch proper, they regard their present center as Bombay and are literate in Gujerati. Apart from one resident Brahmin, they are all of the Bhatiya caste, a merchant caste dispersed from East Africa to Singapore and claiming Kshatriya varna status. As Hindus, they prefer to group themselves in a separate residential community with separate and exclusive wells; their cows wander in the few short lanes of the Hindu neighborhood, where also the women move somewhat freely and can sometimes be observed in their colorful saris, with exposed arms, faces, and waists, like foreign butterflies in a country of blackveiled women. The Banyan community of Sohar today consists of thirty-five to forty persons. Nearly all were born in Bombay, Kutch, or prepartition Sindh; but many are second generation and third generation in their association with Oman and the existence of a Banyan community goes back many generations.

Until fairly recently, there was also a small Khoja community of Ismaili shopkeepers in Sohar, alternatively known as Hyderabadis or Luwatiyas. This whole community in Oman used to hold British passports, but with India's independence in 1947 they had to choose between Indian and Omani citizenship. Whereas most members of the much larger Khoja population in Mattrah opted for Omani citizenship, those of Sohar mostly chose Indian, and have now disappeared from the town (though the Banyans, as Indian passport holders, have remained). Finally, in the memory of the very oldest residents of Sohar, there were also the last members of a once-flourishing Jewish community related to the Bani Israel of India. Of the more recent arrivals, Pakistani labor migrants are beginning to take on the features of an established ethnic category, but still without the full routinization of identity and interaction that would give them the quality of a resident component of the community.

5

"Blood" and Its Correlates— the Social and Cultural Entailments of Descent and Slavery

A second set of identities that in Sohar entails participation in culturally distinctive tradition derives, somewhat indirectly, from the notion of descent in its narrower sense. In speaking of almost any kind of social identity or personal quality, Soharis will frequently make use of an idiom of descent and physical determination. Thus, membership in an ethnic group (or a religious congregation, or the bedouin life-style, etc.) may be represented by them as arising from birth and being determined by "blood." Likewise, any personal qualities or failings may be explained by referring to the purity, or lack of purity, of family and pedigree. While every person (or, among men, at least every adult male) is regarded as being responsible for himself and his own acts, there is thus an underlying theory that the moral qualities and personal characteristics which are revealed by acts are, in some ultimate sense, the consequences of an inherent nature which has an inherited, physical basis. Yet as I have discussed, Soharis do recognize that ethnic membership is a matter of domestic experience and early socialization, rather than physical determination. It is therefore meaningful to distinguish ethnic identity from that of descent in a stricter and narrower sense, and from this narrower concept of birth determination there arise other social groups, namely, those referred to as *qabīla* (tribe) and the stigmatized category of *xaddām* (singular: *xādim*), that is, (ex-)slaves. In this chapter I shall try to describe, briefly, these main groupings that emerge from Sohari conceptualizations of "blood," the attitudes associated with membership in them, and the cultural features of the traditions that are sustained by these identities.*

*A special difficulty arises in this exposition: the concepts by which these social distinctions, and components of the descent ideology, are handled in Sohari discourse and explanations are exceptionally many and various. To my understanding, this elaboration does not truly reflect the complexity and importance of these issues in Sohari life and consciousness but rather reflects their importance, at previous times and in distant places, in the great tradition from which Soharis derive much of their vocabulary and concepts. Certainly, in the context

42

Soharis subscribe to a basic patrilineal ideology of descent and an associated concept of tribe; and such tribes make claims to differentiation with respect to dignity and excellence, qualities that are conceived of as physically embodied in their component members and concretely conceptualized in terms of "blood." But it is also thought that the excellence of a line of (patrilineal) descent is affected by the "blood" brought into the group by their in-marrying wives, so it is always in danger of being spoiled or of having been surreptitiously spoiled in the past. Thus, in the present generation a person's claim to rank is determined not only by his or her paternity but also by the blood that comes from his or her mother, and by the general reputation of purity of blood associated with the paternal lineage. To this extent, descent is simultaneously conceived of as strictly patrilineal—in its group membership aspect—and as bilateral—in its rules for tracing the origins of a person's inherent qualities. Such an apparently contradictory view is less paradoxical, it might be noted, in the context of an ideology that enjoins agnatic endogamy through marriage with a father's brother's daughter (even when such marriages have fairly low frequencies), than it might have been were the descent groups conceptually exogamous.

In terms of traditional and shared Arabic ideals, patrilineal descent entails membership in a tribe, which is corporate for at least some

---

of more formal interviews, senior Sohari men will try to marshal everything they know of traditional, in part literate and scholarly, Arabic lineage and descent concepts, so as to construct an interpretation of Sohari society based on them. It would thus have been possible for me to elicit such a model from "knowledgeable" informants and obtain an apparently authoritative imprimatur for applying it to the description and analysis of social rank and family histories in Sohar. What is more, such constructs and concepts would facilitate a quite elaborate and systematic discussion of Sohar in terms amenable to traditional anthropological "lineage analyses" and would invite comparisons to parts of the existing literature on Arabic and related social structures. Yet it is my understanding that such a description and analysis would be so biased as to be truly misleading and false, in the sense that it would neither reveal the factors that generate the social patterns that may be observed nor report the constructs in terms of which Soharis reflect on their society and represent their social patterns to themselves. I can all too readily visualize a development where an increased anthropological attention to Omani materials might produce a growing literature pursuing this unproductive theme. Thus, when in the present context I neither develop such an analysis nor refute it systematically, it is not because I have overlooked that alternative but because I judge it to divert attention from other and more productive models and issues for the analysis of culture and society in Sohar. For a further development of this theme, see chapter 12.

purposes. In contemporary Sohari society there is little trace of such corporate activity in the lives of most people, but Soharis are definite in claiming that this was different in the recent past, when tribes were an important political reality in town (see chapter 17). At that time, however, membership in the political corporation constituted by a tribe was not only a matter of birth ascription but also for some persons and groups, a matter of transactions and legal status. There is evidence of both clientship relations arising from (collective) debt bondage (see chapter 18) and, more pervasively, the association of the considerable population of slaves with the tribal corporations of their owners. When asked to enumerate his tribe, one person, himself a member of a small but historically distinguished Baluch tribe, carefully listed not only the households of his own agnates but also ten households of ex-slaves. What is more, this legal status of slave was itself likewise conceived as a hereditary condition, determined by descent. A discussion of descent thus leads us in two very different directions: the constitution of descent groups and tribes, and the division of the population into the categories of normal free persons versus slaves, now ex-slaves. As the first set, the descent groups or tribes, are only indirectly associated with difference in cultural traditions, I shall discuss them only briefly before turning to the more complex issue of the definition and constitution of the ex-slave category, associated with a distinctive subculture.

Distinctions of tribe and descent line are both unclear in their demarcation (there is very little ramifying genealogical knowledge) and variable in their content among ethnic groups and lifestyles. For most persons they serve merely as an idiom for pride or claims to prestige for self and family. Among Arabs, tribal identity is most important in the top echelon of society and among the bedouin. Most distinguished is membership in the Al Bu Said group, entailing a right to respect and considerable privilege, reinforced by the probability that the Sultan will have chosen to vest an Al Bu Said with authority and important functions for the state. Likewise, tribal membership is a primary identity for the settled bedoiun of the inner agricultural zone, where groups such as the Makabil and the Shabli tribes (see chapter 19) occupy compact and virtually exclusive territories, have their separate shaikhs, and practice predominant tribal endogamy. In the town proper, on the other hand, ordinary people do not and need not care what their tribe might be. Persons with pretensions to rank and prominence may choose to express their claims in terms of distinctions of tribe and descent, but cannot derive their influence from such sources.

Among the Baluchis, a similar but more constricted range is found: they lack a dynasty, but have some distinguished groups among them and some communities with a fairly intact tribal organization, though most are relatively unconcerned about the larger collective identities defined by descent. Among the Ajams, the same terminology of tribes and patriliny is employed, but with a rather different basis: the origins of the "tribes" are acknowledged to be not a single family but simply derivation from the same district and social category. Thus, the tribe called Awadiya are the descendants of Persian-speaking Sunnis from Ahwaz in Khuzistan in Iran who by various routes, mostly via the south Persian town of Bandar Abbas, have arrived in Sohar (see chapter 18). Ascription to this group today, on the other hand, is by birth and follows patrilineal criteria. Other families, longer settled in Sohar, may have a less clear picture of place of origin in Iran and identify themselves in terms of descent with small, local lineages within the Ajam category. Membership in such groups gives little claim to rank, but they may have considerable importance for the individual of minority status.

How these different identities are in fact assumed and deployed in shaping real lives is a topic to which I shall return later; my concern now is to clarify ideas behind them as components of differentiation. There are essentially two, which, despite any explicit modern ideology of equality, it is unrealistic for any resident of Sohar to deny: the dignity of pure Arabic descent over other kinds of origin, diffusely acknowledged as inherent in the Arabic origin of Islam, and the stigma of slave admixture. Implications of these premises assert themselves in various ways. Members of the Arab ethnic group will on occasion elaborate genealogical claims in the form of incomplete strings of named ascendants, which to an anthropologist sensitized to lineage organizations seem both unsubstantial and purposeless. Another argument is presented by some Baluchis and others that some Baluch lines are "really" Arab, descended from ancestors who at the time of the Prophet were deputed to live and work among the Baluch to bring them Islam. Zidgalis claim descent from Azd, the apical Arab from whom a number of the genealogically ancient tribes of the Oman area have sprung. (He is represented by Zidgalis as having three sons: one remained in southwestern Arabia, one is the ancestor of the Al Bu Said, and the third traveled to Sindh and is the ancestor of the Zidgalis.) Such claims are on occasion contradicted by third parties on subsequent, private occasions: "No, Zidgalis are not of good families. I would sooner marry my daughter to an Englishman, to a Hindu; not for 3 million Rials would I give my daughter to a Zidgali."

On such relatively rare occasions when descent identities are employed destructively against other persons not present, rather than constructively to enhance the claims of oneself or others, the issue of slave admixture is generally brought in: "You can see it on their face, if you know how, even if you do not know their family history. Like Shaikha, the wife of Mohammed—she is not pure Arab, though she looks very white and attractive. Look at her son; he is quite dark. And look at her brother Ahmed; he is pitch black. They are of one father, only different mothers, and Ahmed's mother is a slave. [But that proves nothing about the agnatic half-sister?] Yes, because the father had some slave blood too, otherwise he would never have married a slave." Or, in the words of a group of women reflecting on the eternal themes of humility and justice: "Look at Fatima: though her parents look white, she is of slave descent. Her grandparents were dark, and therefore God made her dark so that her family will remember their true origin and not pretend to be better than they are."

While even the taint of slave admixture is a matter of some significance for a person in Sohar today, descent in male line from slaves gives rise to an unambiguous membership in a distinctive and stigmatized social category, that of a *xādim*. Since this category has reference to a legal status which is now abolished, and since the social attitudes toward members as well as the cultural characteristics of members reflect a particular historical experience, we need to view the status of the *xaddām* in a somewhat retrospective, historical context.

There can be no doubt that Omanis were major agents of the slave trade in the Indian Ocean, and that the prosperity of Oman's coastal towns in the seventeenth through nineteenth centuries depended on this trade as well as trade in spices and other Eastern and tropical African products. Africans were shipped from Zanzibar and the East African coast, and brought via Oman for sale to eastern Arabia, to the Ottoman Empire via Basrah, to Iran and Central Asia, and to India. With increased British supression of this trade, the flow of new African slaves decreased, but the number of successive treaties concluded on the subject between Oman and Britain (1822, 1838, 1845, 1873) indicates the continuation of a certain amount of commerce in slaves despite the increasingly effective British blockade. Semipublic slave markets have indeed persisted in interior towns, especially the Bureimi oasis, till very recently (though these have in part depended on the kidnapping of children from marginal settlements within Oman; see chapter 15).

In Sohar town the failure of new imports led to a discontinuation of markets for the purchase and sale of slaves, but ownership of the existing slave population was perpetuated until abolition, some time around 1955–60. Meanwhile, the encouragement contained in the Koran for slaveowners to free their slaves was also heeded by pious persons, so a category of freed ex-slaves and their issue, resident in Sohar, also emerged progressively.

The legal position of slaves was defined and controlled by Shariah. Being a slave was a hereditary condition, transmitted through descent from the father; an owner's acknowledged offspring with a slave concubine was thus by definition freeborn. There was some confusion among people as to the allocation of property rights to slave children, but the apparently more knowledgeable informants claimed that ownership of the issue of slave parents devolved on the owner of the mother, not the owner of the father. The normal pattern, however, was for marriages to be arranged between slaves belonging to the same owner, and therefore this question did not normally arise.

As noted, slaves were without descent rights in family lines of their own; on the contrary, they were counted as members of their owners' tribes. Thereby they also acquired an indirect ethnic identity: there were Arab slaves, Baluchi slaves, and Ajam slaves according to the ethnic identity of their owners. But to my knowledge, slaves normally spoke Arabic as their first language, regardless of the household language of their masters. While there were fresh imports of recently captured African slaves, dealers and purchasers were concerned to separate persons of exotic language communities, so no African languages, not even Swahili, have persisted among Sohari slaves.

By 1950, the following population components were thus deriving from slave status: (1) a basic population of continuing slaves, all of them Omani born (in some cases they represented the first generation issue of slaves brought from East Africa [see chapter 15], while most had a longer pedigree of Omani association and a majority had a several-generations-long association with a particular family of owners); (2) a growing population of freed slaves, and the descendents of such freed persons; and (3) children of slave women and free fathers, who were legally free persons with descent rights from their father but who by social prejudice were generally regarded together with those of category 2.

With abolition by 1960, these three categories seem essentially to have been collapsed in Sohari consciousness, and today ex-slaves compose a distinctive category of perhaps 10 percent of the total resident population in town. They are still referred to, and often identify themselves, as slaves, *xaddām,* though the term itself is frowned upon by the present authorities and persons are legally protected against being called a *xādim* or being pressed to use the traditional submissive term of address "Habib," that is, "master." Some ex-slaves choose to maintain their association with previous masters through various symbolic means, notably by using submissive greetings, by serving as butchers for the ex-master's household, and by having a special role at the life-crisis ceremonies of the superior family. At the central event of the wedding of a daughter from that family, they assist in all practical matters and bar the entrance when the groom's party comes to fetch the bride, until a gift of up to fifteen Rials is given to the ex-slave. Other slaves chose to repudiate all connections with their former owners, often joining what seems to have been a rather massive exodus at the time of manumission, traveling as labor migrants to Kuwait or elsewhere regardless of age and marital status, and returning only now after fifteen to twenty years, if at all.

Most ex-slaves do not seem to claim any tribal association, and in contemporary society it has little salience. The ex-slaves of the Al Bu Said governor—probably the last to obtain freedom in Sohar— occasionally claim to belong to the highly prestigious Al Bu Said tribe. Such claims produce irritation among other Soharis, who in private refute them with indignation, explaining that they are not "of the Al Bu Said" at all, only xaddām ma ʿà Al Bu Said (slaves of the Al Bu Said).

In the eyes of other Soharis, the ex-slaves make up essentially a stigmatized, internally unsegmented, nontribal, Arabic-speaking group. Though there are no legal sanctions to support it, there are strong social pressures to isolate them as an endogamous unit (see chapter 19). Their African somatic features are taken as a social indicator of their status, and are generally devalued in the population at large ("we are white and they are black"). Indeed, the concepts of descent and purity employed by other Soharis seem to derive less from positive traditions and identifications with Arab genealogies than from the absence of African somatic features in the family. The higher frequency of such traces in the dynasty and most distinguished families (who were most closely surrounded by slaves, slave concubines, and slave-mothered collaterals) constitutes a kind of paradox to more thoughtful Sohari observers, and indeed is sometimes explained precisely in terms of slave admixture and contrasted to the Arabic purity of ordinary persons. But since the genealogies that substantiate such purity are the characteristic feature of bedouin—themselves another stigmatized group (see chapter 19)—this whole field of claims and conceptualizations remains rather unresolved.

Both in their own eyes and in the eyes of others, the ex-slave population seems to be conceptualized as a kind of de facto ethnic group. Indeed, they do exhibit a number of cultural features that are distinctive to them. This is most apparent in their rather characteristic style of self-presentation. Men of slave descent are more informal and careless in their manners; they dress more loudly and act more assertively and aggressively. Women of slave descent are likewise less shy and more assertive and noisy in public than other women; they dress less modestly and rarely wear the facemask. Gait and posture are distinctive, as are the use and modulation of voice. Both sexes also perform acts that are regarded as dishonorable by others: the men assume occupations that are avoided by others, such as butchering; men play music in public for money; and the women sing as public entertainment at weddings.

Ex-slaves entertaining at a wedding.

A close investigation of this whole social category, and the cultural stream associated with it, would be of considerable general interest. On the one hand the historical situation of slavery is so close as to be within the clear memory of living informants, while another sector of freedmen has a considerable time depth. At the same time the ex-slave population shows an unusual spectrum of social rank, from propertyless coolies to both wealthy and well-connected persons. (In the words of one critic: "Some ignorant people used to be afraid of the slaves, and show them respect because they were close to the Wali. Such people were cowardly, and would lick the boots of the powerful ones.") The number of distinctive African survivals in the assemblage that composes their subculture seems small, despite a temporally close and ethnographically fairly homogeneous connection with Zanzibar and the East African coast, and the factors in the host society responsible for imposing or inducing patterns and conceptions of local origin should be more readily identifiable than in more distant historical material. Thus, valuable comparative material might be provided for comparison with research along these lines that is being pursued for the New World (see, for example, Mintz and Price 1976).

Religious Groups

Differences in religion produce significant distinctions of culture and identity. The truly fundamental distinction is between Moslem and Hindu, and is coterminous with that between the Sohari majority population and the Banyan community. These resident Hindus have no shrines in Sohar and perform no collective religious rites; they do, however, have a resident Brahmin among them and practice such domestic rituals as they deem necessary. Their interaction with the Moslem community is limited to commercial and similar instrumental contexts.

The other major division, one more actively emotionally charged, is that between Sunnis and Ibadhis on the one hand and Shiahs on the other. Shiahs differ from the majority community in a number of beliefs and practices, most notably those expressed in their central celebration of Muharram (commemorating the martyrdom of Ali's son Hussein), as well as all those distinctive features that derive from the practice of Shiah law. There is also a certain body of domestic practice and belief that differentiates Shiahs from Sunnis.

Organizationally, Shiahs segregate themselves in exclusive mosques in which they will not allow non-Shiahs. There are two such mosques in Sohar, and the older one is claimed to be very ancient. The congregation further maintains eight meeting houses (*mātam*), which likewise serve as places of ritual assembly but in which outsiders (particularly women and children) may be allowed. Shiahs have their separate graveyards, though lack of available space today causes a certain intermixture of Shiah and Sunni graves. Residentially, the congregations live intermixed, but with a special concentration of Shiahs in the northern and northwestern sections of Higrah, the central, walled ward of Sohar.

The Shiah congregation in Sohar is composed predominantly of Ajams, but includes Arabs, supposedly descended from ancestors in the Gulf area, on both the Arabian and Persian sides. Jaffari Shiahs in Sohar town make up about one-quarter of the population. The total

*A leader of the Shiah community, himself an Ajam (Persian),
seventh-generation resident of Sohar.*

population of Jaffaris in the Middle East comprises most Iranians, as
well as some others, and so runs into scores of millions.

The Sunni majority has a number of small, unattended mosques
scattered around Sohar but also several larger, attended ones, of which
the most important is the *Masjid Suq,* located by the marketplace and in
part endowed with property there. It is the common mosque for the
Sunni Friday sermon and prayer, which ideally should be attended by
all men of the congregation and is in fact frequented by many. Women
are not allowed to attend.

Different Sunni residents in Sohar belong variously to all four major
schools of Sunni law: Hanafi, Shafi, Malaki, and Hanbali. There are
no collective occasions where distinctions of school of law are expressed
among them—they pray together in congregations determined by
propinquity and neighborhood. But there is a close correspondence
between school and ethnic group, reflecting historical circumstances
and the fact that birth-ascribed membership is very rarely changed.
Thus, Baluchis, Zidgalis, and the Sunni Ajams all belong to the Hanafi
school, while most Arabs are Shafi except for families of relatively

recent central Arabian origin, who may be Malaki or Hanbali. These differences in school of law entail only slight differences in the details of private law and ritual prescriptions, and are not directly associated with any other significant cultural differences.

The Ibadhis, though a much smaller group, many of whom are only temporarily resident in Sohar, enjoy the patronage of the Sultanate and are thus rather well endowed. They have several smaller mosques and one large Friday mosque. On occasion the Wali, or one of the *qadhis*, will lead the prayers and give the Friday sermon there, in place of the regular speaker, who is himself an ex-Wali and notable of the Al Bu Said family. Ibadhis are found elsewhere mainly in inner Oman and in some small settlements in North Africa. Their total population is probably less than 200,000; in Sohar they number a few hundred.

To summarize: the distinctions of school among the Sunnis do not occasion explicit, collective expression and so add no significant element to ethnic distinctions. Arabs are divided among the several schools, and among Sunnis, Ibadhis, and Shiahs. Ibadhis and Sunnis normally assemble as separate congregations, but they are free to, and occasionally do, visit and join each other, so no strong differentiation results. There is no objection to intermarriage between them. They bury their dead in the same graveyard. They cannot be very clearly ranked: though Ibadhiism is identified with the Sultan and with Oman, it would be most unseemly to derogate the major, orthodox schools of Islam by invidious comparison, so while membership in any one of these schools or sects may be a source of private pride and conviction, they must appear publicly as equal. Not so the distinction between them and the Shiahs: here there is no mixing or ambiguity, the congregations are entirely distinct; and the Shiahs even have separate events and holidays celebrating their heterodoxy. In fact, a considerable curiosity and mythology surround the Shiah celebration of Muharram among Sunnis, and their all-night readings of the tragic story in the Shiah assembly houses are on occasion attended by Sunni women and their children, in the hope of obtaining cures for sickness or infertility. But beneath such folk pragmatism, deep mutual distrust and rejection smolder, on occasion expressed by men in harsh condemnation that the others are "like animals"—that is, without culture and any kind of valued learning—or "worse than animals"—insinuating unspecified immorality. (Women, on the other hand, are less concerned with these theological matters.) Because of these attitudes, intermarriage between the two main camps is strongly resisted and indeed very rare. But, the characteristic Omani ideal and practice of tolerance are so strong that they may bridge even such deep divisions, as in the village of Sallan, where the Koran school of that predominantly Hanafi Baluch community is taught by an Ajam Shiah woman. There are also occasions when the universality of Islam is embraced and expressed explicitly, as in the *nader* (thanksgiving feasts), given in accordance with individual pledges, in honor of God and with participation of all—Shiah and Sunni, woman and man.

Only the small Hindu community is left outside of this, the widest circle of inclusion, for reasons of mutual convenience and, even more, mutual irrelevance. It would seem that, to Soharis, Islam is so self-evidently true and superior as to be unchallenged by the presence of believing Hindus, while the world of the Hindu merchant minority is clearly one of traffic with people of multiple creeds and Gods, irrelevant to one's own kin, caste, and ritual. This Sohari attitude contrasts rather strikingly with the traditional stance of Inner Oman, which, fired by Ibadhi fanaticism, explicitly forbade entrance to all infidels and exercised the prohibition with great vigor and violence against all Hindus (and Christains) until subjected to the Sultan's administration.

7

Occupations, Wealth, and Social Strata

The division of labor, and associated differences in wealth and class constitute a major set of differentiating factors in the society of Sohar. This division of labor is in a very direct sense the premise and reason for the very existence of Sohar: a differentiation of tasks collectively produces the goods and services which sustain the urban population and draws products and wealth from the surrounding countryside, and foreign areas, in exchange. The economic and social dynamics of this system will be treated mainly in chapter 14. At this stage, I wish merely to describe the range of ways making a living practiced by the different residents, and the consequences of these occupations for the style of life and social positions of persons. It is a striking fact—particularly if we choose to compare Sohar with the agricultural communities so often depicted in anthropological literature—that this diversity of occupations, wealth, and class entails a wide diversity of life situations, cumulative experiences, and social participation. In this sense, it is meaningful and fruitful to question the extent to which different persons in Sohar live in the same worlds and can share common understandings. It would seem that those cultural understandings and values that are shared must be anchored elsewhere than in the concrete subsistence activities (which are so different), the skills and assets (which are so unequal), and the social networks and groups (which are so disparate). It is a considerable challenge merely to attempt to describe this diversity.

It should be noted at the start that most occupations are practiced exclusively by men and are reflected only indirectly in the lives of women through the income, rank, and pattern of domestic absence and presence of the men of their household. Some women work outside the home, but they are exceptions: a few old women make use of their privileged access to the female, domestic sphere of strangers to work as hawkers or peddlers offering women's wear and trinkets for sale in the homes. These peddlers are very popular, since rules of modesty and segregation generally bar women from visiting the market, and limit their movements, so news and variety provided by the

A Banyan (Hindu) merchant in his shop.

peddlers' visits are as welcome as their wares. One widow also tries to continue the vegetable stall formerly run by her husband. Otherwise, women, to my knowledge, work only within the domestic setting: sewing for families in the neighborhood, providing occasional trade goods for neighbors, embroidering men's caps for sale, or assisting their husbands in agricultural work in secluded gardens.

Men, on the other hand, pursue such a variety of occupations that it would have been very time consuming to make a complete inventory of occupations and tiresome to present a listing of them all. Many of them have emerged recently; some are disappearing. There are bank clerks, teahouse operators, taxi drivers, irrigation pump mechanics, house builders, carpenters, shepherds, etc. Quite clearly, the town of Sohar as a social system is not significantly changed by the presence or absence of one of them, or even most of them. Even at this stage of simple presentation of empirical diversity, it should be clear that Sohar is so constituted as a truly complex, urban society that we cannot simply name the range of concrete occupations; we can succeed in depicting the division of labor only by depicting the processes whereby differences in tasks are created and combined. I will try to do this by making a set of concrete, empirical assertions.

First, the diversity of occupations found in Sohar is constantly modified by the technology in use in Sohar at the moment, and by the organizations of large-scale society with which Soharis at any time articulate. The former may be illustrated by the emergence of mechanics after the introduction of irrigation pumps in the place of animal-driven lift systems, or by the disappearance of camel drivers and the appearance of truckdrivers with the mechanization of transport. The latter may be illustrated by the establishment in the years 1970 and 1974 of the first two banks in Sohar, employing about a dozen accountants and clerks, mostly of local origin, or by the development at the same time of a public elementary school system and the introduction of schoolteachers into Sohar. Second, the main mechanism for allocation of tasks to persons is a monetized, active labor or employment market combined with an innovative commercial and entrepreneurial practice. There are thus constant activity to establish piecework or short-term employment contracts, and frequent changes of job to improve wage or other conditions of service; there is much speculation in imports, exports, and real property, and a never-ceasing series of new ventures being launched by Sohar residents. Third, the constraints on the untrammeled operation of this market circulation are: certain sectorial or personal ideals of what constitutes suitable activity for oneself, and some general principles of rank and stigma. I shall return briefly to each of these points in a way that should allow me to draw a picture of the pattern of differentiation in Sohar.

Crew beaching a sardine seine fishing boat.

To a certain extent, it is possible to compose a list of the major, traditional occupations practiced in Sohar. Such a list would have to include: merchant, cultivator, pastoralist, fisherman, soldier, sailor, laborer, and "pariah"—a combination of polluting tasks including smithing and circumcision. But to encompass more of the diversity of activites, one would also need to enumerate craftsmen: carpenters, well masons, weavers, etc. To differentiate significant contrasts in way of life and social rank, one would have to break up categories such as "laborer" and distinguish the ubiquitous and lowly coolie of the marketplace, waiting to be asked to carry a sack here and a crate there, from the stable members of a steadily employed construction gang. But such a further listing cannot even begin to cover the modern occupations that Soharis are assuming in increasing members as Sohar develops the range of institutions and services of a modern town.

The fundamental sociological point is that I can find no evidence that Soharis themselves make the assumption that there is a finite list of "kinds" of occupations, subsuming and organizing all the different tasks that are, or were, performed in their society. This component of a castelike or estatelike perspective on the division of labor is absent: new technology entails new tasks, and the jobs and occupations they give rise to are not assimilated into preestablished categories and social identities. On the contrary, their implications and rewards are pragmatically judged, and persons with very different social identities may seek the same jobs and coexist in the same niche.

The main mode of allocation of tasks is a labor and property market characterized by effective monetization and rapid circulation. A survey of cultivated land indicated that the present holders had obtained about 50 percent of the plots by purchase, and 50 percent by inheritance. Biographies (cf. chapter 15) show frequent, rapid, and drastic changes of occupation. Much circulation of labor is mediated through piecework contracts, short-term labor contracts, or sharecropping contracts. Thus, coolies wander in the market and are called when the need arises, paid today 25 Baisa (about 7 cents) per box and 50 Baisa (about 15 cents) per crate carried. Day laborers *(ajîr)* are hired for appointed tasks, for a short (8 A.M.–1 P.M.) day at 1 Rial per day (about $3.00 in 1974). The main labor of date cultivation, concentrated in two to three summer months, is given out on a season's contract *(hassad)* for a stipulated fraction of the products. Sharecroppers *(sammar)* take gardens for one-year periods on a 50-50 share. Full-time laborers *(bidár)* work on a monthly basis, dawn till dusk, for wages up to 60 Rials per month. Fishing crews are signed on for two- to three-month seasons. Contact between employer and employed is generally made through acquaintance networks, but is *ad hoc*, and there is no right, or expectation, of renewal on either side. Even where the relationship is multiplex, as between the shaikh and the commoners of a settled group of bedouin living in a compact neighborhood, there is no expectation that the shaikh as landowner will prefer propertiless tribesmen as his laborers or favor them with renewed contracts. Goods, capital equipment, and houses likewise circulate freely; much attention is given to changing prices, and there is eagerness to speculate. Auctions are freely resorted to in many connections. Capital for entrepreneurial ventures generally derives from personal savings and private loans; there are few controls of a licensing or auditing character. Thus, while one shopkeeper may keep elaborate books and accounts, the next may be illiterate and totally unfamiliar with concepts or considerations of turnover, value of stock, or rate of return. Yet all of them—laborers, self-employed, employers, customers, buyers, and sellers—meet in these fully monetized markets, avid in their pursuit of profitable transactions and wealth.

However, two kinds of considerations constrain actors in their pragmatism with regard to occupation and commercial involvement: ideas and pretentions to rank and the avoidance of stigma, and ideas of suitability and competence deriving from the person's identity and experience. While there are no formal requirements in terms of education or training for most activities, and many men through labor migration have obtained the most unexpected and diverse training and experience, there are some very fundamental avoidances and affinities between certain social categories and certain occupations.

These affinities are perhaps most easily discussed first; they arise from the differences in activities and style of life which the basic tasks performed in different occupations entail for the person. The different sectors of activity constitute strikingly different worlds: the shaded, sedentary comfort of the stalls of the marketplace, with their speculation, shrewdness, and cutthroat business dealings; the fort and administration, with authority and discipline, prison, weapons, and manliness; the relative security and autonomy of cultivation in the private orchards, laboring with soil and water and growing plants; the idleness and discomfort of pasturing animals in the open, scorching wasteland, till recently threatened by sudden danger in what was a lawless fringe area; the changeable circumstances of working on the violent, unpredictable, but sometimes bountiful sea. As a consequence, there are some ethnic groups and descent groups which because of their cultural values or traditional skills inevitably become very closely identified with one or another of these worlds and forms of activity. Herding on the barren plain is done only by the sedentary bedouin living along its edge, though the main occupation of this population is cultivation, as owners, sharecroppers, or laborers. The Beni Omar Arab mountaineers almost monopolize the *askar* posts in the fort, and thereby can show the toughness, physical bravery, and loyalty that are specially emphasized by their values. Other Sohari residents believe that these mountaineers, as country bumpkins, would be helpless in market dealings and clumsy in public service; the Beni Omar tribesmen are generally seen to embody some simple traditional virtues but to be unsuitable for any occupation other than soldiering. Baluchis likewise embrace cultural values of manliness and valor so they favor the occupation of soldiering, but they are in no way limited to this and they freely engage in a wide range of activities like cultivation, fishing, and a certain amount of commerce. The constrained shrewdness and physical inactivity of the marketplace, however, are not particularly congenial to their style; other groups are more suited to it. This is particularly true for the Banyan Hindu trader caste, who as foreigners are barred from political participation and ownership of real property, and who embrace cultural values that abhor violence and force, and foster and reward success in trade. Much the same may be said of most of the Ajams: though many of them own land, very few are oriented toward cultivation, and even fewer toward martial activities: theirs is a highly urban orientation where trade, speculation, and sedentary crafts are preferred and genteel rather than virile self-presentation is emphasized. A similar orientation is also characteristic of the Arabic-speaking Shiah families. But in both these groups, poverty drives many into menial labor and other occupations not particularly favored. Where these involve tasks that are thought demeaning, however, there

Man of Zutti descent, formerly a blacksmith.

is less reluctance to accept them among the ex-slaves than among other poor people, while the truly stigmatizing tasks are performed only by families of *Zutti* (plural: *Zatut*), an Arabic-speaking traditional pariah group now virtually disappearing.

Underlying these preferences and choices, however, are some more general ideas of rank and stratification which are shared by the population as a whole, and are indeed rather similar to ideas current in most urban societies. As I understand them and would summarize them, five basic standards seem to be used to rank occupations in Sohar: autonomy is better than subordination; physical leisure is better than toil; self-employment and ownership of the factors of production are better than selling one's labor; cleanness is better than dirt; and the chances of windfall profits are better than a more secure but smaller return. But all these principles are somewhat modified by the additional rule that association with the government is prestigious.

A few examples may serve to substantiate these principles and demonstrate their specific relevance and priorities. (a) The low rank of employed physical labor, which traditionally has scored low by all five standards, has become very apparent during the present boom in Oman; compensation in the form of drastically increased wages cannot prevent its disappearance. Two effects are evident: cultivation is reduced in garden after garden because agricultural labor is unavailable, and there has been a general exodus of families from town to garden houses, so women and children can privately tend the domestic animals formerly tended by hired labor, and thus secure the family's supply of dairy products and meat. (b) Domestic service is virtually unobtainable. Formerly performed by slaves, it is presently only exceptionally performed by young boys after school hours and for limited tasks, or by transvestites for exhorbitant wages. My understanding is that domestic service is felt to represent an unequivocal submission and failure of autonomy, and that this consideration has a very central place in the ranking of occupations. (c) The same is suggested by the range of tasks to which Pakistani migrant laborers are put. Coming from areas of great unemployment and low wages, and unconcerned with local prestige scales, they are set to perform the tasks that Soharis most of all wish to avoid: barbering, washing and cleaning, waiting and cooking in restaurants, tailoring, and garage and repair work. The low rank of tailors may reflect this activity's direct association with traditional women's work, but common to all these are their personal service aspects, entailing a denial of autonomy. When Soharis perform analogous services, they do so as small, self-employed teahouse operators, or transform the enterprise into something more like a shop, selling biscuits and Pepsi-Cola, or self-produced sweets, etc. Such enterprises are also characteristically run by Ajams. In the case of garages and such, which overwhelmingly employ Pakistanis and recent Iranian labor migrants (not local Ajams), this may reflect the greater mechanical skill and experience of such migrants over those of most Soharis. But quite independent of that, there is also the service aspect of the task, and very visibly its association with grease and dirt, so inimical to the meticulously clean Soharis. Despite their admiration for everything new, and for technological progress, the dirt entailed in such jobs clearly repels; perhaps the best overall physical sign of rank in Sohar is the degree of immaculate whiteness of a man's garment. (d) Trade generally rates higher than farming, as seen by the practice of some farmers to accumulate funds to open a shop, and by the public emphasis on the merchant role by persons occupied in both sectors. This might seem to contradict the major value of autonomy, since the self-employed farmer might be thought to score higher on this criterion than the merchant, who must serve customers. The Sohari view, however, seems to be that the relation of buyer and seller is one between equals, and not one where the latter serves the former. Simultaneously, the physical leisure of a shop in the marketplace scores higher than the toil of cultivation, and the meticulous cleanliness that may be practiced—and displayed—there gives rank over the sweat and dirt of the gardens. (e) Though soldiering implies government employment, it does not rate more than medium high. This reflects, among other things, the view that it is autonomy and not command over others which is the desirable negation of subordination. Indeed, in Sohar there is a remarkable lack of appreciation of authority and command: they are avoided rather than sought, and, apart from the sovereignty of Sultan and Wali, suspected rather than admired, for reasons to which I shall return in chapter 11.

The choices and priorities of persons are thus clearly affected by considerations besides the simple pursuit of wealth, affecting the pattern of division of labor and the choices of occupation. The general values emphasize the importance of ownership rather than leadership, trade rather than production, composure and shrewdness rather than force and valor. Men seem to seek ways in which they can secure a high level of autonomy while pursuing wealth. The result is a proliferation of small businesses capitalizing on some small item of productive property, personal skill, special network position, or new opportunity. These small enterprises are related to each other preferably through impersonal market rules and far-flung acquaintance networks. Some persons achieve considerable wealth, but their activities through their waking hours, and thus their style of life, are much more profoundly affected by the particulars of the tasks entailed by their chosen or allotted occupation than by their degree of success in amassing the wealth that they seek. Further, as I shall discuss later (chapter 13), there are few fora and arenas where Soharis can display the fruits of their labor and compare their relative rank. In consequence, most of that diversity between Soharis which derives from the extensive and elaborate division of labor is contained in the character of these activities themselves. For the adult male, who earns the bulk of the family's income, an increase of wealth will give him merely twenty white *dishdasha* (tunics) instead of two, fifty similar outfits for his wife to hide under her *abba* whenever she goes out in public, or a larger house but no more visitors to it. Though clearly exhibiting fundamental and relatively dominant capitalist features in its institutional structure, this society is not particularly illuminated by applying class concepts to its form, and class differences in life style do not have the ubiquitous relevance that they have in many other forms of urban life. To construct a sound understanding of Sohar, we need to take none of its patterns and foundations for granted, but should describe and investigate each feature step by step to discover its sources and implications.

8

Neighbors, Townspeople, and Bedouin

Soharis associate distinctions of a territorial nature with a considerable range of social and cultural differences. Stereotypes about others, and people's own feelings of identity and membership, are tied to neighborhoods and to the larger units of quarters or wards of town; and a comprehensive set of differences are associated with the distinction between townsfolk and country folk.

To begin with the smallest unit, associated with the slightest differences, all houses are seen as belonging to a local neighborhood. Whereas adult men will usually regard the neighborhood in which they grew up with a certain nostalgia, they do not seem to identify very strongly with their subsequent places of residence. Women, on the other hand, are limited to the close neighborhood in their movements; and so the quality of their relations to neighbors becomes very important in their lives. Thus, they come to identify neighborhood and circle of friendship, or social clique.

Both sexes, however, recognize strong obligations of a moral kind between neighbors, involving mutual help in sickness and misfortune, mutual protection of property and person, and mutual dependence for maintenance of reputation and standards in the neighborhood. I know several cases where entirely unrelated neighbors look after a cripple or a very aged couple, sharing food with them and spending time in their company. The traditional saying "A neighbor is better than a father and mother who are far away" thus expresses real priorities of everyday social life. But the extent to which such ideals are fulfilled will vary between different neighborhoods, and the particular practices that develop will often show local peculiarities and differences. These peculiarities of style, degree of intimacy, and mutual loyalty and other such features are thought of as characteristic of the neighborhood, and women will describe them proudly or disparagingly as such.

The actual range in variation between neighborhoods is considerable—from completely unorganized to highly supportive—and this does not seem to correlate very closely with, for example, degree of

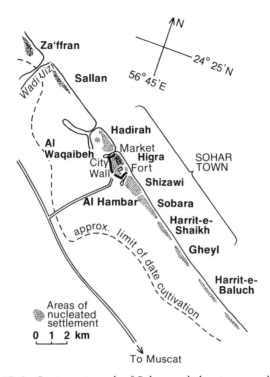

MAP 1. Component wards of Sohar, and closest surroundings.

kinship integration. But even where most effective, the boundaries of neighborhoods are somewhat vague and egocentric, membership is contingent, and the units are generally not distinctively named.

The higher territorial level of quarters or wards, on the other hand, involves clear territorial boundaries and names, and provides both units of administration and of mutual identification and self-identification. The whole central part of Sohar, within the old city walls and embracing both fort and marketplace, forms one such ward, named Higrah (see map 1). North of it lies the ward of Hadîrah, and the practically contiguous villages of Sallān and Zaffrān. South of Higrah are the wards Shizāwi, Sobārah, and Hillat-esh-Shaikh, and beyond them in a belt of practically contiguous settlement lie Gháyl, Hillat-el-Baluch, Swáherah, and a series of others down to the boundaries of Sohar province toward Saham.

Each of these wards contains a population of up to 2,000 inhabitants, and membership is automatic with residence within its territorial limits. Schematically, each ward has a shaikh who is responsible and intermediary between the Wali and the residents: the Wali may summon persons through the shaikh and the shaikh steps in to protect the rights and interests of the resident. Passports are issued by the Wali on the basis of letters of certification from the shaikh. The very ambitious Shaikh Mahmud described his functions and duties as follows:

The shaikh has full authority in his ward. No one can sit down, stand up, go to sleep without his permission. If someone is arrested, the shaikh should not wait to be informed by that person's family; he should *discover* that the person is missing, trace him, go to Muscat to plead his case. If he needs money for a fine or bail, the shaikh should pay that money. He should be as a father is to his child. He should be close to all people: to the boy he is like a boy, he is an equal with the poor man, and with the rich he is the equal of the richest.

Reality is not always that straightforward. The shaikh has no privileged sanctions by which he can support his claim to authority. Nor are all persons unequivocally his responsibility: some descent groups, particularly of bedouin, have shaikhs of their own whose authority depends not on residence but on the persons' descent membership, and persists wherever they may settle. The whole Ajam ethnic group likewise has a shaikh, who exercises similar obligations and concerns for Ajams no matter where they reside. Such shaikhs are fully recognized by the government, but there is nothing to prevent any other person from feeling the responsibilities and assuming the functions described as a shaikh's duties in the previous paragraph: nobody would be required to refuse such assistance from anyone and no person in authority would turn away such an intermediary. As a result, several persons within a ward may be offering patronage—to members of loosely organized families or descent groups, to a neighborhood or several adjoining neighborhoods, or to all and sundry. The resulting factionalism may even be such that the Wali chooses to recognize several coordinate shaikhs of an undivided ward, as is presently the case in Shizawi.

There may have been a time when the ward was a more significant political unit, the authority of the shaikh greater, and the echelons of command more definitive. But we need not imagine a differently constituted system of organization to generate these features: the principles embraced today could reasonably be expected, under conditions of greater external pressure and insecurity, to lead to this greater clarity and coordination. This potential for greater solidarity and importance is also reflected in the way in which persons identify with their ward, and in the way in which they conceptualize its qualities. Despite acknowledged diverse origins, the population of a ward tends to speak of itself in quasi-descent terms as a "tribe" (*qabîla*). In the words of one perceptive commentator: "People speak about their ward as their homeland (*bálad*), so as to be able to brag about themselves." Stereotypes and differences of custom are also ascribed to each ward. Thus, in Higrah, "women do not use the *burqa* [facial mask]," an observation true of some parts of Higrah, but certainly not of all. In South Sallan, a ward as predominantly Baluchi as is North Sallan, "the women have started using Arab dress though they continue to speak Baluchi." In Ghayl, "women use different styles of golden jewelry from us, and they continue wearing the *mafraq* [forehead ornament] though it has gone out of fashion. There also, a stranger will be welcomed in every house in turn; and people feel so much like one family that a man may visit a neighbor's house while the husband is not present!" Blame-worthy tendencies can also be associated with (other) wards; for example, "it used to be that Hadirah was known for most female unfaithfulness; but nowadays you find it most in Shizāw."

Characteristically, most of the traits relate to women or domestic arrangements—that is, are concerned with the sector of the population and the sector of life most locally based. To the extent that these distinctive cultural traits are indeed found and are common to a major part of the population, they may be emergent traits of the social milieu or be historically caused by the especially strong impact of one descent group or ethnic group on the ward as a whole. But by and large, cultural groupings and distinctions discussed above do not correlate very closely with ward units. Thus, most ethnic groups occur in most wards. Higrah is perhaps the most composite, but also shows the most marked internal segregation. The Banyan community is entirely located in Higrah, in a concentrated neighborhood just south of the market. The Beni Omar are likewise found exclusively there, in one large neighborhood southwest of the fort. The northern and western parts of the ward are solidly Ajam, but an equal number of Ajams are found outside Higrah. Central and southern parts contain an unusually high percentage of *xaddām* (ex-slaves), but this group is also found in all other wards. Hadirah is a ward with a relatively strong Ajam representation, and also with a fair concentration of Arabic-speaking Shiahs, but the majority in this ward is no doubt Arab Sunni. In Shizaw about 30 percent of the population is acknowledged as Baluchi and Ajam (some of the latter Sunni as well as Shiah); the rest, apart from a couple of houses of Zidgali, are Sunni Arabs, but of many tribes and origins, some clearly not originally Arabic (see chapter 18). Sobara, likewise, is predominantly Arabic but of various derivations, intermixed with about 10 percent Baluchis. Taking into account other features and distinctions, a similar criss-crossing pattern is found: farmers, fishermen, and laborers are found in all the wards mentioned; merchants are numerous in Hadirah and Shizaw as well as

Higrah; and so forth. Wealth tends to concentrate along the beach waterfront, and is therefore found in all wards and most neighborhoods. Sect and school are, as I have mentioned, scattered; tribes are dispersed over large areas, and families are related and intermarry from one end of Sohar to the other. In other words, the territorial organization defines a set of groups which share limited cultural and subcultural features but cross all the other culture-bearing groups and sections described so far. (See map 1.)

The highest order of territorial division within Sohar—between the zone of settlements along the beach and those inland from the belt of date orchards—correlates with a fundamental cultural division: that between persons who define themselves as "townsmen" (hāder) or "bedouin," respectively. These, perhaps most comprehensive, two cultural cotraditions in Oman need to be seen in a wider geographical and historical perspective before I return to the specification of those traits which conceptually and actually differentiate them in contemporary Sohar.

Fundamentally, the dichotomy as understood and largely practiced in Oman is that between two distinctive lifestyles and cultures: the town-based, sedentary civilization of cultivators, merchants, and craftsmen versus the dispersed and nomadic society of the pastoralists of the deserts and mountains. Today the dichotomy is perhaps most clearly exhibited in inner Oman, as in the case of the town of Bahla and its environs, where my wife and I did some brief and preliminary field work (see Barth 1978a). Bahla itself is a sedentary community of about 8,000 inhabitants, largely cultivators who live in compact hamlets of substantial mudbrick and plaster houses, cultivate by irrigation, and depend directly on the central institutions of the marketplace and the governor's fort. Their whole settlement, including the agricultural land and date orchards, is surrounded by an enclosing fortified wall. Outside live the bedouin, actually of two main kinds. The first are camel nomads, regarded as true bedouin, who are highly mobile in a relatively irregular pattern of pasture use whereby different sections of the household often are located far apart. These nomads frequently have no tents, but live in temporary shelters of grass and reeds, acacia branches, or date fronds. The second kind are breeders of small stock, called shawāwi, who are often quite stationary or move within a small territory, generally in the mountains. These shawāwi never have tents, and may live for extended periods in the open, simply in the shadow cast by an acacia tree, or they may construct small huts of brush, date fronds, or even stone. The household does not normally subdivide residentially. The shawāwi frequently also engage in some cultivation of whatever annual crops can be grown in their area.

In many cases the contrast in ecologic adaptation and productive regime between the townsmen and bedouin may be less categorical, though the social and cultural distinction persists. Thus, some of the (camel) bedouin in the Bahla area, and most of those further south in the Sharkiya, actually own or rent date groves, and settle for three summer months close by them, while tending and harvesting the crop. Nonetheless, both sides regard the division as an insurmountable chasm between two worlds; we found only one case of intermarriage in Bahla—between a bedouin girl and a silversmith, who as producer of silver jewelry for the bedouin market has unusually many and close relations to the nomads.

In the Sohar area today, three categories of bedouin are found. (*a*) A small number of true camel nomads—largely impermanent visitors of the Druˢ tribe in inner Oman—make use of otherwise unused pastures on the dry wasteland between the irrigated zone and the mountains. Previously, these same or similar groups would come only more infrequently, as marauding bands infringing on pastures used by others, preying on peripheral settlements or defenseless persons and groups, or even attacking major settlements. (*b*) In the mountain zone of the province of Sohar are true *shawawi*—partly the Beni Omar from which the Wali's *askars* (guards) are recruited—living on their own lands in traditional fashion. (*c*) Most of the category "bedouin" in Sohar today, however, are now settled cultivators living in palm-frond compounds (*barastis*) of the same construction as those in Sohar town, but without the enclosing compound wall, in fairly dense settlements in an almost contiguous belt along the inner edge of the date orchards. This population belongs to the tribes traditionally dominant in that zone, and seems as late as twenty years ago to have practiced a subsistence and a life style predicated on their Bedouin traditions and the opportunities provided by their location close to the sedentary zone and the port towns of the Batineh. While the Sohari category of "bedouin" is conceptually epitomized by the roving nomad of the desert, it is this latter, sedentary population that represents the category in actual, everyday experience.

The distinctive cultural features of this locally prevalent bedouin population have been undergoing a rapid transformation during the last generation, as the bedouin have been drawn into the spreading political and social milieu of Sohar town. Their subsistence, as noted, has been based on mixed farming and raising of small stock, but till recently camel keeping—for transport rather than animal products— has been an important component in their economy. Apart from dialect and various features of domestic custom, what distinguishes the bedouin most clearly from the town population is their much stronger and better integrated tribal organization. Agnatic descent groups live territorially compactly, practice close family endogamy, and maintain

Bedouin compound in the inner zone of settlement.

an effective political organization based on tribal membership and the office of tribal shaikh. This organization has served them till recently to safeguard life and property within the community and family, and to extract tax on transit through their territory. In return for such payments, they used to be responsible for the security of caravans by providing guides from border to border of their tribal lands. In relation to the sedentary communities along the coast they also served as a general buffer between townsmen and the more mobile, marauding tribes of the interior.

Some data on bedouin marriage patterns and family organization will be given in chapter 12, and a more dynamic view of cultural change within the groups is provided in chapter 19. At the present point, it is sufficient to note that the two life styles of bedouin and townspeople are conceptualized by Soharis as radically different and the bedouin style is stigmatized as unsophisticated, old-fashioned, and essentially uncivilized. On the other hand, bedouins are not denied certain human virtues by the townsmen, and are even somewhat idealized and admired by the men for their bravery and honesty. In the words of Ali:

Bedouin customs are different, and very bad. They cook food in the same pot, day after day, without washing it out. They wear the same clothes, day and night, for a week without washing them [that is, ignoring both dirt and the ritual pollution that arises from intercourse]. As *persons*, on the other hand, they are good, better than most of these so-called civilized people of Sohar town. If their families [that is, wives and children] quarrel with their neighbors, they do not involve themselves—the men are polite to each other. In Sohar, if one child fights with another, the mothers will quarrel. And if a woman tells one bad word that a neighbor has said to her, then the husband becomes angry and abuses the other's husband. Always, they meddle in the affairs of their neighbors and make trouble. . . . The townspeople are too interested in making and grabbing money, not in living the right life. A bedouin will see someone else doing well, and yet continue to mind his own business and not be dissatisfied. Among townspeople, if one man has something, or does some good business, they want to become his partners so as to get the money for themselves.

9 Man and Woman

In the preceding five chapters, I have sought to map out patterns in the cultural diversity of Sohar by identifying the various social categories or identities that are associated with distinctive syndromes of cultural traits and thus entail participation in a distinctive cultural tradition, and by characterizing the salient features that compose each such tradition. The last set of identities to be discussed in these terms is gender. Without doubt, gender is most fundamental to the organization of social interaction in Sohar; observing the differences between the sexes in dress and equipment, activities, and social participation, it is attractive to regard them likewise as differences of cultural tradition. But while the association of ethnic groups with distinctive cultural heritages, the identification of bedouin's and townspeople's lifestyles as contrasting cultures or subcultures, or even the acknowledgment of the ideology, cosmology, and law of a literate sect or church as a distinctive cultural tradition may require no special conceptual effort, there are reservations to be overcome in seeing the differences between men and women in comparable terms. Most importantly, we tend to think of gender identities as realized not in separate group memberships but in dyads of complementarity and mutual dependence, where each pair is engrossed in shared concerns rather than the realization of distinctive identities.

In the present context, I wish to explore the extent to which men's culture and women's culture in Sohar can be conceptualized, in the literal sense, as distinctive cultural traditions within a wider plural situation. I shall try to identify the syndromes of cultural traits that distinguish the two, the social organization that characterizes each cultural tradition, and thus their conditions of persistence and reproduction—a theme that will be developed further in chapter 20. It is striking that gender identities in Sohar exhibit features analogous to those of the other culture-sustaining identities I have discussed above:

1. they divide the whole population in explicit categories of ascription and self-ascription;
2. each identity entails participation in a shared body of culture

ranging from the overt diacritica that signal membership to substantial bodies of knowledge, skills, standards of excellence, and
views of the world, the self, and the society; and
3. there is a pervasive pattern of social organization whereby the two
    genders largely pursue different activities in segregated, homo-
    geneous groups, and thus are profoundly differentiated in life
    situation and life style.

The anomalous position of the *xanith*—the approximately one in
fifty adult males who has adopted a transsexual role—provides illuminating materials by which to test some of the substantive generalizations under these points (see Wikan 1977). Finally, and most significantly for the perspective pursued in this monograph, a conceptualization of gender differences in Sohar in these terms allows us
to exploit the material for a comparative analysis of the conditions of
cultural pluralism in Sohar.

Gender roles, particularly their forms in interaction and conceptualization among Arab women in Sohar, have been the focus of a
thorough description and analysis in my wife's monograph (Wikan
1982), based on the same joint store of field data on which I also have
drawn. This allows me to be somewhat more schematic and narrowly
focused in my discussion that I should otherwise have been. A first
descriptive step in establishing the coherence of gender cultures as
distinguishable cultural traditions or streams will be to summarize her
account of sexual segregation in Sohar (ibid., pp. 51 ff., 74 ff.).

While marriage unites gender pairs in a relationship that takes
precedence over all others (ibid., pp. 231 ff, esp. 240), the actual *time*
that coresident spouses spend together may be estimated typically to
represent less than three waking hours per day (ibid., p. 52). There are
only few and infrequent occasions in which the worlds of men and
women coalesce apart from this elementary family/household context;
the overwhelming part of an adult's active hours are thus spent in
homogeneous, same-sex gatherings. These gatherings are also of very
different scale and structure for men and for women (see chapter 13)
and are partly localized in space that is categorically off bounds to the
other sex. The nature of these differences will emerge as the description proceeds; the essential point here is that segregation is so
thoroughgoing that only small parts of men's and women's social
environments overlap at all, and their experience even of those occasions where they are jointly present will be highly discrepant. In
general, the exclusively male domain corresponds to the public sphere;
women appear in public only as shrouded transients or in temporary,
highly constrained contexts. The men's world, furthermore, forms a
largely open society in which persons move with great facility, whereas
women are divided into smaller, more intensive, and more intimate

segments. But most women are united, ultimately, in a single encompassing network of female society. The only exception here is the Banyan women, who have relations with each other, and some contacts with Banyan men other than their husbands, but no contacts at all with the other women of Sohar. Indeed, they do not share in what is here referred to as a women's culture in Sohar, and to the extent that they are distinct from Banyan men in culture they form an isolate of their own.

The codes whereby the conduct of men and women is judged also differ profoundly, in such ways as to reinforce the pattern of segregation. Where modesty and retirement into passivity are emphasized and encouraged in women, men are required to show assurance—strongly tempered with tact—and conversational and social competence. On the other hand, in the small circles where women may appropriately appear, they are allowed greater freedom of informality and spontaneity, whereas men should perpetually exercise the circumspection, responsibility, and control that are perhaps best summarized in the English expression of "good judgment." Thus, the standards that apply to men are such as to propel them into a public, individuated world where each person is responsible for himself and his every behavior is closely weighed by himself and others, whereas women are discouraged from asserting themselves at all in such fora, but are allowed to exercise and depend on the trust and tolerance of intimate social circles based on more multiplex relationships.

Men and women in Sohar (disregarding, for the present, the whole Banyan minority) signal their identities by distinctive styles of dress—indeed, there is no single item of clothing which is not sex specific and may be worn by either sex, from head cover to shoe. Most distinctive, in that they have no other-sex analogue at all, are the men's *kumma* (skullcap), the women's head shawl, facial mask, and covering *abba* (these last two not used, or rarely used, by ex-slave women), and the women's pantaloons. Each of these items seems to be particularly loaded with sexual symbolism. Women's jewelry and the men's belt and dagger (*xanjar*), to the extent it is used by Sohari men, are likewise distinctive.

Other features of personal appearance are also contrastive. Men may expose their hair, but more traditionally and politely cover their head with a cap; women may on no account bare their head. Men cut their hair short but not infrequently let their beard grow; they comb their hair backward and leave it otherwise free and untreated. Women wear long hair, which they part in the middle, oil fairly heavily, and braid in one long braid. The anomalous *xanith* (transsexuals) are not allowed to assume female clothing but adopt a number of clearly intermediate signals: whereas men's clothes are white, with a rare

Arab Sohari townswomen with characteristic burqa. *Compare the Bedouin* burqa *as shown in the illustration on p. 76.*

variant in khaki or gray, and women's tunics and pantaloons are in strong colors and patterns, the tunic of *xanith* is generally in pastel colors with a swung waist reminiscent of women's; they wear their hair half-long, with a side part, free but oiled; in common with women, they wear cosmetics but not jewelry; and the standards of beauty (skin texture, facial form, colors) which they espouse and others apply to them are those valid for women.

I shall return shortly to other aspects of the *xanith* role. First, I should note some of the salient differences in the embraced culture of normal men and women. Most immediately, these concern a number of skills and bodies of knowledge. Men must achieve the capacity to pursue one or several occupations and thereby support a family. They must learn to deal and bargain in the market, and to have the knowledge and presence to be able to appear and speak in public. Women need none of these skills, though some of them acquire commercial competence by engaging in trade, selling wares obtained through male relatives or agents, and with their clientele limited to women. On the other hand, all women must be able to cook (a skill in which those men who choose

Bedouin women with traditional dress and burqa. *For overt cultural contrasts, compare the women in the illustrations on pp. 75 and 77.*

are considered to excel them, however, and men therefore take responsibility for cooking at collective, festive occasions). Women must
also learn to sew and do fine needlework and embroidery. In due
course, women must learn all that is needed to look after infants and
children.

In other words, these differences, comprehensive as they are, arise
from the pattern of division of labor between men and women, and
thus are tied very directly to the enactment of specific roles. Indeed,
women may engage in "male" activities and thereby acquire "male"
skills and knowledge where this can be done without breach of the rules
of segregation (as in the trade noted above, or in agricultural work in
secluded gardens). In dire necessity they may even emerge publicly in
the practice of such skills and knowledge, as in the case of a widow,
without close agnates, who runs her deceased husband's shop in the
exclusively male-frequented market to support herself and her chil-

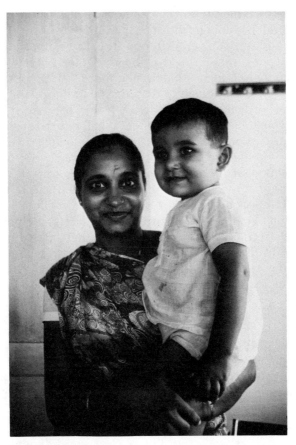

Banyan woman with son.

dren. Men likewise command much of the skills and knowledge of women: they can cook, as noted; they purchase most of women's clothes and jewelry and are thereby knowledgeable of qualities and styles; they frequently wash and mend their own clothes (to make sure it is done properly). The view is shared by both men and women that men are fundamentally more competent than women in all respects: women emphasize that they are untraveled and therefore ignorant; the saying "women are like donkeys, they/we know nothing," cited by both men and women, expresses this folk stereotype of women's ignorance. Thus, men tend to lay claim to superior skills and knowledge in all fields, entailing the view that they command the "whole" culture, and there is really no distinctive store of culture that is held and transmitted by women.

Yet, if one looks more closely one finds that women do not just hold views that are simpler, fewer, somehow "less" than those of men: they entertain understandings and interpretations that are clearly inter-connected and substantively different from those of men. Their views of the social person are distinctive; their judgments of essential charac-ter, in men as well as in women, emphasize other qualities or give different priorities to qualities than do the judgments of men; their explanations of behavior, both desirable and bad, are systematically different from those provided by men. I shall return later (chapter 20) to a fuller discussion of these points, when the contexts of daily life and social networks have been given more adequately. At present, this characterization of the main substantive areas of contrast between men's and women's values and premises gives a sufficient picture of the salient differences in their cultures.

We should also note the *force* with which male and female identities and values are embraced in Sohar. Though there are serious method-ological difficulties in making such judgments, particularly in the case of ascribed statuses, the field work situation provides some obser-vations that may lead one to form opinions. Important clues are revealed in spontaneous interaction by the strength and pride with which a person asserts a certain identity, by the special symbolic acts whereby particular aspects of an identity may be affirmed or repudi-ated, and by the frequency and circumstances under which an identity is abandoned in a sample of life histories. Ethnic identities were often proudly and apparently unnecessarily affirmed; religious membership was embraced with categorical conviction and very rarely changed (though theoretically adults can change sect or school by a free and voluntary act)—in the case of the Shiah minority one may also argue that the identity is embraced despite clear social disadvantages. But such observations are also made ambiguous by the effects of covert social pressures: stigmatizing statuses may be ascribed and enforced by a community or a group with a subtle force that generate the ap-pearance of voluntary embracement.

In the case of gender, identity is initially ascribed by anatomical criteria, but Wikan (1977, 1978, 1982) shows convincingly that its key expression, and thereby ultimate ascriptive criterion, is found in the sexual *act* rather than sexual organs in Sohar. As a consequence, gender identity can be changed by men, who by assuming the passive role in homosexual intercourse become *xanith*. *Xanith* do not thereby fully "become women," but they obtain an ambiguous and anomalous identity in many ways closer to that of women than that of men. We have noted the intermediate diacritica by which *xanith* identity is signaled. Personal names and the personal pronoun applied to them continue to be masculine, but in terms of the dichotomous rules of social segregation they are treated as women: women need not wear

the *burqa* face mask before them and are free to have informal contact
with them, and at weddings and other public occasions where both
sexes are present they move and eat with the women.

Such evidence as we have (see Wikan 1982:172) would indicate that
their cherished identity is that of women, and the standards of behavior and achievement by which they are judged, and judge themselves, are those of women: they are praised and take pride in the
neatness of their homes, the quality of their baking, the softness and
roundness of their cheeks. Perhaps more importantly, the reactions of
men, and their explanations of how boys become *xanith*, seem to
emphasize their own male identity as something precious and vulnerable. The idiom favored is that of an egg: "Once it is broken you cannot
put it together." In the view of men, male identity seems to require—
and clearly to justify—a perpetual vigilance in its defense. According to
their understanding, the *xanith*, in contrast, desires the female identity;
thus Ali was unable to understand or accept my wife's suggestion that a
homosexual urge might perhaps be experienced by the *xanith* as a
burden and an unwanted vice: "No, no, they are happy; that is what
they want." The negative case of *xanith*, and the men's reaction and
explanation of them, would thus indicate that male identity is strongly
embraced by most men.

Women likewise seem to embrace their female identity with contentment and pride, despite the inferiority it entails in comparison with
men. Its diacritical signs are valued and cherished, for example, in
dress, face masks, and jewelry (see Wikan 1982:88ff. for the symbolic
value of the face mask), and its standards and limitations for behavior
and comportment are internalized and experienced as part of one's
person in a conception of uneasiness and embarrassment with anything that is felt to be at odds with these standards (ibid., p. 68ff.).
There are no cultural conventions to facilitate a transsexual option for
women, but perhaps unfaithfulness and prostitution may serve some
as a symbolic repudiation of at least some aspects of the female identity.
If so, it may be noted that such activities do *not* change the woman's
relations to other women, they only affect her relations to her husband
and her kin (ibid., p. 153). In general, women express a compassionate
view that the life of men is one of hardship (ibid., p. 230); women's
values and lives seem to be practiced by them largely because they are
cherished: their gender identity is strongly embraced.

An attempt at depicting the differences in behavior, knowledge, and
attitudes between men and women in Sohar as differences in the
cultural syndromes associated with these two identities shows the
following to be the salient differences between the two syndromes: (*a*) a
level of overt diacritica which serves to signal gender identity, and
which is in part strongly embraced as expressive of the person's true

self; (b) comprehensive differences arising from the allocation of tasks according to gender roles, masked by a general premise of universal male superiority in skills and knowledge; and (c) basic divergencies in values and assumptions held by men and women. Such a configuration of differences suggests hypotheses about how they may arise from differences in the life situation entailed by the separate worlds of men and women, and the particular features of the social organization that connects them. This theme will be taken up in the later parts of this monograph.

10 The Forms of Pluralism in Sohar

The immediately preceding chapters have given an account of the major features of cultural and social diversity in Sohar. The categories in which this description is cast were provided by Soharis themselves, and do not reflect preestablished theories about the nature of cultural diversity and the kinds of social categories that are significant for such diversity.* Thus, through the observations and conversations of field work we were progressively taught what Soharis themselves regard as the major differentiae of social persons. Explicit and named categories of this kind are "Baluchi," "Arab," "Shiah," "woman," "bedouin," "merchant," etc., as these were described earlier. Each of these terms serves at times to identify persons within the community of Sohar, and each entails that the person in question command or be characterized by a considerable syndrome of distinctive cultural skills, knowledge, beliefs, and values. It should be further noted that these terms of current use categorized not whole persons but only logically separate aspects or capacities of the person, that is, *statuses* in the broad sense.

What is more, the terms are ordered in clear sets by Soharis themselves—for example, an ethnic set, a religious set, a gender set. These sets are largely implicit, but can be named and elicited. They underly discourse as self-evident understandings: it makes good sense to say "Is that person Shiah?" and to answer "No, she is Sunni," but no

---

*Indeed, the diversity of identities that entails membership in distinctive culture-carrying groups in Sohar was not one that I had anticipated. I arrived in the field with the expectation that ethnicity would provide the primary, ordering identities and that other statuses implying cultural specialization would exhibit strong and easily identifiable patterns of involution (cf. Nadel 1957, Barth 1960). My vision of what might be the overall picture in Sohar was thus one of a mosaic (cf. Coon 1951:4 ff.) of peoples living together in complex interdependence. The dismantling of this picture and the fashioning of the model which is construed through the chapters of this monograph were my response to empirical findings in Sohar and the needs that have arisen from wanting to understand them and give an account of them.

sense to answer "No, she is woman." In other words, some terms form alternatives in a set, some form other sets of alternative identities. Chapters 4 to 9 are organized to explicate such sets of identities or, as one might conceptualize them, "dimensions" of social and cultural diversity in Sohar. Some of these dimensions are clearly named and distinguished by Soharis themselves. As one careful methodologist among my informants explained: "You will ask: Which religion?—Moslem. Which school (mazhab)?—Shiah. Which teacher (Imam) do you follow?—Jaffar." Likewise, one may ask which peoples live in Sohar, and be told a list of ethnic groups. Other sets or dimensions have no label—the dichotomy of townspeople versus bedouin does not correspond to a concept of "way of life" used to refer to this difference—and some are apparently only diffusely acknowledged—there is no use made of a concept of free man in contrast to ex-slave, and no overt acknowledgment that the descent principle entails an ascription of ex-slave identity that is equivalent to that of tribal membership. Yet also in these cases, I am prepared to argue that the dichotomization of townsmen and bedouin, and the uses made of the concept of "blood," justify my claim that these are dimensions of differentiation employed by Soharis themselves, and that the occupational categories likewise provide the terms for a class-subculture or stratificational native model.

Is it also possible to argue that these categories together provide an adequate and complete ordering of the cultural diversity that obtains in the community? In the sense of encompassing all the distinctive customs, competences, standards, or symbols current among persons in Sohar, the answer is certainly No. Soharis themselves recognize this and see each other as having had a diversity of experiences and stimuli that entail differences between them and that may entail continuing membership and participation in collectivities outside of Sohar with distinctive cultural orientations and traits. They also employ concepts of "character" and inherent psychological "nature" for what they see as individually motivated variations in standards and styles of behavior. Nor are even these categories and dimensions fully exhaustive of major patterns in the diversity. To complete a synchronic model of the distribution of cultural differences, I should have to add two additional major dimensions: one might be called "generation," and the other "degree of modernization." When I have chosen not to focus on these last two, I have done so for distinct reasons: relative age, though clearly conceptualized and referred to by Soharis in connection with differences in behavior and orientation, yet comprises a continuum through which all persons pass. If the actors themselves conceived of this as life stages, or age classes, they might consolidate the cultural correlates of each stage as a syndrome with some degree of stability. As it is in Sohar, I suspect a list of the cultural correlates of age to be ever shifting in its content, an epiphenomenon without an internally predicated dynamics of reproduction.

As for "degree of modernization," one might imagine a consolidation of certain cultural stances and values, for example, between a traditionalist and a modernist faction. If such exist in Sohar, they are so discretely articulated as to escape my notice in the field. As far as my data go, there is a universal embracement of progress and all things modern which is in harmony not only with present state policy but also with the widely embraced premise of tolerance and a positive evaluation of increased knowledge and welfare. Though people do in fact differ in their command of "traditional" and "modern" cultural items, these differences do not, by the data available to me, correlate with any other clear factor than cosmopolitan exposure.

It is thus my definite feeling that my description of Sohar, and the categories used by Soharis to conceptualize local cultural diversity, in fact capture most of the patterned differences and most of the range found among Sohari residents. An inventory of this diversity can therefore now be said to have been completed. I must then address some general ontological and epistemological questions. To report on the observed patterns in the cultural diversity of Sohar, I have constructed—or accepted from informants—some kind of descriptive "entities," for example, Baluch, Arab, Sunni, Shiah, woman, man, *xanith*. How are these best to be conceptualized for the purposes of analysis? Like the Soharis themselves, I initially saw them as parts of social persons, as major *identities* in which residents of Sohar partake. I could continue to inquire into the "cultural correlates" of these identities, and proceed to analyze each, according to its character, as ethnicity, religion, class, gender role, etc. But to try to fashion an analytical perspective whereby the "whole system" of diversity is encompassed, let me now shift my attention from the level of identities as parts of the social person to the level of just what it is that a person participates *in*, by virtue of these identities.

To say merely that persons participate in "groups" or "collectivities" by virtue of such identities may be begging some questions and also failing to confront others. It is, after all, cultural diversity that has been my point of departure and remains my ultimate focus. Let me therefore emphasize, as I have through the bulk of my description of them, that each category (Shiah, Baluch, woman, etc.) refers to and entails a characteristic syndrome of *cultural features*. The features of each syndrome are distinctive; but all the syndromes have certain general properties or characteristics in common.

1.) Each syndrome has a continuity through time that transcends the life span of persons: each persists through the enrollment and socialization of personnel who *embrace* and *reproduce* the syndrome.

2.) Each syndrome has a distinctive distribution beyond the community of Sohar, with territorial and social boundaries unique to itself. Thus, the Jaffari Shiah syndrome of traits is identifiable in congregations of Shiahs found in Bahrain, Iran, and southern Iraq, but not in Yemen or Pakistan. Local variants of customs like those of Sohari Baluch are found among Baluchis on the Makran coast in Pakistan and Iran, but not among the northeastern, Marri Baluch and nowhere among non-Baluch. The syndrome of knowledge, skills, and values characterizing Sohari merchants is reportedly replicated in Bandar Abbas on the Gulf coast of Iran and indeed probably in all the port towns of the Arabian Gulf, but not among persons engaged in trade in Inner Oman (Barth 1978a), and so on.

3.) Each syndrome is also sustained by a characteristic social organization, not only descriptive of its pattern of enrollment but also instrumental in organizing the various behaviors entailed by the syndrome. We can describe this social organization of each category in terms of which persons of the category interact and organize their characteristic activities: the social organization of Jaffari Shiism, of Batineh women, of Gulf merchants, of coastal Baluchis. The syndrome of cultural traits which each such category shares is presumably sustained by these distinctive forms of organization: no living Jaffari Shiism without mosque, *matam*, and imam; no women's culture in Sohar without segregation, marriage, neighborhood circles.

By virtue of these shared characteristics of the cultural syndromes with which we are dealing, it would seem that they can each be legitimately conceptualized by the general anthropological concept of a "culture." Such a usage seems to receive explicit sanction by Radcliffe-Brown (1952): "In a particular society we can discover certain processes of *cultural tradition....* In complex modern societies there are a great number of separate cultural traditions. By one a person may learn to be a doctor or surgeon. By another he may learn to be an engineer or an architect. In the simplest forms of social life the number of separate cultural traditions may be reduced to two, one for men and the other for women" (p. 5).

To emphasize their particular character, they might more graphically be called "cultural streams." A syndrome such as those here described is probably never fully reproduced through time—it changes as old ideas are forgotten, new ideas are adopted and embraced, and new accommodations are made to the changing circumstances of life. In this indeed, they are like all other cultures: changing in content, but with a continuity that in the short or intermediate run allows us to say that it is the same stream undergoing incremental change. But in the community context of Sohar, personnel variously participate in a plurality of such "streams"—the same person is an active participant in being Baluch, Sunni, cultivator, etc.

What is more, some or most of these identities and participations are subject to possible change or choice, and even the patterns of enrollment whereby persons are *ascribed* an identity—and thereby led to embrace the values of that cultural stream—may themselves change.

In dealing with these cultural streams, we are thus dealing with something that changes both its content and its boundaries—a methodologically very questionable situation. Yet, do we not expect this to be inherent in the ontology of all culture? I see no alternative but to recognize the phenomenon and try to handle it as best we can, rather than abstract such properties away so as to improve our methodology at the expense of empirical relevance or adequacy. This issue will be raised again in conclusion, when the reader may be in a position better to judge the fruitfulness of the conceptualizations that I have adopted.

In this fashion, each syndrome of traits will be spoken of as a "culture," a "cultural tradition," or a "cultural stream," and I shall speak of a Shiah culture, a Baluch culture, a merchant culture, a women's culture, etc., in Sohar. The advantage of having such a common mold for the conception of each is that it facilitates generalizations about their differing conditions of persistence, their interdependence as coexisting traditions in a community, and their change, which are the themes on which I shall focus my analysis.

If this is a defensible usage, then the total situation in Sohar is truly one of cultural pluralism: both in the sense that a number of cultures coexist and in the sense that every person participates in several, though far from all, of these cultures. This second aspect of pluralism may cause some unease to readers, as it is at odds with the conception of a culture as a "whole" way of life and the "sum total" of learned behavior. Yet other accepted usage, such as the "two cultures" of C. P. Snow (1969), logically entails the same plural memberships, if we reflect on its implications in the context of complete persons or communities. Nor are we dealing with "subcultures" in the sense of local or sectional variants of a common prototype "whole" culture. Baluchi and Ajam culture in Sohar may appear as subcultural variants in relation to those of Baluchis in Makran or Persians in the Gulf area, but not in relation to each other or to the culture in which women in Sohar partake qua women. And there is certainly nothing "subcultural" about the Shiah or the Sunni great traditions that inform the respective congregations in Sohar. The only danger I see in this "part of life" concept of a culture is that it may tempt us to split the life of communites and persons into too great a multiplicity of ever-smaller sets of distinctive traits, each considered separately from its wider context. Therefore, it is important that each cultural tradition here identified should exhibit the coherence of a truly separable tradition, anchored in an explicit social category of ascription and identification, and that their *interrelations* should be constantly in focus. It is only to the extent that these features of boundedness and continuity can be specified that we can expect the syndrome's conceptualization as a distinct culture to be fertile.

Let us pause yet longer to contemplate what it is we are doing—and how much of this we need to do—when we choose to conceptualize Shiah, Sunni, townsperson, bedouin, Arab, and Baluchi in Sohar each as enrolled in a separable culture. First, we are clearly adopting an *ideational* concept of culture (Keesing 1974, see also the more extensive discussion in chapter 16). "Culture" is not synonymous with an observed assemblage of cultural things, but is only one set of factors that shape these things, together with such other factors as environment and social processes. As it has been itemized in the descriptions of the preceding chapters, culture embraces skills, knowledge, idioms, symbols, and standards: all that ideational equipment which people "inherit, employ, transmute, add to, and transmit," to borrow a felicitous phrase from Firth (1951:27; cf. Singer 1968). But for my present purposes I cannot be content to employ this general concept of culture as a device to (help) explain behavior or to interpret the import of acts (Geertz 1973:10). My ambition is to differentiate the strands, the separate traditions of cultures with their different histories and different prospects, so as to make an inventory of the local distinctive conditions of perpetuation and change and their interdependence and dynamics.

This may mean taking a single event or cultural thing and identifying distinct aspects of it, assigning each aspect to the context of a distinctive cultural tradition. To contrive a concrete example: We wish to be able to say about a particular piece of needlework that it is simultaneously an expression of women's culture in Sohar and an expression of Baluchi culture. Women express their gender role, assert themselves in terms of standards of dutifulness and neatness, and may supplement their own or their family's income by producing such needlework. At the same time, the design, technique, and color of certain items are distinctive features of Baluchi culture. We are justified in identifying those apsects that are relevant to our description and understanding of one culture, and leaving the other aspects aside for the time being. But we can also ask questions about the possible nature of interdependence between the two cultural traditions which is exemplified in the particular case. Presumably, women will embroider in Sohar, and thereby express their gender identity and transmit their conceptions and values, even if all Baluchis disappear. It may not be equally true that the esthetic vitality and distinctive decorative ideas that are characteristic of Baluchi culture will continue to assert themselves, if the role of women in Sohar changes in such a way that they discontinue their embroidery.

This focus on the distinct cultural traditions as the objects of major interest must also affect how we phrase our questions and descriptions. Thus, in the plural context of Sohar we should not ask how culture is "shared" between persons, but instead investigate the processes of "enrollment" and "embracement" whereby persons come to participate in a tradition. This means looking at the same things, but from a different perspective, that is, not with whole persons as the primary units. It does not mean that we can ignore microevents, or the integration of persons as systems—quite the contrary. It means that we try for a while to solve our equations with respect to the "y" of cultural traditions rather than the "x" of persons.

If this discussion has provided some perspectives, at least in provisional and general terms, on the questions of the nature of coherence of each syndrome of cultural features and the nature of continuity within each tradition, it has left unresolved the question of the nature of wholeness or integration of *all* of Sohar as a society and as a cogeries of cultures. How do we most fruitfully conceptualize the ways in which what we have separated as cultural traditions are in some respects made interdependent and integrated through the lives of people in Sohar, and the operation of Sohar as a community?

Again, I shall construct a conundrum to represent the problem concretely: If a Navaho family—or two Norweigian anthropologists—arrive in Sohar, they cannot be said by their physical presence to have become part of the "society" there. Their beliefs and behavior are unilluminating for an understanding of the beliefs and behavior of long-time Sohari residents, and it would seem unfruitful to define any local "system" of Sohar in such a way as to embrace them as a component, sector, or subsystem of that system. Yet, as they stay on, this seems gradually to become less unfruitful—presumably because we assume that interaction between them and old Soharis has increased and that they have mutually affected one another: old-time residents of Sohar have accommodated to their presence, developed knowledge and stereotypes of them, indeed been drawn into certain experiences and confrontations that may also have modified their views of themselves and each other. Particular features of the once-irrelevant beliefs and behaviors of the strangers may have been particularly consequential in this, and are thus crucial to the understanding of the new modified beliefs and behaviors of a number of Soharis. Likewise, the changing knowledge, attitudes, and behaviors of the erstwhile strangers are increasingly revealing of the social and cultural systems of Sohar.

At what point are we justified in recasting our conceptualization of Sohari social organization, and Sohari cultural pluralism, to embrace that Navaho family? What processes are we assuming, and should we be able to demonstrate, to be taking place to produce this justification?

Can our criteria here be made relevant and produce insight into the relationships between Arab, Ajam, Baluchi, Sunni, Shiah, man, and woman? Indeed, which of these processes, and which additional processes, are illuminating as a model of how Sohari interactional and ideational diversity hang together?

The questions I am raising are clearly related to those raised by, for example, Redfield (1956), Singer (1968), and Marriott (1959), in their vision of the production and reproduction of multiplicity and unity in the Indian civilization. But the empirical facts of the Sohari case seem to be very different from those depicted by them; and partly for this reason the more specific concepts and procedures developed by them seem inapplicable in Sohar. By no effort of imagination can Sohari pluralism be depicted as a great and little tradition mingling and fusing in the life of a community. Nor can we think of our task simply as the investigation of "the social structure of a civilization" (Redfield 1962; Singer 1964). The activities that constitue the several traditions in Sohar are not, as they may perhaps be in the Indian civilization, embedded in an embracing ritual and symbolic system of cosmological scale and ambition. To the extent that Sohar is a "society," its character seems too open, its composition too fortuitous, and its structure too uncompelling for its unity to be taken for granted and its processes to be conceptualized with reference to that unity.

Nor does it seem that we can turn to the literature on ethnicity to solve this problem. As I have described, Sohar certainly exhibits the social organization of cultural differences entailed in the concept of ethnicity (Barth 1969); but it also contains cultural differences, and whole traditions, *not* so organized, and we are interested in understanding *all* the forms of difference and their conditions of perpetuation and change. Drawing a lesson from the perspective of ethnicity, we shall be concerned to understand the boundary processes between each of these traditions, but will not prejudge their forms or degree of uniformity.

The next step must therefore be to turn to the materials so far presented, and try to systemize them in such a way as to bring out their overall patterns. Any marked patterning may then be used to raise questions as to the nature of constraints underlying the pattern, and construct empirically falsifiable hypotheses about processes that may be at work. I have described a number of social categories, which appear as parts of social persons and entail identifiable cultural traditions. Furthermore, I have discovered these categories to be associated in a limited number of sets of alternatives, most obviously by identifying the alternatives to questions of the type: "Is she a Shiah?"—"No, she is Sunni/Ibazhi/Hindu." We could thus identify certain dimensions of social and cultural variation, within which a person can occupy only *one* of the alternative positions.

A Sohari might also quite sensibly have answered to that specific question "No, she is a Baluch," since it is common knowledge that no Baluchis are Shiah, they are all Sunni. This reveals a secondary and partial patterning of the identities: all possible permutations of identities from different sets are *not* found among the social persons of Sohar; there are some constellations that do occur and some that do not.

Figure 1 systematizes all the significant categories I have identified, ordered in their appropriate sets and cross-correlated to show their constellations in persons in Sohar today. The first set comprises language/ethnic categories. These are distinctive and readily separable in Sohar; the only difficulty that arose was to limit their number, since additional ethnic groups are represented as transients and guest laborers: Pakistanis, Indian medical personnel, Egyptian teachers, Western experts, etc. The five categories included are exhaustive of stable and long-time residents of Sohar. The second set shows "blood" or descent rank. The distinction between ex-slave and freeman is clear enough in conception, though the status of particular persons may sometimes be unclear. Under "commoner" I have grouped a great number of de-

	ARAB	AJAM	BALUCH	ZIDGALI	BANYAN	HIGH	COMMON	EX-SLAVE	IBAZHI	SUNNI	SHIAH	HINDU	MERCHANT	CULTIVATOR	SOLDIER	FISHERMAN	LABORER	HERDER	TOWNSMAN	BEDOUIN	MAN	XANITH	WOMAN
ARAB						X	X	X	X	X	X	O	X	X	X	X	X	X	X	X	X	X	X
AJAM						O	X	?	O	X	X	O	X	X	?	X	X	O	X	O	X	?	X
BALUCH						O	X	?	O	X	O	O	?	X	X	X	X	O	X	O	X	?	X
ZIDGALI						O	X	?	O	X	O	O	X	X	X	?	X	O	X	O	O	O	X
BANYAN						O	X	O	O	O	O	X	X	O	O	O	O	O	X	O	X	O	X
HIGH	X	O	O	O	O				X	O	O	O	X	X	X	O	O	O	X	O	X	O	X
COMMON	X	X	X	X	X				X	X	X	X	X	X	X	X	X	X	X	X	X	X	X
EX-SLAVE	X	?	?	?	O				X	X	X	O	X	X	X	X	X	X	X	X	X	X	X
IBAZHI	X	O	O	O	O	X	X	X					X	X	X	X	X	X	X	X	X	X	X
SUNNI	X	X	X	X	O	X	X	X					X	X	X	X	X	X	X	X	X	X	X
SHIAH	X	X	O	O	O	O	X	X					X	?	O	?	X	O	X	O	X	X	X
HINDU	O	O	O	O	X	O	X	O					X	O	O	O	O	O	X	O	X	O	X
MERCHANT	X	X	?	X	X	X	X	X	X	X	X	X							X	O	X	X	O
CULTIVATOR	X	X	X	X	O	X	X	X	X	X	?	X							X	O	X	X	O
SOLDIER	X	?	X	X	O	X	X	X	X	X	O	O							X	X	X	O	O
FISHERMAN	X	X	X	?	O	O	X	X	X	X	?	O							X	O	X	O	O
LABORER	X	X	X	X	O	O	X	X	X	X	X	O							X	X	X	X	O
HERDER	X	O	O	O	O	O	X	X	X	X	O	O							O	X	X	O	O
TOWNSMAN	X	X	X	X	X	X	X	X	X	X	X	X	X	X	X	X	X	O			X	X	X
BEDOUIN	X	O	O	O	O	O	X	X	X	X	O	O	O	O	X	O	X	X			X	O	X
MAN	X	X	X	O	X	X	X	X	X	X	X	X	X	X	X	X	X	X	X	X			
XANITH	X	?	?	O	O	X	X	X	X	X	X	O	X	X	O	O	X	O	X	O			
WOMAN	X	X	X	X	X	X	X	X	X	X	X	X	O	O	O	O	O	O	X	X			

FIGURE 1. Combinations of statuses represented in Sohar.

scent groups of variable influence and importance; but though claims
to "better" blood are differentially present among them, there is no
context in which such claims can be socially confirmed, and my understanding is that the vast majority of the population would agree that
they are collectively of ordinary commoner kind of descent group.
There is in Sohar no emphasis on special descent status as Sayyid
(descendant of the Prophet) or Ashraf (noble). Yet it does seem
justified to single out a small group of "high" families, mainly composed of the members of the Al Bu Said dynasty, as a separate category.
On the other extreme, for lack of numbers and visibility in the contemporary context, I have ignored the presence of the stigmatized
category of Zatut. The third set of religious communities is unprob-
lematical. The Sunni community comprises all four orthodox schools
of law within the congregation. Ibazhis and Shiahs each have separate
mosques. Hindus are not allowed to have temples for worship, but they
do have separate wells for ritual reasons, and are undeniably socially
recognized as a distincitive religious community. No other religious
community exists as a stable part of Sohar. The fourth set is the one
most dependent on the anthropologist's judgment rather than on a
clearly distinguished schema of the actors. Differences of wealth and
socioeconomic class are only diffusely assigned and confirmed; it
therefore seemed most illuminating to focus on occupational categories to identify the main distinct traditions in this general domain.
But the particular grouping of occupations in the six main categories
listed is somewhat arbitrary and reflects my appreciation of the most
important differences in life styles, skills, and standards found in
Sohar. The fifth set is comprised of the simple dichotomy of townspeople versus bedouin, of explicit and fundamental importance in
Sohar. Finally, the sixth set distinguishes men, *xanith* (transsexuals),
and women.

Each person in Sohar can occupy only one position in each of these
sets; that is, the categories within each set are alternative. The empirical
patterns in the combination and noncombination of categories *between*
the sets are tabulated in figure 1. Theoretically, one could imagine a
range of possible systems from completely free combinability between
sets to one where categories were combined in persons only in standard
constellations, as when a person's religious affiliation was firmly predictable from his occupation or ethnic group, and vice versa. The latter
would correspond to a sociologist's ideal type caste organization, the
former to an ideal type open society. On such a range, Sohar places
itself about two-thirds of the way toward the open pole, that is, most
statuses do occur in combination, but some combinations do not occur.

What may this entail for boundary maintenance and persistence of
the cultural tradition associated with each category? If organized in

restrictive constellations, one would find certain associations to hold universally, and this might entail a disappearance of a boundary between some traditions through their persistent fusion in persons. Something of this may be reflected in the tendency of Soharis to think in terms of an equivalence or coalescence of the Shiah and the Persian traditions, calling both indiscriminately "Ajam" and ignoring the approximately 10 percent Arab Shiahs and the approximately 10 percent Sunni Persian speakers. In the case of the Banyans, in fact, a fully standarized constellation obtains among Banyan ethnic group, Hindu religion, and merchant occupation: apart from male and female, only one category is occupied within each set, and indeed Banyan females cannot in any case be said to partake in Sohari female culture, since they live in complete isolation from non-Banyan women. Yet, there is no difficulty in separating "merchant occupation," "Hindu religion," and "Kutchi language" conceptually. What is more, even if there were no others in Sohar participating in the cultural tradition of merchants, there would still be no grounds for assimilating it and Hinduism and the Banyan language and domestic customs with each other, because the three have distinctive regional distributions as traditions; persons combining the three will still be participants in three distinctive cultural traditions. To understand the conditions of persistence of boundaries, we therefore need to look at the larger-scale distribution and social organization of these collectivities, not only the local organization and combinations of statuses. Likewise, even if Sohar were to move toward the opposite pole of a truly open society with a random statistical pattern of combination of statuses between sets, this would not preclude the persistence of plural traditions: there would still be a Sunni and a Shiah tradition, even if Arab, Ajam, and Baluch were equally prominent members of each congregation and all the different occupations were represented in each. Full freedom in the combination of categories between sets does not logically prejudge the relationship of categories *within* each set, on which the nature and persistence of each tradition depends.

Let us next look more closely at what these relationships may be, that is, at the internal structure of each set of alternative identities and cultures. There seem to be several ways to conceptualize these relations, the most salient being the logical and functional interrelation of alternative cultures, and the interactional mode that characterizes incumbents of alternative identities. Under the first, traditions may relate to each other in a fashion that may be called: (1) complementary (composing distinct but interdependent parts of a whole task or life style), (2) distributive (a limited set of items is allocated between them, so any increase to one entails an equivalent decrease to the others), (3) optional (changes in one have no direct entailment for the others), (4) emblematic (symbolically contrastive, as diacritica), or (5) contradictory (incapable of being sustained or accepted simultaneously). In their mode of interaction, the incumbents of alternative identities may be (1) cooperative (as in division of labor), (2) competitive (that is, engaged in the same pursuits, but in a zero-sum/constant-sum situation), (3) non-articulating (interactionally without direct relevance to each other), (4) counterposing (differentiating symbolically without engaging in com-petition for the same objects), or (5) antagonistic. As one can see, there is a rough isomorphy between the kinds of relations that may be distinguished in logical-functional terms, and in the typology of modes of interaction.

The coexisting traditions and identities in Sohar seem to exhibit the whole range of these modes. Indeed, at first flush they may even be thought to exemplify the types, ranging from the complementarity of men's and women's culture and their cooperative relationship in gen-der and household roles to the contradiction and antagonism between Sunni and Shiah. But a slightly more discriminating inspection shows this to be false: the two major religious divisions certainly also use a series of emblematic devices to counterpose one another, while a number of the beliefs and practices of one are simply irrelevant to the other, that is, optional and nonarticulating. Man and woman, and their cultural differences, are certainly emblematically counterposed as well as ordered by complementarity; many differences between ethnic groups are simply optional and members of different groups do not articulate in terms of them, while other contrasts are highly em-blematic. What is more, within one set the alternative identities and traditions relate differently to each other. Thus, if Sunni and Shiah may be conceptualized mainly as contradictory and antagonistic, Ibazhi and Sunni represent optional, nonarticulating alternatives, while Hinduism is so far beyond the pale as to appear nonarticulating in a rather different sense. Thus, the sets of alternatives do not subdivide the population at all into homologous segments, and alterna-tive identities and cultural traditions do not even show the same mixture of modes in how the relations between them are articulated.

Indeed, I would suggest that the effort to construct a logical or typological structure to encompass the organization of diversity in Sohar may be a way to characterize some of the patterns, but it provides no way to identify an overall social structure or the determinants of such order and pattern as prevails: it is in the process of embracement and reproduction, and the factors that canalize them, that a degree of order and pattern is generated. The mental models of cooperation, antagonism, complementarity, and emblem may provide templates for actors with respect to some dichotomies in some contexts, and will thus obtain reflections in the material; but this can best be depicted in a model of process, whereas no premise of a hidden, underlying structure can do justice to the complex, open, and turbulent society and plurality of cultures which we confront in Sohar.

Why then should there be any pattern and order at all in such an open system of cultural pluralism? Mainly, I would suggest, because of the most compelling context of coexistence for the component cultural traditions or streams: (a) they are pursued and realized by persons who have multiple commitments, that is, who are incumbents of several identities, requiring them to practice several traditions in the framework of one life and existence; and (b) they are all of them practiced by a body of persons who cooperate and maintain relations with one another while also maintaining distinctive values and attitudes. In this lie the main constraints that generate pattern and order, and in this Sohar also may appear as a microcosm embodying key problems and processes of a pluralistic contemporary world. It is in the praxis of daily life, where Soharis cope with these conditions of their existence and shape their individual lives—and thereby inevitably but partly inadvertently also shape their aggregate society—that these formative processes may be observed most closely. Before pursuing further the dynamics and reproduction of cultural traditions, we must therefore turn to a close scrutiny of the minutia of individual lives and interaction as they unfold in everyday life in the town.

Part 3

Daily Life and How It Shapes Society

11

Standards of Behavior and the Management of Self

In the description so far of the various cultural traditions in Sohar, I have made no a priori assumption that, taken all together, they make up an integrated whole in any logically or morphologically compelling way. On the contrary, I have taken it to be a matter for empirical discovery to ascertain what their interdependencies are. Their separateness as cultural traditions would be drasitically reduced if it could be shown that the traditions are mutualy entailed by each other as parts of a coherent whole, and/or that the social groups which partake in the different traditions form homologous segments within a unitary organization. So far, the evidence has suggested that the latter is only occasionally and insignificantly true, as in the case of the patrilineal "tribes," whereas the former may be the case to some extent between the traditions within some sets, particularly those characterized by complementary relations.

However, even where this degree of structural integration is absent, it does not follow that each tradition can be understood in isolation from the others. The many distinctive cultures practiced in Sohar are part of one encompassing system to the extent that they blend in the lives of persons—who invariably partake in several of them—and to the extent that they become connected through the interaction of persons partaking in different ones. To depict the structural and dynamic relations of the cultural traditions, we must therefore depict social life as it actually unfolds in Sohar, that is, the whole social context within which the multiple traditions coexist. A close observation of the praxis of social organization in Sohar should reveal both the extent of morphological integration between cultural traditions and the processes by which they are interconnected.

How can one best analyze social organization to bring out these features? The focus of my interest has been stated: how the major identities of persons are interconnected and may affect each other's expression in the life and behavior of the person, and how persons with different identities interact. The focus of my description of social organization should follow from this: I will depict the ground rules,

97

and the overt forms, by which persons comport themselves and make decisions concerning themselves—how they meet, interact, and form relations. In such description, I want to maintain a simultaneous attention to what individuals are doing and how the separate cultural traditions are brought into play. Consequently, I shall devote chapter 12 to domestic life, kinship, and affinity, chapter 13 to the networks and groupings of everyday interaction, chapter 14 to the activities of the marketplace and the consequent circulation of wealth and labor, and chapter 15 to careers and the constitution of whole persons. But first of all, in this present chapter I need to give attention to some ground rules governing social interaction in general and the comportment of the individual person in Sohar.

POLITE BEHAVIOR

What strikes the participant observer from the very first moment in Sohar is the fantastic "tea party" politeness of all social interaction in town. It can be sensed immediately—and in striking contrast to most of the Middle East—on the first confrontation with the market scene: the thronging mass in the narrow lanes of the marketplace does not bump and jostle, but moves with a grace and an awareness of one another as in a dance or theater performance. The level of noise is like a soft murmur, shopkeepers and customers alike maintain a conspicuously low-keyed, soft-spoken calmness of manner. Even the auction scenes, though swift and dramatic, take place without histrionics, shouting, or acrimony. And as the observer enters into more private interactions and intimate relations, this impression is only strengthened: each new scene exihibits, in its distinctive way, the same qualities of tact and manners, attentiveness and niceness. The basic value stances of people show corresponding features of reflective tolerance of variation, of change, of the state of the world, of the behavior of others.

The main focus of the present chapter will be this code of politeness, tact, and constraint that Soharis exercise in the company of others, and what it entails for the life of Soharis, both individually and collectively. At first glance it might seem that this gives too much prominence to the surface phenomena of etiquette over the more fundamental rules governing behavior. However, it is hardly possible to exaggerate the extent to which this code pervades all action, and its positive evaluation by Omanis. Nor does it seem, as one progressively investigates its social implications, that it lacks structural consequences. The argument I shall pursue is that this ideology of politeness, as it may be called, provides directives for behavior which profoundly affect the courses of interactions and the kinds of encounters and groups that emerge.

Thus, major features of social organization can be generated from the distribution of rights and duties on statuses only if one takes the transformation rules of politeness into account.

The main features of this ideology are best revealed in the everyday acts through which the ideology is expressed. Most prominently, the code demands self-control rather than the control of others; the appropriate behavior toward others is a tactful and constructive attentiveness to their situation and their susceptibilities. This indeed may be the essence of all true good manners; in its Omani practice it is carried to unexpected lengths. Thus an orthodox Sunni may choose to greet a Shiah acquaintance courteously, with the hand-on-heart greeting used between Shiah co-religionists. Multilingual facility is utilized to address a person in his mother tongue—indeed, this seems almost the only practical use to which a prevalent multilingualism can be put in a community of persons universally fluent in Arabic. Another aspect of this politeness and tact is the restraint that is exercised in sanctioning others: criticism is avoided or undercommunicated, in both the presence and the abscence of a person or group concerned. Even quite fundamental antipathies, such as those between Moslem and Hindu or Shiah and Sunni, are not apparent in the graceful encounters between members of the opposed congregations, and condemnation of the other is only rarely and moderately expressed. Behavior that is felt to be morally and personally repugnant, such as the homosexual prostitution practiced by transsexuals (chapter 9; Wikan 1977, 1982), is tolerated without any show of indignation, and the transsexuals are not visibly discriminated against in any way. Even from persons who clearly had the greatest confidence in us and our discretion, it proved very difficult to obtain information about others which might be judged compromising. The major exception to this tactfulness regarding persons concerned physical appearance. Soharis were quite prepared to devalue African racial features of dark skin and kinky hair in a way that could jar modern Western susceptibilities.

These features of daily etiquette appear to express a common and basic stance of tolerance and noncondemnation. Abdullah, waxing nostalgic about the old days and ways, described with great pleasure the traditional joys of picnicking under the date trees as the first dates matured in the summer, some youths climbing the tall trees to collect fresh dates while others crushed coffee with a rhythmic, melodic beat in the mortar: "But now, young people no more have time for this. They buy Pepsi-Cola and want motorcycles instead." My attempt to commiserate on the declining quality of life brought an immediate clarification: "No no, each way is good—for those who practice it."

Even when clear conflict is present in a relationship, good manners prevail. When two of our closest friends, Abdullah and Rahmeh, felt strongly insulted and distressed because their daughter and son-in-law slighted them during a brief home leave and came to them only on the second day, arriving belatedly and staying briefly, they expressed only the slightest of recriminations for this and generally sustained a polite show of friendliness and satisfaction (see Wikan 1982 for an extended discussion of this particular case). Indeed, it is not just anger or disapproval that should be suppressed: any strong show of emotion is best controlled as unsettling and impolite. Thus when we observed a mother and married daughter meeting under happy circumstances and for the first time in several years, the two greeted each other with the formality and restraint of distant acquaintances.

NORMATIVE PRINCIPLES

What are the crucial normative principles on which such patterns of behavior are based? We face a certain methodological impasse in seeking the answer, since the actors themselves, by virtue of the very code that interests us, are constrained from expounding it. To state the rules of elegance and grace is always inelegant and difficult because they are never routinely explicated in that manner. To illustrate them by one's own successes would be to destroy those very successes; to praise the successes of others in such explicit terms would be both unsubtle and fawning. Our main source of evidence must remain the concrete kinds of examples briefly noted above, understood in the full context of their circumstances. But generalizations that derive from such evidence will be entirely cast in *our* modes of conceptualization. And how can the anthropologist, less sensitive than Soharis to the low-keyed subtleties of their style, know that he has identified the main components of the case correctly and, equally difficult, provide convincing documentation of it for the reader?

In the course of field work, some firmer evidence did progressively emerge to support and clarify the wealth of implicit material. With respect to the basic importance and valuation of the ideology, a widely celebrated proverb is instructive: "The ornament of a man is beautiful manners, while the ornament of a woman is gold." Other proverbs occasionally explicate aspects of the code, though usually in the context of real-life dilemmas or realism.

Second, life stories and incidents were sometimes turned into morality tales to instruct me in the ways and values of Oman. For example, the life story of the now aging, highly respected imam of the Market Mosque was told to me:

For a number of years after he was entrusted with the administration of the *waqf* (the mosque property and income) he used part of this property for his own shop, and let the mosque deteriorate, never spending money on its repairs. Many people thought he must be using the income for his own purposes only. So it continued, year after year. Then suddenly, he rebuilt the whole mosque, all new. For all those years he had been saving up and reinvesting the *waqf* income. He never told anybody, nor did they ever criticize him to his face. But now, those who distrusted him must say "What a good man!"

Third and most importantly, a few of my wife's and my own close friends, who understood and were willing to involve themselves more deeply in us and our interests, were even prepared to violate the style they cherish by reporting on themselves and others, and explaining the relevant rules to us. My closest friend, Ali, even explained some of his most personal concerns and dilemmas in such terms.

The essence of this ideology lies in its emphasis on the dignity and individuality of the person—that both of others and of oneself. Vis-á-vis others, this entails showing respect toward everyone, regardless of their power and rank; not challenging their credentials or presentation of self; not criticizing their performance; not asserting oneself at their expense; offering them precedence before oneself. But this should not take a form that detracts from the dignity of one's own person: one is responsible for oneself and one's own fate, and should go about one's work and one's life with competence and assurance; one should avoid confusion, weakness, or any uncontrolled emotion; one should be in command of one's situation and perform one's part so that others can rely on one; one should avoid bragging and self-praise and let all one's talk be responsible and true and discrete.

When situations arise that disturb the tenor of politeness and manners in a gathering—as when others are vulgar or insulting or when accident or crisis strips away pretences—it is for each to manage his own behavior in the best possible way, rather than to direct or defend others. In other words, the failure of others does not absolve the actor himself from observing the constraints and niceties of manners; it gives him no license to respond in a manner different from normal politeness. To answer insult or vulgarity with abuse or any other breach of etiquette is compromising to the person no matter what provocation he has been given.

With this emphasis on good manners goes an ingrained assumption that there is a "correct way" of doing everything—valid, that is, for oneself, but optional for others, who may be pursuing other styles. Repeatedly in the commentary of Soharis this was associated with the ideas of education and civilization. Sohari men particularly seem to embrace the view that bad manners are an expression of ignorance; to know what is right is to do what is right. Education will enable persons to construct an ordered and correct life for themselves, by under-

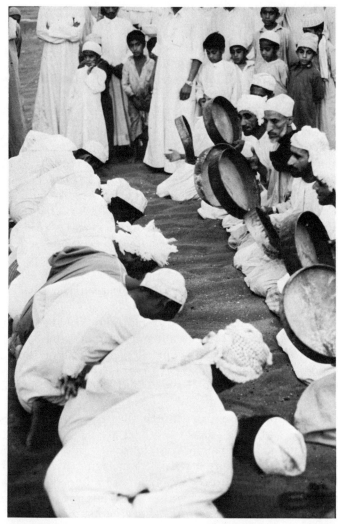

Men engaged in pantomime songs to tambourines during a wedding celebration.

standing the dangers of the various vicissitudes of life, and taking the correct precautions. Luck and chance have little place in this view of man, and misfortune elicits only very moderate compassion, while there is no greatness in tragedy. More important than intentions are appearances, since they are indicators that good manners are indeed mastered and being observed.

EFFECTS ON PRESENTATION OF SELF

Good manners may demand the expression of hierarchy and precedence in certain clearly defined contexts; otherwise, the basic requirement is an egalitarian practice of mutual respect and individual tactfulness. This tactfulness entails that persons are socially accepted and confirmed in the roles which they assume, that is, the selves which they present to the world. In this respect, the ideology is closely in harmony with the ethics of Islam, which judges a man by his acts and not by his beliefs or intentions. But if, by the operation of Sohari tact, you become what you claim to be, what claims can you make without violating good manners and becoming assertive, crude, or braggardly? As I noted in connection with wealth and class, there are other goals in life than good manners which persons seek for themselves and the achievement of which they admire in others. Of these, wealth seems the most prominent. But claims to achievement in this as in other fields must be tempered by the code of good manners—most strictly in the case of men, who are also the economic managers of the household.

What then are the permissable uses of wealth which can make its presence conspicuous? Mainly the building of a commodious house in cement, as an increasing number of Soharis are doing. Where resources are somewhat limited, one starts by constructing only the outer compound wall in cement, leaving the house itself in traditional thatch *(barasti)*—perhaps inadvertently revealing the priority of making wealth known over enjoying its fruits. In the case of the most prosperous and ambitious, on the other hand, the buildings also include a spacious, separate guest room *(majlis)*, even equipped with ceiling fans for the future date when Sohar will be provided with electricity. But fear of ostentation and other constraints mean that the guest *majlis* stands unused and empty—an announcement of wealth but not a means of hospitality or other social activity. Indeed, the elaboration of hospitality into a practice of merit-giving or influence-producing feasts, so nearly ubiquitous in one form or another in the Middle East, is practically absent. Even the extremely infrequent *nāder* (thanksgiving feast) must be performed under the emphatic cloak of honoring God rather than the giver. Only the wedding feast is the occasion for a truly conspicuous dissipation of wealth on the groom's side. Small wonder then that grooms have been so remarkably uncooperative in supporting the Sultan's recent ordinance forbidding bride prices of more than 300 Rials ($900): though done to make marriage more possible to the average, impecunious man, it also robs him of this one and unique occasion for public ostentation.

Wealth may be discreetly sensed in the clothing of men. Immaculate whiteness of clothes has been noted as an important signifier of rank.

Besides indicating a nonmanual occupation, perpetual immaculateness in these hot and dusty surroundings is difficult to maintain
even for the most sedentary. Its importance is indicated by the fact that
men choose to wash their own clothes, or if possible have them washed
and ironed professionally in the market, rather than entrusting their
wives with the task. Clothing thus becomes an item of conspicuous
consumption of some magnitude; besides, it serves as an expression of
the man's self-respect, the commendable attention he gives—and has
the leisure and resources to give—to his own personal dignity. It seems
to me plausible to see the rather excessive and finicky attention of
Soharis to their health and its protection in the same light.

The clothes, and even more the ornaments, of women, generally
worth about $3,000 in gold alone, are a far more flamboyant expres-
sion of wealth. But this, after all, is wealth earned not by the woman
who exhibits it but by her husband, whom she honors in wearing it, and
he can hardly be blamed for being impolite and ostentatious thus to
express his respect for his wife.

In most other ways, the ideology of politeness encourages a gracious
but rather puritan style. How else can a man seeking to live by, and win
repute by, such a code present himself to others? Beyond practicing the
required tact, grace, and attentiveness to others, only by showing in all
his demeanor that he possesses the personal qualities entailed in this
politeness: constraint, calmness, control of himself and his own situation, responsibility. Though forthcoming and courteous, he had best
show moderation in all things. Sohari men present themselves to the
world as consistently reserved: moderate in praise, restrained in criticism, inhibited in emotional expression, lacking in both indignation and
positive involvement. Though invariably hospitable, there is, particularly among men, an underplaying of the giving of hospitality and
among all a striking lack of acknowledgment of its acceptance, while
individual gifts are always inconspicuously presented and indifferently
received. Again particularly among men, levity and merriment are
eschewed, even among close friends and equals; the demonstrative
relaxation of jest and banter is avoided, and disapproved where it
occurs among youths. Joking is showing disrespect; significantly, the
only extended incident of joking and ribaldry which I observed involved as the main protagonists a somewhat marginal shaikh and a zutti
blacksmith. Among women, on the contrary, relatively uninhibited
sexual joking often takes place between friends, according to my wife's
observations. Indeed, women are in a rather different position from
that of men in their practice of politeness and tact, since their social
world is so very differently constructed. (A fuller discussion of this
issue will be pursued later, chapter 13.)

The ideology of politeness not only systematically censors a person's

presentation of self and thus the encounters and sequences of interaction that emerge but also systematically affects the person's management of his assets and his life. I have said that the tact exercised by
others allows a person to *be* the self that he presents to the world. Each
person therefore recognizes that it is his *practice* which will matter, and,
depending on the material resources at hand and his strength of
character, he acts accordingly. But what is sought is not the superficial
impression and the transient projection of an image: it is the long term
that counts, and the social person that emerges through perseverance
and plan, as with the imam in the above-quoted morality tale. This
perspective on the self was made entirely explicit for my benefit by Ali,
describing how he came home to Sohar at the age of twenty-three after
eleven years abroad, and set about creating the Ali that he wished to
become (see chapter 15). In his first, faltering moves, he took the advice
of his father, but then progressively followed his own course, even
against the judgment of his father, whose confidence and support he
thereby quickly lost. Nor did this failure of loyalty from his father
absolve Ali from fulfilling his part of the relationship and giving his
father one-quarter of his income each month. But with the resources
left to him, and all his time and tact and intelligence, he went about
systematically forging a life and its foundations, demonstrating with
patience and shrewdness the polite integrity to which he aspired. All
his decisions and dispositions were, to the best of his ability, cast in
harmony with the dominant ideology of politeness.

AGGREGATE EFFECTS

If many or most people in Sohar do this, as their overt behavior
seems to indicate, the aggregate consequences on their society should
be logically derivable and empirically identifiable. I shall focus on the
three aspects of behavior: *(a)* nonsanction of others, *(b)* nondefense of
self, and *(c)* nonassertion of self.

(a) The requirement of each person that he exercise tact and sustain
others in their chosen performance, so basic to Sohari politeness,
entails an absence of diffuse collective sanctions on the behavior of
individuals. An example from my wife's material (Wikan 1982, particularly pp. 143 ff.) may highlight this best. In the circle of her closest
friends—a group of very polite and virtuous women—was one married
woman who was an active and not very discreet prostitute. Though
such activity is regarded as shockingly immoral and the most serious sin
a woman can commit, there were no apparent sanctions against her in
the circle of her friends, no avoidance of her company, and no fear of
being associated with her. As these women would point out in response

to my wife's queries, she had done nothing bad toward them that could occasion such reactions on their part. Even their husbands, fathers, and brothers, though fearful of the possibility of immorality by their own women, were constrained by the ideology of politeness from sanctioning their neighbor or requiring of their women the rudeness necessary to snub her and disassociate themselves from her. The neighbors were sure that no word of her activity ever reached her husband: to tell him would be embarrassing, tactless, and shameful. This also left him the option of feigning ignorance of his wife's infidelity, an option that he chose, for reasons known to him alone, though this was probably a pretense. In the absence of reactions from him, as the person wronged, there seemed indeed to be no negative sanctions against her. Idle talk and gossip being likewise impolite and compromising to the person who practiced it, there was not an active public opinion formed behind her back which might build up to produce serious consequences for her in the long run. No doubt a great number of people were aware of her activities, but the constraints on speaking about it prevented any kind of collective indignation from emerging. A similar situation could be observed in numerous, less extreme cases. Both logic and observation thus clearly indicate the absence of clear public opinion and serious diffuse sanctions in the community as a whole.

Within the family and household, a similar restraining effect can be observed on the strength of sanctions and control of others. Anderson (1982) very perceptively describes a distinction found among Pakhtuns—and also, I think, among a number of Middle Eastern peoples with a strong code of honor and etiquette—between the "polite" code followed in interaction in symmetrical, largely public relations and the "rough" code adopted in complementary and especially intimate relations. No such distinction can be made in the Sohari situation: the ideology of polite behavior permeates all social relations. Though perhaps more difficult to practice consistently in these intimate relations, where mutual vulnerability and emotional involvement can be overpowering, it yet severely restrains the kinds of expression, and effects the kinds of interactional sequences, that take place in the privacy of the home, and therefore also the character of domestic relations.

When Ali's father-in-law, into whose household Ali moved at marriage, kept the whole bride price for himself and provided his daughter Fatima with none of the customary gold jewelry, and in addition appropriated the monthly installments that Ali, absent on labor migration, sent his wife, there was no polite way whereby Ali felt he could do anything about it ("I was a new man, in a weak situation"). But a year later, when the father-in-law under similar circumstances again kept two of Fatima's monthly remittances, Ali on his return did feel he could inquire what had happened to the money. The father-in-law explained that he had been short of money at the time and needed it to replace the tires on his Land Rover, which allowed Ali to reply calmly that it would be convenient if he paid it back now. Though this hardly suited the father-in-law, he yet felt he had to start paying the sum back in installments. When the second installment failed to eventuate, and Ali had the cheek to remind him of it, all the father-in-law could say was "Ali, your character is changing. You used to give freely, as the Koran enjoins," to which Ali reports, probably with *l'esprit d'escalier*, to have retorted: "But then I should give to the poor and the needy, and not the likes of you."

A similar constraint should also govern husband-wife relations, and, from everything we were able to observe, seems to do so. Though Latifa's husband once, in a sudden fit of impatience with his wife, smashed a portable radio against the wall of their room, he strives to be always polite "so Latifa will not say/think I am bad!" She, on her part, never speaks up or acts badly toward him, but sometimes will not speak to him at all "for half an hour or an hour." Even in their behavior toward small children, parents and other adults try to practice the niceties of politeness, and avoid as much as possible the embarrassment of having to scold or punish to control misdemeanor.

In this way, tact and politeness may be seen to permeate all life and limit the modes by which one appropriately can attempt to sanction others in an encounter or affect the repute of others not present in an encounter.

(b) Omani politeness entails that impolite behavior, even overt insults directed against oneself, does not absolve the person thus abused from observing all the constraints of politeness. In its implications, this would mean that a person cannot defend his own dignity against attack, lest he loose it by his own acts. And so it would seem to be, as manifested by the reactions of Soharis. A slight, an insult, or a challenge to honor leads not to counterattack but normally to withdrawal. During or after the event, no mobilization of support and no effort at retribution take place. Indeed, men seem even to refrain from seeking the moral support of their closest intimates by reporting such insults to them; women, in their differently constituted networks, seem to feel slightly freer to elicit sympathy from intimates after the event. The pattern of restraint can be observed most strikingly in public interaction, where persons deftly extricate themselves at the first sign of vulgarity or insult or, where this is not practicable, suffer it passively or try to ignore it. When neighborhood children completely destroyed one of Nizam Ahmed's rare attempts to use his *majlis* (guest room) for a solemn and self-important exercise of hospitality by hooting and crying catcalls outside the windows, Nizam first tried to ignore it, then excused himself and went outside, only to see the culprits disappear down the street. He then returned to the pretense of ignoring their existence (rather than, for example, posting a member of his household outside to keep the children away or seeking to frighten them with threats of reprisal), but they again took up their antics. Likewise, when the clearly senior woman of a group was denied the seat of honor beside her own grandson in the front of the car by a frivolous and overassertive younger woman, she did not protest and appeal to her grandson or the others, but in indignation confided to her granddaughter afterward that she would never again go anywhere together with that trollop (Wikan 1982:156).

In defense of distinctive rights in a relationship, on the other hand, recourse can be had to others, but then in their capacity of objective third parties and not as partisan support. Thus, when Fatima felt personally badly treated by her husband at the beginning of their marriage, she told no one, not even her own mother. But when she wanted her right to a house of her own, as a last resort she dressed in her best clothes and declared to her husband Ali that they should go together and visit *his* father. Whether from the threat of shaming him before his father or through the confirmation she thereby produced that her demand was justified, this led to her husband's agreement and immediate action. In all other kinds of cases, and often also in conflicts between spouses, the appropriate person to turn to is the Wali, or alternatively the shaikh of the quarter or the ethnic group, or perhaps the imam. So when Abdur Rahman heard that his wife's half-brother had defamed his honor by questioning his paternity, the result was no form of self-help from Abdur Rahman's side, but a court case in which the brother-in-law was acquitted for lack of witnesses.

Yet even the most polite performance and the most virtuous person must surely be in danger sometimes of being spoiled by slights, insults, or merely inadvertent involvement in unseemly scenes. What can a Sohari do to repair such damage when he cannot fight back? There is really no single answer to this, other than vigilance and foresight. So in making his dispositions and decisions, a person must ever have an eye to what might eventuate in any situation, and avoid those situations that are frought with risks. It is best not to enter into transactions of any kind with persons previously experienced or imagined to be "rude," or take forms of employment in or near Sohar (but not on labor migration far from home) that entail potentially degrading activity or even reduction of autonomy and its associated freedom of maneuver and withdrawal. "Otherwise, you only get into trouble. I have worked, I have taken care of my life, I have a job and a family, and no one can speak a bad word against me. I would be a fool to jeopardize this by keeping bad company."

Once the damage has been done, all one can do is sever relations. Despite a long and close friendship, Yusuf adopted a "nonspeaking" stand toward his neighbor when the latter in an exchange criticized him for not repaying a quite trifling amount that he purportedly owed. After ten years of ignoring the existence of his closest neighbor, some people may think him rather unyielding, and "not speaking" even to the extent of not greeting a neighbor is thought to border on impolite behavior, but such withdrawal is still, barely, within the limits of what a person may be allowed in his defense of self. After all, "if two bottles knock too hard together, both will be broken—and then, who can mend them?" Characteristically, the result is an absolute reduction of social activity, rather than its mobilization, around a conflict.

(c) To assert oneself (other than by an opulence of snacks in women's hospitality!) is bad form; to show off and do anything resembling strutting or bragging is distinctly shameful. This means that there is little encouragement to seek the attention of others, even by excellence in performance; and persons are not propelled to seek out arenas for activity. The general absence of such arenas entailing contests has been noted—with the very important exception of the marketplace (as will be discussed in chapter 14)—and there is very little encouragement for the more improvised and ad hoc creation of audiences, larger gatherings, or public events. Even the Wali acts with becoming modesty and moves about discreetly. Only the present Sultan has chosen to act at variance with this constraint in introducing a series of holidays and celebrations focusing on the leader and the nation in a fashion parroting that in the Near East. These innovations have been enthusiastically taken up by Soharis as progress and modernization, so for the national holiday in 1975 one could even observe, among other gaudy decorations, a green and white plyboard gate bearing the message: "The Ajams of Sohar congratulate Sultan Qaboos on National Day." But these are very new and still very inconsequential forms of assertion.

Since there are no important countervailing pressures on Soharis against withdrawal, and any association with others can give social repercussions, a "safe" policy of restraint becomes the simplest and most favored solution, particularly among men. The person who wishes to win the respect of his community can "sit in his house." With justified pride in self, many men will announce: "I go to the market, I go to the mosque, I return to my house. I say *Sala'am Aleikum. Bas* [that's all]."

The aggregate society that is generated from such principles and practices will have precisely the unfocused, dispersed character so noticeable in Sohar. It is not that factions do not exist, news does not become known, or gossip and other "impolite" behavior does not take place at all. But the assertion of factional division and support is ever so muted, many persons genuinely are never reached by news that would indeed interest them, and gossip and scandal are communicated by indirection and suggestion. Others are rarely mobilized in confrontations and contests; even less are leaders or spokesmen of public opinion or interest groups ever thrust forward. Practically no matter what else may be happening, the dominant tenor of interaction is its grace and politeness.

POLITENESS AND HONOR

The standards of conduct outlined above provide the ideals against which a person's worth is measured and by which he seeks to compose himself and his life. They must provide the measure of what Pitt-Rivers (1965) has defined as honor: "the value of a person in his own eyes, but also in the eyes of his society. It is his estimation of his own worth, his *claim* to pride, but it is also the acknowledgement of that claim, his *right* to pride" (p. 21). In this sense, what I have been discussing in this chapter is the Sohari code of honor; its central importance to the understanding of Sohari social life is then perhaps more readily accepted.

But this Sohari version of a code of honor raises a number of perplexing problems. Many of these have been clarified in Wikan's explicit and penetrating analysis, with particular reference to gender roles and women's conceptualizations and behavior (Wikan 1982:141ff.). Sohar confronts us with a code of honor that inhibits the articulation of public opinion about a person's worth, expressed in judgments of criticism or praise, ridicule and scorn or deference. It likewise dampens the assertion of one's own honor, the demonstration of individual excellence, the expression of claims to pride, and even denies a person's right to some forms of pride in himself. Further, it forbids any form of violence to cleanse one's name, indeed any strong action of a person in defense of his own honor. Even when eliminating those false paradoxes that arise because our implicit conceptions of honor are unnecessarily colored by the particulars of its Mediterranean version, emphasizing a bellicose assertion of virility, real problems do remain. We need to understand the connection between the person's private image of himself and the public tact that is exercised toward him, and we search in vain for a convincing identification of those strong sanctions that would seem required to explain the pervasive practice of politeness, consideration, and honorable restraint in the population. Ali tells how an elderly, good woman whom he had known since childhood, one day looked gravely at him and asked: "Ali, are you a man?" He thought about her words and their possible import all night, and the next day he proceeded to reverse his long-term dispositions and essentially change the course of his life. The story may be apocryphal, but in any case, why should he care what the woman thought of him? If he did not heed what may have been a cryptic critical judgment, she would nonetheless have been constrained by the ideology of politeness always to treat him respectfully and not speak badly of him behind his back. Searching for a control or contrastive case, I am reminded of a meticulously clean and distinguished-looking figure, a member of the dynastic family, who occasionally wanders in the marketplace and converses about listeners' letters that he writes to the Arabic program of the BBC. There were clear signs in his behavior that made me suspect him to be mentally unbalanced, but I was unable to observe any sign in the polite throng that he was less than what he pretended to be, and I never heard a derogatory comment behind his back. What then has Ali, or anyone else, to fear by *not* being honorable?

The empirical, if not theoretical, resolution to this puzzle seems to be that a person's own feeling of dignity is of great importance to him or to her, and that, though politeness can largely be trusted to prevail, the person is concerned about what others *really* think, in their heart or hearts. This is what drives the person to such perfectionism in style, and distress at the unseemly. Men, who must move in an open society and participate in a multitude of brief and superficial encounters, are particularly exposed to such problems. With this perspective, we can more readily understand and empathize with the male view that the self is so vulnerable, rather than so safe, in this in so many ways gentle environment. The practice by others of politeness creates for each throughout life an isolation that breeds in each man the loneliness of a long-distance runner. And so each is led to practice the aloofness, the noninvolvement, that harmonizes with politeness and reinforces its practice.

12

Household and Kinship

Family and household provide the ultimate basis for all social reproduction, and we may expect the patterns that are predominant in this field to have profound consequences, directly and indirectly, for the organization and maintenance of all the cotraditions that are found in Sohar. Very briefly, it is true to say that family and household in Sohar show a markedly "urban" or "modern" structure, in that they are characterized by a pattern of relatively small and exclusive units. They are groups into which their members retire to partake of a private and largely internal social life. Thus, households are not open to the larger society or invaded by its members, except for certain priviledged persons and times. Nor are they intricately embedded in larger kin groups and networks. In all these respects, their forms approach those found in modern Western industrial societies, and to some extent other major urban civilizations, and differ from those of most primitive and tribal societies. But it would be entirely premature to conclude that these similarities in form arise from similarities in kinship values or the mode of functioning of households in relation to labor markets and physical mobility. The ideological basis for the forms of Sohari household and family are distinctive and also inconsistent in ways that pose dilemmas and contradictions, so the arrangements that people make are often the outcome of compromise and are at odds with some of their ideals and interests. Consequently, an analysis of these forms is a relatively complex matter, and would require a quite extended discussion. Recognizing this, I shall identify only *some* of the main values and circumstances that generate *some* of the major resultant patterns. To provide the descriptive data on which such a partial analysis can build, I shall proceed from the more overt surface patterns and inward toward the more fundamental interconnections.

Households in Sohar each occupy a distinctive physical space, which is laid out in a relatively sterotypical basic pattern. The distinctness of the unit is marked—both materially created and symbolically expressed—by a compound wall about eight feet tall, with a single gate that can be locked. This wall should be impenetrable. If it is built of palm thatch—as is most common—it is possible by putting one's eye to the cracks to peep through; but to do so from the outside is very bad manners, whereas persons inside sometimes do peep to observe the public scene outside.

The compound area is square, and will contain an open court area and enclosed rooms. The latter should provide distinct areas for sleeping and inside living, for a kitchen, and for bathroom and toilet facilities. The toilet is generally just a walled-off sandy area in which the sand is occasionally cleaned and changed, used mainly by women, whereas men use the beach or the gardens. There is also usually a veranda area or a raised sitting platform for outside living and sleeping; in the hottest summer months the family may even move out into the open streets and lanes, or to the beach, for sleeping. In addition, there is often optionally a separate *majlis* (guest area) just inside the gate, screened off from the inner court.

The compound is unequivocally identified with a domestic unit. While this group may be temporarily joined by close kinfolk who stay as houseguests, its real membership is clearly delimited. Every Sohari must be a member of one, and only one, such domestic unit. Persons who are absent on labor migration are generally counted as members of the domestic unit. This reflects both the absence of any other basis for identity of the absent migrant within Sohar and his continued economic contribution to the household.

While the delimitation of each domestic unit is definitive, no single criterion is entirely satisfactory to define its constituition. Its component members hold private and usually some joint property. Income for its maintenance is normally produced by its members, but substantial subsidies may also be provided from kinsmen outside, while some income of its members may be kept privately for themselves. Thus, every woman has her locked chest *(sanduq)* into which may enter gifts or income she receives; boys and men contribute as they see fit from their earnings. Joint cooking is likewise no sure indicator, since neighbors both cooperate and redistribute dishes, and sometimes contribute persistently by providing for old or disabled neighbors. Commensality is a matter for individual decision: while it is common in elementary families with small children, the presence of several mature males generally entails segregation of the sexes during eating. Apart from the periodic but rare presence of visitors as houseguests, the clearest definition of membership is given by sleeping arrangements, expressed by the locking or barring of the gate at night when all are in.

Small sample censuses were made of households in several parts of Sohar: the predominantly Arab ward of Sobara, the predominantly Baluchi ward of South Sallan, and the predominantly Bedouin ward of Hambar. In each, a neighborhood was mapped in detail for household composition, providing the data for table 1.

TABLE 1. HOUSEHOLD COMPOSITION IN THREE AREAS OF SOHAR

Item	Sobara		Sallan		Hambar	
	Number	Percentage	Number	Percentage	Number	Percentage
Incomplete household	3	7	4	6	1	3
Solitary couple	4	10	10	14	3	10
Elementary family	14	35	26	38	15	50
+ additional dependants	10	25	4	6	1	3
Polygynous household	1	2	2	3	5	17
Patrilateral joint households	7	17	10	14	5	17
Matrilateral joint households	1	2	13	19	0	0
Average size	5.9		4.7		4.8	

One may further note that 42 percent of the households censused contained 4, 5, or 6 persons, and far the largest number of persons lived in households of 6 members, whereas the largest single household contained 15 members. Of the 703 persons included in this census, only 5 (men) lived alone. Other features brought out by the tabulation are: (a) the notable frequency of matrilateral joint households among Baluchis, arising from their custom of uxorilocality upon marriage (of the 14 such households, 11 contained 2 married couples and only 3 contained 3 married couples); (b) the only moderate frequency of patrilateral joint households, despite the clear ideology encouraging such residence (of the 22 such households, 19 contained 2 married couples and only 3 contained 3 married couples); (c) the higher frequency of polygynous households among bedouin, and (d) the ban on stranger, nonkin membership in the household reflected in the absence of any such unrelated person from any of the households enumerated.

It is clear that the central, constituting relationship in a household is that between spouses. Those very few persons who live alone are widowers or male transsexuals, while incomplete households are the result of death or divorce, and are either a temporary phase or a brief final phase in a faimly's history. Men who become single will seek to remarry, or leave on labor migration, or if they are old they may choose to move in with a married child or some other close relative. Women of marriageable age are not allowed to reside separately or remain single. When her second, beloved husband died, leaving her widowed with three young sons, Said's mother pleaded with her father, the shaikh, to allow her to remain single and support her children by sewing. She moved her house close to his, yet after a few year's grace for the sake of the children, he gave her, against her will, in marriage to a third husband.

Defacto incomplete households result more frequently from the absence of the husband on labor migration. The frequency of such absences among men in Sohar in 1974–75 was running at about 25 percent. Though most of the migrants are single young men, the absence also of many married men poses difficulties to household arrangements. "If a woman has three or four children, like a son who is thirteen or fourteen years old and understands what is happening, then the husband can leave her, but not otherwise. Someone must be responsible for her; she must not be left alone. . . . If someone climbed over this compound wall, came in, and she was alone, could she fight him? He could steal and take away anything he wished." But the more pervasive fear among men arises from the increased opportunity for sexual misdemeanor by wives which results from the husband's absence. "The wife's infidelity is a *great* shame for the husband. But it only happens because he is stupid. He is responsible; he should think. He must prevent her from doing such things. If he is away, he must set another person to watch her, make reliable arrangements." The common solution adopted in the situation of labor migration is residence in a joint household, whereby close relatives take on these supervisory functions for each other: among Arabs and Ajams in the form of patrilateral joint arrangements, among Baluchis either virilocal or uxorilocal residence. Characteristically, such joint household arrangements rarely comprise more than two married couples, as noted. This is especially true of those involving agnates: such households never comprise a father and all his sons, but only that son or those sons who are urgently in need of the father's—and mother's—supervisory services because of their own absence. The effective factor that generates joint households is thus not the patrilineal ideology, to which lip service is frequently paid, but the special conceptions of male and female gender roles combined with male absence on labor migration. Indeed, the informant cited above on residence arrangements even had the (incorrect) impression that the Shariah defines a married woman's *right* to her own house, and thereby justifies the strongly preferred, and predominantly practiced, pattern of elementary family households.

The distinctness and isolation of the household is very clearly shown in the conventions of limited access to the domestic space, and in rituals performed on entry and exit from this space. A home may be entered only by some few outsiders in clearly defined capacities, for example: (1) neighborhood children, at the times of day when the husband is absent or when other visitors are present; (2) the closest kinsfolk, with greater constraints on high-status than low-status persons; (3) visitors, that is, persons either who have been invited or who stand in reciprocal visiting relationships to each other (such visits are made by women only when the adult males of the household are absent, and by men only when they are present); and (4) a few special-status strangers (elderly women who operate as itinerant hawkers and offer wares for sale, astrologers and magicians (*basîr*) who sell charms and other services, or beggars).

All these persons must observe certain rituals at the threshold. They must knock and call at the gate, and not enter until invited to do so (this requirement is relaxed for small children and between neighboring women on an intimately friendly footing, when males are absent). Males must also before entering make a warning call (*hudd*!) to alert those occupants of the house who might not have noticed their call for permission to enter. The members of the household, on the other hand, emphasize the *exit* from the house. Men dress to cover their chest and arms, which may be exposed in the privacy of their home, and don their caps. Women cover their face with the *burqa* (mask)—which may be pushed up on the head in the home—and drape themselves in a shawl (*lézo*), while if they plan to go more than a few yards along the lane, they also assume the full *abba* (cloak).

Within the household all persons are related in terms of either close kinship or marriage. There is no way by which a man and a woman who are not so closely related that they are constrained by the incest taboo can reside together except by entering into a legal marriage. Thus, all the relationships between household members are such as are cast in terms of Islamic family law, most significantly husband-wife and parent-child.

As codified by Islam, marriage is a highly unequal arrangement. The wife is the legal ward of her husband, while she has the right to obtain all necessary material support from him. The husband also has uni-lateral monopoly rights to his wife's sexuality. The jealousy that may be aroused in the wife through the husband's entry into plural marriage or his extramarital relations with prostitutes and transsexuals is recog-nized by Soharis, but provides no legal basis for complaint from the wife. A few cases were recorded of first wives abandoning the husband on his entry into a second marriage, but these dissolutions of marriage reflect a realistic accommodation to strong individual feelings and no legal rights on the part of the wife. Extramarital relations on the part of the husband when away from home are accepted by the wife as an inevitable result of a man's physiological constitution and needs.

In regard to authority, a similar inequality obtains. Strictly speaking, a wife should not leave the compound without her husband's explicit permission. Though she has a legal right to visit her parents—once a week, fortnight, or month according to the distance involved—even this can be withheld by the husband if he can show sound reasons, and the visit should, in any case, take place according to his arrangements and specifications. The wife's purchase or sale of real property held in her own name can likewise take place only under the direction of her husband as her legal guardian.

Children are in a similar legal position vis-a-vis their father: for girls, this lasts until these rights and obligations are transferred to the husband upon marriage (the rights revert to the father or closest adult male agnate in the case of divorce or bereavement); for boys, it lasts until puberty, and in practice considerably longer unless they depart from the household on labor migration. The husband and father likewise is invested with ultimate authority in all normative and moral matters, and the final power of decision in all questions concerning wife and children, as well as the responsibility for their behavior and training. The duty to "educate" his wife was very explicitly stated by a number of husbands, and acquiesced to by their wives; even the woman's moral integrity reflects, in the view of many men, ultimately more profoundly on him than on herself. Thus, Ali could state categorically that even the shame of adultery recoils on her husband rather than the woman herself: "It is not her responsibility; it comes from lack of education. How can she know the right from the wrong when her parents and her husband do not show her and look after her?"

The exercise of these comprehensive powers and responsibilities by the head of the household is profoundly shaped by the requirements of politeness and grace in all his demeanor. A man should be in command of his situation without making an unseemly spectacle of his authority and power: he should be obeyed because he is respected and admired by his family, not because his sanctions are feared. When Ali discovered that his first wife's mother had a past history of sexual misbehavior, he immediately divorced his wife rather than involve himself in the concerns and risk his own failure in imposing other standards on her. And in discussing the immoral activities of another married woman, her acquaintances explained to my wife that it was better for her husband to remain passive than to try to lock her up in her house; besides being fruitless, the latter course would only aggravate matters by drawing attention to the scandal. Even vis-à-vis small children, parents are signally reluctant to assert active authority in response to rebelliousness because of the loss of poise and grace that such reactions entail. This is carried to such lengths that young mothers, to forestall the embarrassment of their infants' simply crying, have adopted the deplorable measure of feeding infants up to the age of one or two years the opium product *suqūr**. To shape a marital and domestic relationship so that it can serve to enhance the esteem of a person in his or her own and others' judgment, the fundamental requirement seems to be that it should allow each party to act gracefully and be respected by the other, not that it exhibits a well-orderedness that derives from tyranny, no matter how effective.

The recurrent pursuits that the household is called upon to organize are the provision of food, clothing, rest, and shelter for its members, and also their provision with the resources that they need to enter into social relations outside the domestic unit. These pursuits have two faces: the preparation and consumption that take place internal to the household, and the external relations by which household members engage themselves with the outside in production and exchange. Gender roles are complementary with respect to these two faces, rather than being based on division of labor in terms of specific tasks. Women normally do all housework and men are responsible for all work that relates the household to the outside, but most tasks can be done by either sex. For example, cooking is women's work only to the extent that it is done in the home and for domestic use; for larger feasts and all collective occasions, men are the cooks. Inversely, if production takes place within the home, it is done by women. The main work done in the home is sewing and embroidery; secondary trade in cloth is also pursued. This activity has considerable magnitude: one woman in every four provides herself, or her whole household, with considerable income from such work. Likewise, when agricultural production is organized within the household, women may work in addition to the men, but they never do so for strangers, as contract labor.

The activities of the household and its members follow a standard pattern through the day. People generally get up before sunrise; a meal of bread with tea and/or milk is eaten, whereupon the men depart for work—in their own fields or shops, or as employed labor. (Fishermen, on the other hand, depart very early and return around 9–10 A. M.) The main meal of the day is taken after noon prayers and consists generally of fish stew and rice; men generally return home for this meal. The afternoon is more variously utilized by men, including some period of leisure, before they rejoin their families for a supper meal after sunset and evening prayers.

These routines generate a characteristic pulsation in the home through the day: starting out as an exclusive private place for the family, it becomes available as a major social arena for women from the

*After the Sultan's recent prohibition of this practice, mothers reportedly have started giving their infants sleeping pills for the same purpose.

time men depart until they return at noon. Midday is again an exclusive period for family life, while in the afternoon occasional male use takes precedence over female use, and the presence of a man in the home inhibits access for neighboring women.

The activities performed by husband and wife as their respective responsibilities in household pursuits make them participants in very different social worlds. This is perhaps best conceptualized by using the metaphor of "social space" for the persons, places, and occasions in which each is expected to be involved. It then becomes clear that, though their roles may be represented as complementary, the social space in which husband and wife move are so different, and have so little overlap, as to be more adequately characterized as disparate or even discrepant. The privacy of the home is occupied by them jointly; otherwise, men must and do move in farflung, open networks, constantly confronting strangers and facing the option of whether to transform these strangers into acquaintances and associates, whereas women move in a small space both physically and in terms of persons, among close neighbors and close relatives, largely outside the normal space of the husband.

I have stated that the husband is responsible for all external relations of production and exchange. This includes all the family's purchases, except the small fraction that comes by way of the itinerant hawkers: men purchase the fish for dinner and select the vegetables, gravely judge the quality and select the colorful patterns in cotton and silk for their women's clothes, or surreptitiously show the merchants small samples that have been sent with them. Women are entirely barred from the market, or, more correctly, most women are, both by their own feeling of shame and by their husbands' or fathers' prohibition; and a majority of women will never in their life have seen the interior of the market or the contents of a shop. Occasionally, older couples, especially bedouin, may be observed together in the market, or even a mother and daughter together unchaperoned; the merchants report an increasing number coming year by year (in 1976, "so many" was specified as 4–5 among the 200–300 customers of a busy day). As noted, in January 1976 one woman also operated as a merchant to support herself and her children. Given the nature of her situation, her courage and fortitude in attempting this was clearly accepted and admired by both customers and merchants in the market.

The responsbility to earn an income also requires men to enter into a number of other relationships, and rewards the man with the widest networks and consequently the greatest range of options in transactions and careers. Service and assistance, as well as occasional small and even larger windfall profits, are also obtained through network connections, which must consequently be cultivated by men to enable them to perform their roles adequately.

The same need also arises from the husband's duty as his wife and children's legal guardian: to protect his family and their interests, obtain the news, information, and judgment that is needed to avoid unfortunate involvements and mobilize the shaikh or other *wasta* (mediator) at the right time, choose good sons-in-law and obtain desirable brides for sons, etc., he can use the largest possible range and variety of connections. Add to this the experience of labor migration, and a style of socializing in which information about everything from the price of Chinese crockery in Dubai to the name of a driver in the Ministry of Information and the kind of jets now being bought by the Iranian Air Force, and perhaps a picture of the complete man and his social space will emerge: a person perpetually husbanding particularistic informaion and managing himself and his network of connections in a pragmatically bounded, potentially infinite social space.

Women, on the other hand, are in their own judgment ignorant when measured by these standards. But such standards have no meaning in the social space that they occupy, and also are inconsistent with the ideals of behavior applied to women. They have been taught from an early age not to orient their behavior toward a wider audience but to develop inward-turning poise and modesty (Wikan 1982:148) that are appropriate and adequate in their role. Engaged in tasks internal to the household, and barred from moving unauthorized and unchaperoned outside the immediate neighborhood, they are automatically constrained to operate within a world of a different character from that of men.

A marriage thus unites two persons of different cultures (see chapter 9), trained to command very different skills and occupying highly discrepant social spaces. Their legal rights are unequal to the extent that one is a ward of the other. Yet what unfolds between them is no simple reflection of these facts. The actual relationship that emerges between husband and wife in Sohar is both high variable and characterized by qualities that may seem surprising and unexpected under the circumstances. Let me try to collect the major premises that inform the relationship, and generate from them the major characteristics that emerge.

(1) The conventionally appropriate roles for husband and wife are such as to make them functionally highly interdependent on each other. (2) As members of opposite sexes in a society prominently based on sexual segregation, much of their time is spent apart from each other. (3) As a consequence of premise 2, such interaction as takes place between them is limited to private situations. (4) Their formal rights

and powers over each other are highly unequal; likewise, their social worlds are of highly discrepant scale—and the domestic context in which they interact is a major sector of the wife's social space and a very small fraction of that of the husband.

Starting with this last premise, what then becomes the actual balance of defacto influence between spouses? The privacy of the domestic groups robs the man of most of the advantages that his much greater social network might otherwise have provided him. He cannot mobilize it and bring others in—essentially, spouses meet in solitary confrontation. And here, the discrepancy in scale between their respective worlds has unexpected implications. It is logical in theory, and apparent in practice, that the arena of the domestic unit is immensely more important to the life of the wife than to that of the husband. Consequently, she is far more prepared than he to escalate a conflict to protect her essential interests, while he is tempted by his freedom to withdraw from the scene to avoid the discomfort of battle, and write off a loss that concerns only a small corner of his life and activities. In most everyday matters, consequently, husband and wife tend to meet roughly as equals; and many couples seem, as Unni and I observed through close friendships, to exercise a fairly balanced control over each other in matters of mutual concern.

The inequality of jural powers is also modified by the mutual interdependence of spouses and the segregation of their nonprivate social spaces. Not only is the husband limited by the pervasive standards of politeness and elegance in how grossly he can assert his powers without loss of esteem, but he is also dependent on his wife for the provision of tangibles and intangibles which he needs to play his role in *his* world, as is she on him. She needs the clothes, jewelry, and consumables to act graciously within her small circle of friends. He may choose to look after his own clothes, but he needs other domestic services of food, rest, etc., from her, and he needs her cooperation in the modest but essential hospitality he practices. But far more important, he needs the essential intangibles of cooperation, modesty, respect, and submission from her to avoid the dishonor vis-a-vis the world at large of being a man unable to handle his own family. He needs her loyalty to forestall the slightest indiscretion, in circles to which he has no direct access, which might destroy the public image that he has so laboriously built and protected. He needs her faithfulness to avoid the subjectively devastating dishonor of her infidelity, the ever-present nightmare of the Sohari husband. As a result, spouses in Sohar seem essentially locked in a relationship of mutual vulnerability, unable to secure the cooperation of the other by safeguards and negative sanctions, and heavily dependent on a constructive reciprocity of doing right to the other, so as not to give the other cause to default.

The outcome, finally, of this effective equality of control, mutual vulnerability, and privacy of interaction is the emergence, often apparently quite swiftly, between spouses who meet as strangers on their wedding night, of a degree of intimacy and personal sensitivity quite subtle and profound. Tolerant and noninterfering in those parts of the other's life that are his or her sphere of legitimate separate assertion, they yet seem to succeed often in being close and genuine in their joint sharing of involvement in mutual matters. (For more extensive case materials depicting such qualities in the relationships of spouses refer to Wikan 1982.)

The preceding discussion should have demonstrated that an analysis—indeed, even on adequate description, of the husband-wife relation—cannot adequately be performed with data deriving only from within that relationship itself. The features and qualities of the relationship arise from the concerns, activities, and characteristics of the parties as whole persons, not just as husband and wife to each other. Among other concepts, I hve sought to use the metaphor of "social space" to capture some of those aspects of their disparate positions outside the relationship dyad which are most influential in shaping their opportunity situation, and thereby their behavior within it.

Nor can a description of the husband's and wife's roles be derived directly from a set of norms—whether as premises, ideals, or principles—concerning the legal and customary rights in marriage, the segregation of the sexes, the nature of patrilineal identities and loyalties, etc. It is only through the more comprehensive consideration of the life situation of men and women, taking account of *all* their diverse identities, activities, and interests, that one can depict and understand their problems and solutions in the management of their selves, in the praxis, commitments, and binding choices they make. Even where a particular practice seems to have a considerable degree of harmony with a particular feature of ideology, as in the tendency to form patrilateral joint families, there are other and wider considerations (*in casu* the fear of unfaithfulness) that are mainly effective in generating the practice.

We are thus forced to recognize that life in Sohar, as presumably in many places in the world, is genuinely problematic to its practitioners. Persons are not provided with a recipe of customs or patterns which offers an integrated solution to their major existential problems. The values and goals embraced by any single person need not be particularly coherent in a logical or cognitive sense, and even those that seem to exhibit a reasonable degree of such coherence may turn out to be highly incompatible and irreconcilable in practice. Therefore, the shaping of one's own roles and one's own life is a complex and continous matter of deliberation and management. This is not to say that the frustration of man's desires, and the need for foresight and deliberation, cannot be equally prominent features of the experience of participants in more uniform and culturally more closely integrated communities, but merely to observe that such cultures do apparently more often provide more unequivocal frames of reference and more limited ranges of options, in a number of concrete situations, than those that confront persons in Sohar.

Just as the husband-wife relationship cannot be understood in isolation but must be seen in conjunction with the other relations and activities of whole persons, so also the relevance of husband-wife relations is not exhausted by showing how they are expressed in the behavior of women and men as spouses. They in turn have a much wider relevance, affecting and generating various features of social organization outside the relationships of husbands and wives. I shall discuss these effects in three important fields: the degree of emergence of corporate descent groups, the relationships of affinity, and the social organization of neighborhoods.

I noted in chapter 5 the absolute primacy of an ideology of patrilineal descent, and the presence of a set of in part large and populous agnatic tribes as units of reference and identity. Even the Baluchi practice of uxorilocality at marriage implies no modification of this ideology: it is not the identity of future children as members of their father's tribe that is at issue, but the welfare of the bride, faced with the major transition of her life and in need of parental support in the Baluchi view. Yet, despite this unchallenged dominance of patriliny for the transmission of identity, and a pervasive rhetoric of descent, corporate descent groups do not emerge today on any level of segmentation, and the significance of descent groups seems to have been quite limited in Sohar Town, at least for the last few generations.

What might be the circumstances and processes that explain such a situation? We may seek them in (a) the prevailing patterns of property and work, (b) the politics of support, and (c) the sources of male esteem.

(a) The existence of some form of inheritable and potentially joint estate or the enticement or necessity for sons to join their fathers in larger cooperating work teams are generally recognized in the anthropological literature to provide the factors that may generate corporate descent groups and the growth points for their elaboration. Both factors are to some extent present in Sohar. Land, fishing vessels, and other property may be held collectively, and are inherited by Islamic law in a pattern favoring agnates, and boys over girls in the proportion 2:1. Second, both agriculture and fishing are best pursued by larger cooperating teams than the single person, and a traditional pattern of underemployment would presumably encourage persons to seek partnership in labor where they held shares in other factors of production or had other claims on those managing the team. To judge the importance of these factors, however, we must see them in the context of the total patterns of circulation of land, property, and labor. When we do this, other cross-pressures become apparent.

Apart from the allocation of occasional lands or wealth to pious purposes (whereby it becomes *waqf*, that is, mosque property), it is common for persons to die intestate with their property intact. In such cases both the difficulties in arranging an equitable permanent division of property between heirs and a certain emotional sensibility among the bereaved favor the postponement of partition. Consequently, a convenient unit of land use—a "garden," in the local idiom—often may be owned by three, four, five, ten, or even up to twenty persons. But the consequences for men of joint holdings in such shared estates are generally divisive and alienating rather than integrative. Public authorities, ultimately the Wali, underwrite the rights of ownership and protect titles, and so joint owners rarely need to unite in defense of their rights. Internal management decisions, on the other hand, are frequent and recurrent; to cut down or retain trees, to make investments in irrigation, which crops to favor, how to reconcile horticulture and the keeping of stock for milk and meat—all these questions become frustrating matters of joint decision or the basis of conflicting interests and judgment. Men therefore generally hold the view that such joint holdings are highly unsatisfactory. For women, on the other hand, the arrangement has distinct attractions. Though they are generally the smaller shareholders, their share is important to them in that it is generally administered by a brother, as joint owner, and not, as are their exclusively owned properties, by their husband. Consequently, their income from such shares is not so readily appropriated by their husband; and the existence of share interests in gardens provides women with the occasion/excuse to visit these places, thereby increasing their mobility and bringing them together with relatives. Males, on the contrary, prefer to sell their shares in such gardens to a coowner, and use the proceeds to purchase an exclusive plot of their own. Rather than encouraging the corporate emergence of descent groups, such agnatic joint holdings tend to create divisions among male agnates, become increasingly selective and incomplete, particularly in male membership, and ultimately dissolve.

As for joint task groups uniting close male agnates, the considerable occupational specialization and division of labor that characterize Sohar militate against this practice. There is an active labor market for short-term contracts and for specialized services. One man-hour is thus in no sense the equivalent of another, and it is distinctly poor management practice to use a son or a close agnate for tasks that would be more competently performed by a short-term specialist. Nor can the shop of a merchant in most cases assimilate more small boy assistants. As a consequence, there is no marked incentive of an economic or practical nature for the emergence of nuclei of agnates as work teams in most activities in Sohar.

(b) The politics of security and support likewise take a course that militates against the realization of agnatic corporate groups. For over a generation, the basic defense of life and property has effectively been provided by the state authorities; also before that, the Wali and the purely territorially based formal structure dependent on his authority were the major forces behind law and order. Yet even today, though ownership titles may be guaranteed by the public authorities, few claims are based on notarized title deeds and there are no institutions that automatically secure every person full equality before the law. In other words, in Sohar today, a person may need to mobilize political support to secure his interests. Where might he then turn? Most persons will have the options to seek the support of (1) a locally based group (neighborhood, small community, etc.); (2) an occupational group or similar common-interest category; (3) a descent group or tribe; or (4) one or several men of influence. Under various circumstances, each of these courses is possible, and is or has been practiced, but under the effectively centralized conditions of Sohar today, they are very unequally practicable and attractive. (1) Neighborhoods and wards used to coalesce in defense when suddenly attacked by marauding bedouin, though the scale of attack was often such that this was only a momentary response to effect a coordinated flight to a stronger, fortified position, notably the main fort of Sohar. Indeed, the emergence of the village of Sallan as an entity independent from Sohar town coincides, according to local accounts, with the defensive fortification of the mosque in Sallan for service as a place of refuge. Today there does not seem to be any occasion, other than a fire, when a person would mobilize a neighborhood as a collective. (2) As for occupational or similar common interest groups, there is no collective organization in the form of guilds, brotherhoods, or unions in Sohar. The only case in this category known to me was a spontaneous attempt by the sardine fishermen (pp. 32f.) to present a collective petition to the Sultan to have the Wali's decision on fishing rights overruled. Their reluctance to make any show of collective pressure and their individual fears of emerging as identifiable leaders or troublemakers were striking, and reflected the potential dangers inherent in such political mobilization in a political system as highly centralized as Sohar. There are thus, for example, some very clear common interests and desires among the merchants of Sohar's marketplace—and an awareness and some degree of realistic sensitivity to such public opinion on the part of the Wali—but any emergence of a constituted pressure group would certainly lead to drastic countermeasures. There can be no doubt that the information-gathering systems of the Walis have always been particularly keen observers of any such currents. (3) In the past, descent groups, tribes, and tribally based coalitions were sometimes mobilized, not only as collective interests and pressure groups but also in mass action. This was true not only of the bedouin but also of the population of Sohar town, as attested to by numerous traditions of concrete cases. The conflicts described in such accounts seem to have arisen mainly over homicide and revenge, or over land—both types of conflicts which are today emphatically the concern of the public authorities. Any attempt to mobilize agnatic support in such conflicts today, as pressure groups and not in self-helf, would surely lead to severe countersanctions from the state, and so no longer provides an occasion for corporate action. Possible advantages today of belonging to a large or wealthy descent group and tribe may arise from the diffuse support on many sides which a person can thereby obtain. But this will depend on the person's network connections, and is never a matter of corporate membership and obligation. Characteristically in Sohar today, even in kinship matters the agnatic group does not live by its corporate charter: though shares in the bride price obtained for a girl should by custom be given, at least in symbolic amounts, to all her male agnates up to and including first cousins, this is in fact practiced only selectively with those agnates with whom one is on friendly terms. For example, the Dabdub minimal lineage in Sobara is composed of four sets of siblings related as agnatic cousins. In the case of the marriage of maidens X and Y among them, agnates' shares of the bride prices were distributed to the boys as follows: for X, 100 Rials to her two brothers, 45 R. to one set of two cousins, 30 R. to another cousin, and none to a set of three cousins; for Y, 50 R. to her brother, 30 R. to one set of two cousins, 40 R. to another set of two cousins, and none to the set of three cousins. The amounts are adjusted to the ages of the boys in question, but mainly depend on the strength of friendly relations.

(4)The main advantage that may today ensue from membership in a large or wealthy tribe is that it may give a person access to an influential shaikh who can plead one's case before the central authorities. But agnatically based support and protection thereby become submerged in a general network of connections and relationships, and the political distinctiveness of descent groups and tribes dissolves. In any disagreement or conflict situation, the best course (see chapter 3) is to mobilze a *wasta* with influence. It becomes a matter of no consequence whether such a *wasta* can be called because he is the senior of one's family or tribe, or one's employer, or the shaikh of one's ward, or a wealthy or particularly reputable neighbor. As long as the product of his influence and his willingness to wield that influence is reasonably high, he will be mobilized. There is also a hidden caveat in this situation. Since all conflicts are ultimately resolvable by the Wali, and indeed a great number of them find their solution in his court, it is vitally important to have *wastas* who do not challenge the central authorities by emerging with any kind of semi independent and seditious power base. Their effect derives from their ability to speak well and wisely in court, to defuse the confrontation, and to vouch for the good behavior of their charge in complying with the Wali's wishes and admonishments. Both parties are therefore best served by mobilization on an ad hoc basis, from case to case, and without the emergence of patron-client relations that would entail a stable following, and consequently autonomous power base, for the *wasta*. Only by avoiding such stability can men exercise influence without offending the authorities, and thus best serve the interests of their ad hoc dependents. To the extent that men of influence involve themselves on behalf of members of their own tribe, they therefore tend to act emphatically as proxies for the central authorities rather than as spokesmen for their agnates. Add to this the fact that many of the issues that arise are divisive for descent groups and families, so leading men of the group may be involved in designing compromises rather than in being active spokesmen for any one party. Consequently, political activities will tend to reduce and obscure such collective identities as may be present, rather than to activate and express them.

(c) The final, and perhaps most profound, constraint on the emergence of corporate descent groups strikes at its very roots or growth points, such as the linkage between father and son. The public esteem accorded to a man depends above all, as I have discussed (chapter 11), on the dignity and social competance he exhibits: his mastery of his own situation, his wisdom and self-management, his autonomy and integrity—in sum, his "character." This is not obtained and demonstrated through a young man's association with his father; rather, it requires his deep and demonstrated independence of his father. It is furthered if he carves out his own separate career and is economically independent, instead of working for and with his father. It is demonstrated best if he lives in a separate household, so he can act as the responsible head of that household. It is safeguarded if he establishes himself at some distance, spatially and socially, from his agnates, where he can escape the quandary of simultaneously owing respect and obedience to his father and needing to demonstrate independent responsibility and judgment. In other words, every boy's ambition to win esteem, will propel him out of his paternal household and agnatic group and into the wider society as an independent operator.

This is directly reflected in most men's careers, and in the patterns of choice and arrangement that prevail in the town of Sohar. When boys in their early teens, or even before, have left Sohar on labor migration so consistently as to produce a mass exodus of this age group, it reflects employment opportunities as they have been in Sohar. Despite this employment situation, most of them have returned a decade later, when they have firmly established themselves as independent adults, and managed to secure some kind of employment. By their own accounts, the decisive factors that made them leave were domestic or personal.·People speak of "the need to gain experience" and "to be responsible for oneself." The actual moment of departure is frequently associated with the loss of the boy's mother, through death or divorce, when conflicts with stepmother and even with father are acknowledged to occur. Abdullah (whose biography will be briefly sketched in chapter 15), as an orphan brought up by his uncles, felt free to speak directly of the conflict that made him leave: "They made me work hard without recognition. I decided the only way to make them respect me was to succeed independently." Indications of the same cause are usually hinted at in other life stories where the father was alive, while any kind of support from father or other agnates, then or later in life, is given little emphasis.

Choice of location, at marriage and later, is likewise affected by economic and physical circumstance. Urban congestion and an active real estate market would tend to promote a considerable dispersal of persons in neolocality, regardless of what preferences they might have. But these preferences, indeed, are dominated by the same personal circumstances and interests, and are such as to promote dispersal. Despite the clear advantages for potential labor migrants in maintaining joint agnatic households or close propinquity, the actual trend is the opposite; and in cases where people explained to us the personal considerations in their choices, or where the process of decision making was observed (see, for example, the story of Ali, chapter 15; Wikan 1982:254ff.), settling at some distance from agnates was favored. Regardless of location and availability, the predominant pattern of actual mobilization of support is one where most younger men are reluctant to turn to their fathers and closest agnates for help, and prefer to prove their ability and realize their autonomy by dealing directly and independently with the larger, open society and its institutions. (These generalizations do not hold, it should be noted, for the bedouin settlements along the inner fringe of Sohar town. The bedouin case will be discussed below, chapter 13 and chapter 18.)

MARRIAGE CHOICE AND RELATIONS TO AFFINES

These same circumstances and concerns dominate the choice of spouse and the quality of interaction with affines. The formal right to enter into a marriage contract is held by the prospective groom himself and by the prospective bride's guardian, her closest adult male agnate. Young men will be influenced, to varying degrees, by the opinions and advice of their parents, while a girl's guardian may choose to give consideration to the preferences of the girl—if she expresses any—and her mother. (These matters are treated extensively in Wikan 1982, esp. chapter 10.) Soharis recognize and increasingly protect a girl's right to refuse to enter into a marriage that she definitively rejects. The formal bars on marriage formulated in the Shariat are observed; membership in the opposed congregations of Shiah versus others (Sunni or Ibazhi) is likewise a very serious impediment, though cases of intermarriage do occur. Membership in different linguistic/ethnic groups is much less of an impediment. Thus, in the mixed, predominantly Baluchi ward of South Sallan, a count of 84 spouses gives the frequencies: Baluchi-Baluch, 66; Baluch-Arab, 9; Arab-Arab, 7; and Ajam-Ajam, 2. There is no ideological or noticeable statistical skewing in these interethnic marriages with regard to sex; that is, male Baluchis marry female Arabs as often as male Arabs marry female Baluchis, etc. Prejudices are considerably stronger concerning marriages between freemen and ex-slaves. In continuation of the owner's right to marry his female slave, making her free, men do sometimes take an ex-*xādim* bride.

To marry thus may make trouble in the family, but no one can stop him. Thus the son of the shaikh of Sallan married a *xadim* (as his second wife) despite the protests of his father and mother. But people said: "If he wants to do this, what can anyone else do about it?" What is more, she is quite light in color.... If a man wishes to give his daughter in marriage to a *xādim* but the rest of his family objects, the case may be brought up before the *qadhi*. By recent practice, if the girl says before the *qadhi*: "Yes, I know he is a *xādim* and yet I want to marry him," then the *qadhi* will allow the marriage.

The degree of relatedness between spouses in the urban population shows the following frequency distribution (total sample = 365):

Agnatic First Cousin	All First Cousins	All First and Second Cousins	"Strangers"
5%	11%	14%	86%

These frequencies are the result of cross-pressures. On the one hand, there is a strong and clear ideal preference for agnatic-cousin marriage and close-kin marriage. Such unions are correct and desirable according to Islam, and they show a concern for—and thus affirm the value and purity of—family and blood. Ali also emphasized another aspect of the prevailing agnatic categorizations and ideals: "It is good to marry an agnatic cousin because that way, if you do something for your wife it is like doing it for yourself, since she is of your own family." To the extent that mothers influence the selection of marriage partners, they seem rather consistently to favor close-kin unions, presumbly because such unions link persons within the mother's preexisting network, where her participation and interests are directly involved.

On the other hand, men see clear advantages in an opposite policy of marrying strangers, as do marriageable girls. The reasons are summed up in the argument we repeatedly heard formulated by grooms (referring to prospective in-laws more than brides): "Strangers respect you more." It also proves much simpler to control and limit the degree of one's involvement with unrelated affines subsequent to marriage: one can maintain distance without the unseemly estrangement, conflict, and breach that may become necessary with parents-in-law who are relatives.

As may be seen from the actual frequencies, these latter considerations clearly prevail in the urban population today. This is true of all ethnic groups except the bedouin category, which exhibits very different frequencies, for reasons and with consequences that will be discussed later. Critically interpreted by unsympathetic Banyan onlookers, the prevailing pattern causes indignation: "Omanis do not, like Indians, look to character, suitability, and whole family background in choosing a husband for their daughter. Just now, there was a father who sold his sixteen year-old daughter to an eighty year old who is blind and cannot walk, just because his bride price bid was the highest."

After marriage, a wife has the legally protected right to visit her natal family regularly, with a frequency adjusted to the distance she must travel—once a week, once a fortnight, a few days a month. But this does not entail any necessary involvement by the husband with his affines; it is sufficient that he makes his wife's visits possible by delivering and fetching her, or having someone else accompany her. If he must meet with them at all, it is sufficient that he observes public standards of politeness (see Ali's biography, chapter 15). What is more, a married daughter herself has no strong obligation to visit her parents, just a right to do so if she wishes, as has been clarified repeatedly in the Wali's dismissal of cases where parents have complained of not being visited by their married daughters. Indeed, many young brides swiftly transfer their primary loyalties to their husband. One distressed mother observed: "When a daughter marries, she transfers all of her affection to her husband. That is not right. There should be one part for him and one part for her parents." (See Wikan 1982: 231 ff., especially 240, where a close portrayal of one such step in estrangement is given, and a full analysis of its causes is provided.)

The aggregate picture of marriage and affinity then, is one that shows a wide dispersal of marriage connections through the population, yet without entailing significant functional ties or alliances. This is so because as a rule the marriage arrangements have been made not by groups but by individual persons (the groom and the girl's father) without such purposes in mind; their effects are negated by the groom's reluctance to let close affinal relations develop; and the very basis for alliance is frequently removed by the bride's swift emancipation from any close and active relationship to her parents.

OVERALL PATTERN

The combined effects of all these processes and cross-pressures is to establish the majority of conjugal pairs as independent households, *not* ascriptively embedded in any effective wider networks. On the conceptual level, the whole population is familiar with and subscribes to an ideology of patrilineal descent, a division of the majority of the population into named tribes, and an idea of responsibility and leadership of such tribes in the offices of shaikhs. Some people also command a considerable amount of genealogical knowledge, entailing a kind of map of a bilateral kinship network. Finally, new marriages are carefully negotiated, and people are entirely familiar with the idea of creating alliances by marriage. But the social activation of bilateral and affinal networks and relationships is optative, and generally not opted for, while the activation of patrilineal descent groups is not even an option, since through a lack of internal loyalties and contacts such groups do not in fact emerge as corporate and potentially mobilizable bodies.

Methodologically, it is important to emphasize that this is a picture that emerges only if one analyzes the material in such a way as to question what the behavioral entailments of categorical relationships are. In fact, most persons will be found to cultivate active intercourse with (some) kinsmen; they will have occasional dealings with an elder or shaikh of their tribe; they will seek to manipulate some marriage or other so as to create a "connection." But it does not follow from this that it is kinship that creates the active social relations, that descent determines group membership and patronage, or that marriage signifies alliance. My point is that these particular forms of interaction are not *entailed* by the categories of relationship that I have identified. And I am not merely pointing to an occasional failure of a relationship to entail a certain type of interaction to support my claim; on the contrary, if we critically inspect the whole set of relationships we will find that *most* of them are not activated in this way, and that those that are activated are, on most occasions, not decisive. We cannot read simply from the saliency of some kinsmen in a person's network to the importance of kinship for interaction; we must also count the number of identical relations that fail to be important for behavior. Likewise, one cannot extrapolate from the purported normative entailment of relationships to their effective or functional importance in actual social life, or vice versa.

My own interpretaiton of the data from Sohar is that other processes than the ascription of kinship positions are involved in the shaping of the social networks of persons and the patterns of social intercourse that emerge. Social life in Sohar is based on the basic segregation of the sexes, and on the separation of men's and women's activities so that they occupy partly overlapping but mainly discrepant social space. Therefore, despite the establishment of primary identification and loyalty between spouses, husband and wife move mostly in separate social networks which they separately develop and cultivate. With the onset of maturity, members of both sexes tend to break loose from the social anchoring entailed in their natal family position, in the sense that they build up their own social networks rather than entering into any major set of preestablished links. Thus, each person in Sohar, it seems to me, enters a fairly open and complex society where his or her prospects are only weakly predetermined and where most social relations and achievements are not ascribed but emergent: for the women, deeply affected by her marriage; for the man, constantly negotiated, built, and dismantled. Sohar is a highly differentiated and inegalitarian society where persons command very unequal resources and suffer unequal inpediments, partly as a result of birth ascription and partly as a result of what they through their own activities have progressively accumulated. I have already shown what resources and impediments are entailed by the main sets of ascribed positions, and what are the standards of excellence whereby performance and its results are judged. To depict how social life is shaped—and thereby how the enrollment, transmission, and change of cultural cotraditions are determined—we also must consider the particular configuration and form of the arenas and other foci in which social interaction is consummated and people's activities and fates are consequently determined.

13 Social Scenes and Networks

To depict how social interrelations are patterned in Sohar today, and to understand the factors that bring this about, let us perform a mental experiment on the data. Proceed from the premise, established in the preceding chapter, that each person's network—that is, the particular set of other persons with whom he or she recurrently interacts—is based on that person's own selection among the opportunities that occur. Imagine, then, a person's being launched into this society. Where and how will such a person start building up a network, and what are the options and possible policies that he or she may pursue? In real life, of course, nearly no one starts this way; yet thinking of it this way clarifies the opportunity situation that everyone is in with respect to increasing or changing his or her network. Next, let us provide our imaginary person with the different social characteristics of persons in Sohar (sex, wealth, religious affiliation, etc.), and observe the different opportunity situations these differences entail and the ways in which contacts and choices are consequently channeled. Finally, if we now imagine many or all persons going about their interactions and selections in the ways we have deduced, will it all mount up to or aggregate into a pattern such as that which one can observe in Sohar today? If so, we will have reasonably identified the factors and processes that reproduce the forms of social life in Sohar. If not, we may be wrong in some of our premises or supposed facts about Sohar, or we may have identified contemporary factors that are markedly changing that form.

NEIGHBORHOOD

Moving out into the larger society, a person's local neighborhood provides the first and most accessible, indeed in some senses obtrusive, set of potential parties to relationships. The urban neighborhoods in Sohar, both on the ward level and even on the more local level, consist of a highly mixed group with respect to most social characteristics. The majority of neighbors will be strangers, without any ascriptive connection with ego, though some of them will normally be cotribesmen and kin. In view of the standards and guidelines for demeanor (outlined in chapter 11), how can one as a person best go about managing oneself and one's relations to such a set of others? Let us first look at the problem from the point of view of a man. Because it is so difficult to protect one's own person from the harm caused by aggression or vulgarity in others, the most important thing is through foresight and good judgment of character to avoid involvement with potentially embarrassing others; neighbors pose the greatest threat to this because of one's great exposure and accessibility to them. This was most clearly put in Ali's advice to his wife, Fatima:

> A while after we moved in here, Fatima told me a bad thing that one of the neighbors had said about another neighbor. I said to her: "Have nothing more to do with them, neither the one who spoke nor the one who was spoken about—just sit in your house and mind your own business." . . . Yes, it is difficult to do this without being impolite, and you cannot just turn them away if they come. But there are ways of showing it: you put out the mat for your neighbor to sit on, then busy yourself with other things—clothes, cooking, or something. Let her sit there alone and wait for a while. Then serve her coffee only. She will notice, and leave and not come back. And *you* need not visit her.

However, these strangers and as-if strangers that surround you are both recipients and a reservoir of human compassion in times of need; to them you show your sense of responsibility and your faith in fellow Moslems when the occasion arises. But if you once enter into a close relationship with a neighbor, it can be discontinued only by the compromising enmity of a nonspeaking relationship (cf. p. 000). Thus, the policy of genteel isolation is the safest, creating social distance where physical distance is absent.

Such a policy is practicable for men, who have a large radius of activity and innumerable options for interaction. Characteristically, their networks will contain only a few, more or less judiciously chosen neighbors and a majority of persons resident elsewhere. Women, on the other hand, with their restricted radius of movement, have really no such option. Their neighborhood is essentially their "whole world," and so neighbors of necessity provide the main parties to their life, besides husband and a few, irregularly accessible, close kin and affines.

Wikan (1982:113ff.) describes and analyzes in close detail this world and its implications. Outstanding features are the prevalence of next-door relationships, with little regard for ethnicity, rank, or age. Latifa, at present the hub of a circle of women in an unusually integrated neighborhood, where more than half were kinsmen and affines, thus anticipated even celebrating the ꜱEid at the end of Ramadan with strangers in her new neighborhood when she moved hardly 100 meters down the street to a new house. In this situation, then, women find their social membership ascribed through the fortuitous circumstance of residence, and consequently strikingly secure. The extent of intimacy is subject to control, but the rules of tactfulness essentially assure that each woman will be accepted as she chooses to present herself, and accorded a place in the neighborhood's circle of women. I shall return below to particular features of these circles, and the behavior that unfolds within them.

Men, on the other hand, seek out of the neighborhood into the open, and far less secure, wider society. They come into contact with real strangers, about whom they may know nothing and who may know nothing of them; they must trust in their ability in self-presentation and in their own judgment of the character of others. The main institutional framework of the town gives shape to the options with which they are faced.

MAIN ARENAS AND FORA FOR MEN

These are most conspicuously the public or semipublic fora where men are congregated, especially the marketplace, mosque, Wali's fort, town club, and various cafés. There are also some special occasions that create temporary foci, such as public parades and processions, weddings, *nāder* celebrations. In contrast, restricted or private fora are few and sparingly used. Most houses contain a *majlis* (male visitors' area), sometimes quite spacious in the case of wealthier men and shaikhs; but these are rarely used and then mainly for certain formal occasions such as greeting at major holidays, negotiating marriage, etc. Only the *majlis* of shaikhs, where many people have legitimate or necessary errands, are regularly in use. For these reasons, most interaction between men takes place without the benefit of a special space set aside for that purpose.

The market is unequivocally the major place where men are found and can be approached. When serving a summons to the court, the Wali's peon goes there, not to the man's home, to inquire after the man. Through most of the day, this all-male arena will contain at any one time perhaps 1,000 persons, and its 200 shops will welcome anyone, stranger or familiar. People congregate at auctions, or even such undramatic events as the unloading of trucks or small boats, as uncommitted spectators; they are free to overhear or join most conversations. Being in charge of all their household's purchases, they always have a legitimate errand there; and indeed looking for a particular other person is also regarded as a legitimate and sensible reason to come to the marketplace.

Typical scene from a market lane.

The mosque is also an open and perpetually accessible focus of interaction: every Moslem is welcome to join the congregation, and he has business to transact there since he is under obligation to pray. But there are many mosques, divided among the major sects with regard to how proper prayer should be performed; they are scattered, and are irregularly attended by relatively small numbers other than on Fridays; and conversation in the mosque is not as free and open to participation as in the marketplace. Shiahs, on the other hand, have in addition their *matam* buildings, which function less rigorously as a place not only for worship, and which on special occasions serve the congregation essentially as community houses.

The Wali's court functions most days to bring considerable numbers of persons to the fort; those with errands there will spend a considerable time waiting, in a crowd. But socializaing in this throng is quite subdued, and persons who have no business there are not present. The gatehouse of the fort is more informally accessible, and serves as a meeting place for a variable, but small, group of mostly elderly men.

The club is a recent government creation, amalgamating what was formerly subdivided into five local and autonomous community centers. It receives a small government subsidy and organizes recreational and cultural activities, and elects its own officers. Members pay a small monthly fee; there were in 1974 about 300 members, but a far smaller attendance at any particular meeting. Some members, especially those elected to office, spend a great number of their free afternoons there.

Finally, there is a small assortment of cafés. Among the shops of the market are a few very modest, traditional "tea shops" serving hot and cold beverages, waterpipes, and perhaps simple meals of eggs, etc. A couple of slightly larger "restaurants," still very primitive in equipment and services, are modeled on similar establishments abroad, familiar from labor migration. With growing traffic in overland transport lorries, there is also a "hotel" next to the fuel pump, which has an electrical generator and is consequently lighted in the evenings, has cooling facilities for soft drinks and some food products, and serves meals at five or six tables.

Otherwise, Sohar provides people with the public roads and paths, inside of town and in among the orchards, where they may chance to meet and where they may hope or fear that they are being observed. The beach along the waterfront serves as a major thoroughfare, and also (since so many houses face the beach) as a possible route when searching for persons around sunset, when the marketplace is closed. At that time, small groups of Indian merchants can be seen there, taking their evening stroll—though they observe regretfully that they cannot do so with their wives, and even to do so with one's children draws sufficient attention, so it is better to refrain. Their desire to promenade as a family can be indulged only on rare occasions on Fridays, by arrangement on the precincts of the government experimental farm. Finally, the outpatient's clinic at the newly established hospital, during its morning hours of opening, invariably draws a large crowd of both sexes (in segregated areas).

With these opportunities, how does a person proceed to seek social contacts and establish a social network?

Children, as they move out of their mother's closest presence, use the public space of neighborhood streets and lanes, and the adjoining beach, as well as the compounds of the neighborhood during the hours when the men are absent. They form local cliques, composed of both girls and boys up to the age of about eight years, at which time the girls become increasingly restricted in their movements. Even though boys may continue for some years longer in such a neighborhood network, their normal passage into a long phase of absence on labor migration creates a discontinuity, so few of these relations last into adult life. With the contemporary innovation of local schooling, which postpones their departure considerably and creates the opportunity for youth groups to develop, this may change. Some of the discrepancies between old ideals and new practices are revealed in the story of Ali's brother. When we were first in Sohar, he was about fifteen years old, and was supported by Ali with 15 Rials per month to go to school. He did rather poorly, and Ali declared: "I will support him only till he is grownup, then every man must be responsible for himself, and seek education and use his time to gain knowledge, not fritter time away smoking and drinking and talking and fighting about nothing." One and a half years later, Ali could rather gleefully report:

He had bad friends, drank, and quit school. I offered to let him live with me—poor boy, he has not his own mother—but no. I made him think about what he wanted to do for a living; he wanted to be a driver, but never got down to that either. So I arranged for a group of soldiers on leave to abduct him. They caught him in our father's garden, took him to a recruiting station and said the government had heard complaints about him but that he would be excused if he signed up for the army. So now he has finished six months' training, and is stationed in Jebel Akhtar.

Men, on their return to Sohar and for the rest of their lives, are free to seek contacts and relationships in all these different fora. But if they value and wish to cultivate their public esteem and pride in self, by the standards summarized above in chapter 11, their movements and choices become highly circumscribed. The market is an opportune place to go, as it is impersonal and uncommitting, provides easy access to and easy withdrawal from interaction, and serves as the center for collecting news and information. The mosque is also a relatively safe forum, since interaction there is particularly constrained to be polite because of the sacred character of the location. It is also well suited as a place to exhibit responsibility and morality, if one has sufficient command of Islam and good manners. It is probably the place where the art of conversation is most highly cultivated—with little pragmatic consequence but considerable effect on public esteem and self-esteem. The club functions, in a more secular way, to similar effect; its role as an organ of government policy, to further education and modernization, is particularly legitimizing. Cafés, on the other hand, are less suited to enhance a man's social position. This, as I understand it, is because visits to a café entail the public exhibition of relaxation and absence of responsibility, and a degree of intimacy with strangers of questionable integrity. Consequently, most men avoid such places, and make a point of how they shun them. Private visits are, in a sense, potentially even more damaging. The formal visits to kinfolk, where both sexes are included and which serve to acknowledge and honor these others, are not included in this stricture. They are indeed very constrained affairs, where the men converse on proper topics of the kinds suggested above (chapter 12), and incidentally supplement their information on the present location and work of various Sohari acquaintances, while the women and children are largely silent. Truly private visits, in small all-male groups, on the other hand, are most automatically assumed to entail behavior or activities which should not become public—or else the meetings would not have been held in private. Thus, men, when questioned, would often adamantly deny having a group of close friends whom they saw in their free hours, with the emphatic *"Abadeh!"* (never/not al all). With justified pride in self, many men will announce: "I go to the market, I go to the mosque, I return to my house. I say *Sala'am Aleikum. Bas!"* Ali sought to explain the situation to me: "I do not like to mix with impolite people, or drink together with people. Actually, I buy a little liquor sometimes, but I say to people who offer me that no, I do not use it. Sometimes with some people, I will stay there when they drink, but not take any myself. I have just *one* friend with whom I drink a little, because he is a truly good person."

SOCIAL NETWORKS OF MEN

Given these attitudes and sensibilities, it is difficult to obtain extensive data on social networks that differentiate closer friends from a wider network of associates and acquaintances. In the case of those few with whom I was most familiar, I know some who seem indeed to have practiced the limitation of contact with others which they claimed. Ali, on the other hand, named twenty persons as friends. These were all very close to him in age (twenty-five to twenty-seven years) and were largely similarly employed (in governmental or municipal services, business firms, etc). Only four had also been his friends in childhood; one of them a "milk brother," a quasi-kinship bond arisng from having been suckled reciprocally at each other's mother's breast as infants. The friends are variously Arab, Baluch, and Ajam, and both Sunni and Shiah. My impression would be that this is an unusually large circle, but representative in its general composition. There is a strong and explicit ideal of the compatibility that should characterize friends, arising from their similarity: "a friend is to his friend like a patch is to a worn garment—if they are of the same kind, they go together and make the garment look new." But the "sameness" that is emphasized is above all one of first temperament, character, and level of integrity, then, second, age and lifestyle. Kinship, ethnic group and wealth do *not* enter in, and even religious congregation figures only marginally. The apposite saying "if you sit with the smith, the sparks will burn/brand you," is intended as a warning against keeping "bad" company, not particularly to emphasize rank and wealth as criteria of suitability.

It is interesting to note that Ali's circle of friends seems to represent an approximately 10 percent sample of the total male population of Sohar within the narrow age range from which it is drawn. It is doubtful that a significantly larger circle than that could be established, if such careful and discriminating criteria are to be maintained. The wider circle of acquaintances—those whom one greets and can approach with some degree of familiarity in the market—is much greater, and one that most men are actively eager to increase. This is also facilitated by those one already knows, who are generally helpful in mediating contacts. Finally, there is the even larger category of persons of whom one has heard, whom one may recognize, and about whom one is active to gather current information as to employment, location, marriages, etc. But even this category falls short of embracing the whole adult male population of Sohar, so that we, even with a explanatory sentence, sometimes could not establish the identity of one of our contacts with one of our other contacts.

The networks of some of the minority groups are in addition structured with reference to the minority category. Zidgalis, as a small ethnic group, practice a pattern of visiting all Zidgali households on the occasion of weddings or funerals there. Ajams claim the same custom, though with their much larger numbers it is doubtful that this is in fact practiced. But members of the Shiah congregation, by virtue of their special calendrical festivals and their unique *matam* (community houses), develop a stronger familiarity with each other and a greater concentration of their social network within the boundaries of their category. Their reading sessions of the traditional texts of tragedy and martyrdom at *Moharram* are such central events, when membership is solemnly affirmed and greetings exchanged. Being largely centered on the market in their livelihood, this also introduces a duality into their relationships—as commercial rivals but personal and communal supporters. A similar duality is even more marked within the smaller, completely specialized Hindu merchant community: "When I sit here in my chair in my shop, we are enemies. I must always try to know what they charge for sugar, rice. If they say 17 Rials, I say 100 Baisa less. But after 5 P.M., we are friends."

WOMEN'S NETWORKS AND STYLE

The small worlds created for women as a consequence of sexual segregation and the rules of female modesty contain both fewer arenas and fora, and fewer persons than the world in which men move. The options open to a woman as she develops and accumulates her social network are consequently few and simple. The sanctions of others, and her own feelings of modesty and shame, prevent her from entering mosques, the club, or any cafés. Nor can she enter any part of the market unless invited to do so by her husband *and* intensively chaperoned by him or a person entrusted by him. The vast majority of women have never once been there, according to my wife's information (Wikan 1982:51). Nor should women ever linger on their legitimate passage along public roads or paths, or ever address persons in such public places outside the very closest neighborhood. The degree of observance of this latter stricture is variable, decreasing with age and poverty and depending somewhat on personality. Only the outpatients' clinic of the hospital provides an (immensely popular) accessible larger public arena. Essentially, a woman is limited to the close neighborhood and to occasional visits to kinfolk as the only opportunities to establish new social contacts.

Women's networks reflect these restrictions very clearly. Accommodating to the periodic absences of men from the compound, women establish a small set of reciprocal or unilateral visiting relationships, so intense as to involve daily visits, or even several visits a day. The number of partners in the set varies from a pair up to six or eight (plus attached children); some women, for reasons of locality and personality, may even be almost entirely without such companionship. Members of a circle are almost always very close neighbors, in a pattern like that shown in figure 2 for one locality (next page).

The social circles of women are even less homogeneous than those of men. Members differ in ethnic identity, religious congregation, and wealth, and also in age and in the presence or absence of slave background. Nor can one readily see evidence of any particular homogeneity of temperament or moral rectitude—the circle to which my

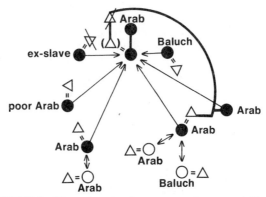

FIGURE 2. Women's network among contiguous neighbors.

wife was most closely attached included, among largely very virtuous women, one flagrant prostitute (Wikan 1982:143). With regard to more public differentia, this large circle, centering on Latifa, contained seven Arabs and one Baluchi; it included one ex-slave as well as persons of distinguished family, closely related to the shaikh of the ward; it bracketed a range of wealth from well above average prosperity to very poor; and it included women ranging in age from twenty to past sixty years.

For the formation of women's circles, it would thus seem that propinquity alone provides a sufficient basis for the formation of relationships; if one of the parties wishes to cultivate neighborly contact, that is enough. This is illustrated most clearly in the case of a newlywed woman, brought into a strange environment and entirely surrounded by strangers: she proceeds to seek contact with her closest neighbors, and is accepted into their circle with no questions asked. This is in clear contrast with male ideals of choosing friends discriminately (see p. 140); but corresponds to an explicit women's ideal of "loving" everyone, and the impossibility of turning away a visitor without thereby being impermissibly rude.

These male/female differences arise as much from the social contexts in which men and women act as from differences in their fundamental views of social obligation and personal honor and integrity. I have already mentioned the importance for men of anticipating the possibility of unseemly incidents and threats to the dignity of one's own person, and avoiding those situations and contacts that might cause damage. The implicit premise for such a view of where danger lies is, of course, the presence of an audience who are not themselves involved, who have not the full information to interpret and judge an incident correctly, whose opinion of one's self will be colored by their understandings of any one particular encounter or experience. This is clearly a correct premise for understanding a male Sohari's situation, moving as he does in a large public arena and in a wide, open social network. But it is *not* true of the social world in which women move. In their small-scale and dense networks, the audience of their behavior largely shares their interpersonal problems and is above all comprehensively informed about them and their past performance. No finesse of self-presentation and politeness can cover up shortcomings in this respect, nor can any passing embarrassment or equivocal incident destroy the picture. Thus, when my wife questioned Latifa and others in her circle as to whether they did not fear for their reputations because they associated with a prostitute, they answered confidently: "Not at all. People know us and they know her. It is only she in this neighborhood who is that way" (Wikan 1982:145). Pressed further, they explained that they would not, however, go by taxi to the hospital with her, as the taxi would pass through neighborhoods where she was probably known, since she roamed everywhere, whereas they were not known, and so she might in that situation harm their reputations. As Wikan points out, this eventuality is of much greater significance to their husbands, whose honor is deeply affected by the reputation of wives, than it is to themselves, who do not seek recognition in this larger world of "public opinion" (ibid., p. 147).

The pursuit of similar ideals of politeness, grace, and dignity in the distinctive life situations of men and women thus allows or encourages somewhat different strategies and rules of demeanor. In the small and familiar worlds in which women live, they can go even further than can the men in practicing tolerance and noninterference, and can more completely avoid the practice of social sanctions against their companions. Likewise, their secure access to a neighborhood circle both frees them from pressures toward social achievement and allows greater spontaneity. The differences in degree that consequently emerge in the interactional styles of men and women may be indicated by a vignette from one of their rare mixed gatherings, a social encounter where a small group of close kinsmen and affines intervisit. Here, males engage in a fairly continuous social conversation, in turn contributing items of knowledge and information on relatively uncontroversial and impersonal matters, and contriving to keep up a fairly sustained exchange. The women, on the other hand, are more quiet, and are content to be silent for long periods. This is also characteristic of all-female gatherings: women are capable of sitting together through very long silences, unembarrassed and confident in an inward-turning complacence (Wikan 1982:123). At other times, however, such female gatherings can be more raucous in their informality, with heavy banter and "teasing" about each others' (legitimate, marital) sexual life. The hospitality involved in such gatherings, on the other hand, is more emphasized than that among men, at least more overtly competitive in its character: women enjoy giving conspicuous hospitality when they are able and the suitable occasion arises; they emphasize prestige foods (in 1974 canned peaches, pears, and cherries; in 1976 fresh fruits!) and also try to keep up with changing fashions in just what is currently prestigious. Women are also more obviously eager to receive hospitality: they help themselves liberally, hoard sweets and fruits "to bring home to the children," and show little of the restraint and disinterest usually attested to by men.

In other words, in their general demeanor women emerge as simpler and more direct, outspoken, and natural—though with a natural grace, consideration, and composure very distinctly Omani. Men, on the other hand, are more socially practiced and aware, they are more skilled at maintaining an impersonal poise and effective social front, and they more often entertain truly long-term purposes and strategies. They also deemphasize the importance of material wealth by being more guarded in its conspicuous use and acceptance, and they explicitly criticize the manners and values of women in giving such things too much emphasis. Finally, they are more committed to conversational forms that are active and edifying, and will occasion criticize women for their unreformed ignorance.

NETWORK AND STYLE OF BEDOUINS

The other status distinction that is associated with marked contrasts in network form and interactional style is that between townspeople and bedouin. The preceeding discussion has focused on townsmen. Bedouin, as represented by the inner zone of settlement between the date groves and the open plain (see chapter 8), are in a rather different opportunity situation and so proceed differently in building and expanding their individual networks.

Let us first look at the situation of bedouin men. I have noted the existence of marked differences in patterns of marriage choice and residence among bedouin. A young bedouin male finds himself initially located in a neighborhood overwhelmingly dominated by his own tribe, separated by an appreciable distance from contacts outside of his own subcultural milieu. His initial network will thus be both local and homogeneous. When seeking marriage, he meets important constraints: townspeople are very reluctant to give daughters to bedouin, and will in the least demand very high bride prices, whereas potential fathers-in-law in his own tribe require low bride prices and public pressures in favor of tribal endogamy are strong (see chapter 18). Also, members of the tribe are allotted postmarital house sites without

demand for payment on the land of the tribe. A combination of factors
thus favors a decision for tribal endogamy and (viri-)local residence.
The resulting structure of marriage links and local community may be
illustrated by the Shabli neighborhood—a small, localized branch of
bedouin with a territory extending along the road between Sohar town
and the hospital. There are thirty-seven married men residing in the
neighborhood; of them thirty-two are Shabli and five are of other
bedouin tribes. The thirty-two Shiblu men have thirty-four Shiblu
wives and three non-Shiblu wives; the five strangers living among them
are all married to strangers, and have not been given Shiblu daughters
in marriage.

Looking out from the household, the bedouin man finds himself
embedded in an ascriptive network of relationships involving bilateral
and affinal ties, and shared tribal membership. These relations entail
both important obligations and substantial advantages; they are not
easily escaped by creating social distance. As a result, bedouin men
tend to choose their companions and pursue their various activities in
ways that reinforce, rather that repudiate, these ascriptive relationships. Between spouses, this means that the networks of husband and
wife are far more congruent than those among townspeople: both
spouses center on a considerable neighborhood of shared kinfolk.

The characteristic features of bedouin male and female interactional
styles are quite consistent with this network picture. Women move
more freely in a larger neighborhood context, and are also more

A bedouin shaikh's majlis *in the inner zone of settlement.*

self-assured, though reserved, in public settings, among bedouin than among townspeople. Bedouin men are more spontaneous and more direct than townsmen—crude but honest, by town standards (see chapter 8). These are features that persist, in attenuated form, as distinctive local customs of wards along the shoreline which are supposed to be of predominantly bedouin origin (for example, Ghayl; see chapter 8).

It is also interesting to note a certain parallelism in the situations and networks of bedouin and town women, and a corresponding parallelism in the effects of this on the behavioral style through which esteem and self-respect are pursued. The networks and world of bedouin, and particularly of bedouin men, are much larger than those of women in town; but at their core they share the features of local density and ascriptive security which men in town lack. The argument that her situation allows a woman to be more relaxed, self-assured, and spontaneous in contexts where it is appropriate for her to interact is thus also applicable to the situation of bedouin men, with results that are reflected in the townsman's judgment of bedouin men as more uncivilized, parochial, and ignorant than townsmen.

GENERAL NETWORK FEATURES

If we try to visualize the aggregate network of social relations that characterizes the population of Sohar as a whole, some clear qualitative features stand out. Basically, it has an open and dispersed character; it is not centralized, hierarchic, or segmented. Though the Wali is beyond doubt the central focus of public decision making, this is not reflected in any pervasive orientation of people's interpersonal networks. Likewise, though the marketplace provides a territorial focus for much interaction, it does so by virtue of concentrating a major fraction of the male population spatially, and not by organizing webs of social relations around key persons. Though the networks of different persons differ greatly in both size and structure, this likewise does not entail any marked centralization or hierarchy, since the greatest difference is between the male and female halves of the population, and the large networks of men are not hierachically ordered. Nor are there marked features of segmentation. The networks of women show such a tendency—though even as between women, relations have a considerable degree of serial character, since a neighbor's neighbor often falls ouside one's circle. Minority status also introduces a certain concentration of relations inside the minority, as does tribal membership for bedouin. But there is no evidence that these tendencies are strong enough to produce an overall network that shows marked lines of lowered density or cleavage. The obverse of this feature is the absence of very high degrees of connectedness in the network. Among men, an appreciable fraction of the adult male population of Sohar may fall within a person's network. But if A knows B and B knows C, the probability that A will know C is not much greater than it would be if A did *not* know B, nor will the relationship be greatly affected by the presence or absence of such a double linkage. I have argued that these features come about, at least in part, as a product of the ideology of politeness and tolerance which Soharis embrace, from their pursuit of self-regard through autonomy and the wish to be accorded respect by others, and from their reliance on centralized political and legal institutions for security and the protection of individual rights.

The result is a relative weakening of the social control exercised by primary groups, and a pattern where the flow of information, to persons and about persons, is largely embedded in an unfocused interpersonal network. With the added specific cultural constraints on the communication of gossip and scandal, the direct impact of ascriptive relations and primary groups is only further weakened. The result is a community with many of the qualities of a large-scale, "urban," and impersonal society. This entails some degree of freedom for the person to assume and shed social identities as an act of individual choice—with important implications for the persistence and disappearance of plural cultural traditions.

14

The Operation of the Market

Whereas most social interaction in Sohar takes a course that allows the person to remain relatively unchallenged in the position and capacities in which he presents himself, because of the pervasive observation of tactfulness, market transactions are subject to another set of ground rules, and market processes are preeminently the cause of swift changes in a person's status. This does not mean that Soharis allow themselves or others to be tactless and ill-mannered when haggling—such exchanges are pursued with much greater decorum than is generally observed in Middle Eastern marketplaces. Rather, Soharis do not see disagreements and direct challenges to the value of material objects and services as being impolite; such matters are regarded as objective, impersonal, and particular. Anyone is free to have an opinion and to question the judgment of others, and to enter into a transaction is a voluntary matter. At the same time, Soharis admire both hard and shrewd business practice, and see a person's success in securing favorable deals, and profits, as a key measure of the person's competance. They are therefore generally eager to enter into such contests and often unbending in their pursuit of them, as if a point of honor were involved. As a foreign expert engaged in the development of the fresh fish marketing system observed: "If you say the price is fixed, 150 Baisa per kilo, and weigh out exactly one kilo, they pay without arguing. But if you offer a whole fish of obviously more than a kilo and let them have it for that price, they say no, 75 Baisa, and get angry if you don't come down to their price. And they would do the same if you had said 10 Baisa—offer 5 Baisa and be sure you were trying to cheat them."

Thus most people enter into the spirit of the market, and very many, both men and women, try their hand in trading when the opportunity arises or can be created. All manner of goods, real property, services, and labor circulate in this way within the population. But Sohar is above all an ancient and contemporary trading town, with the merchant as its prototypical citizen. The mode of transaction and the operation of the market are therefore most appropriately depicted by

A merchant—one of the traditional apothecaries—in his shop in the market. Compare the Banyan merchant in the illustration on p. 55.

an initial focus on the activities and enterprises of the professional merchants of the *suq* (market).

The majority of merchants in the Sohar *suq* are general merchants, offering essentially the same range of wares in similar boothlike premises: open-fronted shops ranging from 5 to 25 m² in floor space. The more active traders have storage space at the periphery of the main market area for their stock. The actual character of the enterprises differs much more than the appearances, however. The one I know best is that of a Hindu whom I shall call Baba Ji, no doubt one of the most successful in the whole *suq*. Baba Ji opened his shop in Sohar early in 1973, with 10,000 Rials (approximately $30,000) in capital from an Ajam partner. Their agreement was that Baba Ji would be responsible for the shop and run it autonomously according to his best judgment, and would take 50 percent of the net profits for his labor and expertise, while 50 percent would go to the Ajam for his captial. For this reason, and because Baba Ji is a literate and well-educated person, he keeps careful accounts and has a very clear and explicit picture of the operation of the shop (whereas his Ajam partner, himself a very successful businessman and speculator, had difficulties understanding that money in the till is not identical with net profits!). Goods are mainly purchased through agents in the port of Dubai, who charge a flat 2 percent on their turnover. Transport is by truck, over 200 miles of roads of variable quality; direct expenses plus 3–4 Rials per trip are paid to the independently operating truckdriver. A subsidiary source of supplies is Muscat. Agents from wholesalers in both ports visit Sohar regularly and also accept orders by mail, and Baba Ji himself visits these centers occasionally to discover new products or styles early. Baba Ji's own provision on the goods varies with the nature of the wares and the opportunities offered by the market, but, generally speaking, it ranges from about 10 percent on durable and dependable wares like rice up to 100 percent on more unpredictable commodities like cotton prints. (At the time I was looking into this, he could show me six-month-old bales he had been unable to sell because the design had not appealed to customers—but he was still offering them at full retail price because his competitors had not yet decided to cut *their* prices.) Turnover in 1974 averaged 200 Rials per day, or the equivalent (apart from the less active first three months in 1973) of 70,000 Rials per year. On this he made a net profit (after deduction of rent, wages for one shop assistant, etc.) of about 10,000 Rials, or $30,000, a year. This gave the Ajam partner a 50 percent return on his captial, while it allowed Baba Ji, by living frugally, to save 300 Rials, or nearly $1,000, a month.

In addition, Baba Ji was making a marginal profit on money changing, and beginning to profit from reinvesting his own savings in some fast-turnover goods. He also holds money for safekeeping, though after the establishment of two banks in Sohar in 1975 the volume of such deposits with merchants has been drastically reduced. Nonetheless, there are still profits to be made from such deposits—one of the coolies in the market keeps his life's savings, 750 Rials, with Baba Ji. In the course of four months, Baba Ji had the luck to make more than 50 percent profit on this sum: he invested it in sugar at 8 Rials per sack just before the sudden rise in world sugar prices in 1974, and was in the process of retailing the sugar at the rate of 13 Rials per sack. The owner of this captial who has place it for safekeeping is not informed of such transactions, nor has he a claim to any interest on his deposit. But after a success like this, Baba Ji would tend to give him some kind of gift or concession, to encourage the customer to leave the money with him. Finally, Baba Ji also serves as wholesaler for several village shops in the outer districts of Sohar province, and for some female hawkers engaged in door-to-door selling. To such persons he will give discount concessions, letting them have cloth at 3.250 Rials a bale, which they, and he himself, retail at 4 Rials a bale (but which he has obtained at about 2 Rials a bale).

Baba Ji's shop operates mainly on a cash payment principle, with monthly accounts for the steady customers who prefer this arrangement. This is the typical pattern of most transactions, but some of the older Hindu shopkeepers extended credit through the year to customers who are farmers, with settlement of accounts after the time of delivery of their main cash crop of dried limes. Such shops do not charge interest on debts, but recover some of their capital costs by charging slightly higher prices, on the order of 1.700 Rials per maund of rice instead of the prevailing 1.600 Rials cash price. This arrangement makes it easier to attract and retain customers, but it has the disadvantage of tying down larger capital—on the order of 30,000 Rials for profits only slightly greater than Baba Ji obtains on his 10,000 Rials. The other drawback, of special importance to members of a minority group largely without Omani citizenship, is that "their profits are only in their books. If something happens they can't take it out." An acute awareness of this insecurity also limits somewhat the diversity of investments and enterprises into which the Banyans choose to enter. Omani regulations prevent non-Omani citizens from holding real property in Oman, and also now require every company to include an Omani in partnership. But even if it could be arranged, Banyans are reluctant to make investments in property: "I am not interested in putting my money in stones. You never know the future. Look what happened [to the Asian merchant minority] in Uganda!"

Merchants from other ethnic groups tend to show greater diversity in the range of their activities, even when they are of clear "minority" status, such as Ajams. For example, probably the wealthiest person in Sohar is an Ajam who has built up his fortune from nothing by speculation, retail trading, and export enterprises. Perhaps his largest single source of income today derives from his control of the exports of dried limes from Sohar to the Gulf, particularly Basrah. He handles 30,000 maunds, that is, 1,200 tons, of the product per year, at a value of 3½–4 Rials per maund, which represents an annual turnover valued at more than 100,000 Rials ($300,000), out of which he makes about 15,000 Rials ($45,000) profit. With a variety of other sources of income, other merchants in the *suq* estimate that he may make double that amount in total income annually. Yet no deal seems to be too small to interest him: with the sudden rise in sugar prices, merchants who expected the rise to continue were eager to secure stores. So the wealthy Ajam came around to Baba Ji's shop with the sad story that he had no sugar for his customers at the moment, and could Baba Ji help him out with a couple of sacks? Baba Ji answered apologetically that he himself was running out; failing to convince his colleague and competitor, he bluffed him by throwing him the keys to his godown, saying: "Go look for yourself!" Indeed, his passion for business and profits is in excess of what Soharis generally regard as justified: "He is a miser. Look at him, how poorly he dresses; he spends nothing and only accumulates. . . . After he dies, his children will start spending the money."

Toward the other end of the range of wealth and success is Ibrahim. His father was an agricultural laborer at 15 Baisas (5 cents) a day when Ibrahim was a boy. As soon as he reached his teens, Ibrahim went as a labor migrant to Kuwait, worked hard and saved, returned to Sohar to marry, and took a job in a local merchant's shop for a year and a half. Having learned the elements of shopkeeping, he borrowed from friends and relatives, 50 Rials here and 100 Rials there, invested his own savings—he does not know how much captial—and started his own shop. He keeps no accounts, can make no estimate of daily or monthly turnover, estimates his stock vaguely to be worth about 900 Rials (whereas the adjoining merchant says it must be more like 2,000 Rials). He occasionally goes to Dubai or Muscat to fetch goods, but mostly relies on what agents offer him locally, and he chooses his range of wares by looking at what other merchants offer. As to profits, he does not know what his shop brings him, but so far he feels that he has prospered, he has been able to pay back some of the loans, and he hopes that God will let him continue.

Though times are prosperous today, prosperity is not assured. There are both exits and entrances to the college of traders, as evinced by the number of men who can report an interlude as shopkeeper in their life stories. Some have experienced bankruptcies, or more often declining profits and turnover, so they have had to use up their working capital for subsistence. Others have suffered accidental losses. As late as 1972 there was a great fire in the *suq* which destroyed many shops, with losses of current stock worth 6,000, 7,000, and 15,000 Rials in the case of some of the more prominent merchants. If a shop is wiped out by such a disaster, some ex-merchants seek other employment, whereas others reestablish themselves ("Never mind, he borrowed stock from the agent in Dubai; in two years he will have earned it all back again!"). As Soharis see it, it is all a question of talent or knack (pointing to the head), and is very dependent on individual qualities, though these are expected to occur more frequently and more strongly among Banyans and Ajams than among Sunni Arabs or Baluchis.

Indeed, the circulation of wealth may well have been considerably more rapid in former times, when both insecurity and the risk of natural accidents were greater, and profits on successful trading ventures could also be much greater. Abdullah spoke wistfully of the opportunities for profits as late as 1960, when he imported some drums of oil from Kuwait, worth 5 Rials there, and could sell them in Sohar for 70 Rials each. The enticement of fabulous profits has no doubt been a significant component in the very high evaluation given to trade as a vocation in Oman. Saving to establish oneself as a merchant and the great profits and wealth that will then accrue seem to be a central theme in Sohari consciousness. Even the ruling Sultans have been propelled by trading ambitions; the motif of the merchant prince is ever present in the history of this coast. Ahmed Al Bu Said, the Sohari founder of the present dynasty (since 1749), was famous as a particularly successful merchant and shipowning prince (Kelly 1968:10 f.), while Iman Seif bin Sultan (1679–1711), of the preceding Yaareba dynasty, became so wealthy through trade and purchased so much of the land in Oman as his private property that at his death he owned approximately one-third of all the date trees in his dominions (Miles 1919:225–26). The same drive, on a less grandiose scale, seems to permeate society down to the meanest *dallal* (middleman) who secures a gross of canopeners that some merchant or other has been unable to sell at the expected price, and circulates through the *suq* eliciting competitive bids in a private auction, hoping to turn a penny of the deal.

In this way, then, the merchant career comes to be particularly closely integrated with the organization and profits of the full range of other occupations and sources of income, not only because these affect the customers' purchasing power and thus the chances of profitable trade but also because personnel and accumulated capital are constantly moving in and out of the trading sector. In these terms, we must also look at the wider labor market, and the rapidly changing level of wages and nature of enterprises. Though unequipped with the data that could sustain any kind of economic analysis, I may nontheless be able to identify some of the main lineaments of important social processes.

First, the life and career of everyone in Sohar have been profoundly affected by rapid inflation, and even more rapid rises in basic wage levels, over the last generation. The pay for day laborers—the cheapest category of essentially unskilled labor—has risen as follows: 1960, 20 Baisa; 1970, 200 Baisa; 1974 1,000 Baisa (approximately $3.00). These wage levels have most strongly affected agricultural activity, which is highly dependent on seasonal labor and traditionally has been organized through various specialized labor contracts (cf. pp. 58f.) by managerial proprietors. As the result of the costs of labor, the costs of local agricultural products have risen so they no longer can compete with imported goods: vegetables from the Lebanon (when they were available) were cheaper than local produce, and a foreign expert adviser on date cultivation abandoned his mission when he discovered that American-grown dates could be supplied to Sohar at competitive prices with those required to pay for the production from the date groves adjoining the marketplace. Soharis agree that agricultural production generally has been declining, formerly cultivated land has been abandoned, and existing date groves have been neglected over the last ten years. But as well as labor shortage and the costs of such labor as is available, they also cite oil pollution of irrigation water as a significant cause of this. In evidence, they point out that the decline in production coincided with the spread of diesel pumps in replacement of the lift systems operated by animal traction.

As a result of these circumstances, the value of agricultural land has risen less than most other items. Such land has consequently also proved a less attractive object of speculation, and landowners have found themselves increasingly stranded in a stagnant sector of the economy, and thereby also peripheral to the interest and awareness of Sohari society. Only those favorably situated in relation to urban development, particularly along the beach, have benefited from the rise in the value of building sites there (from 5 Baisa to 200 Baisa per square foot in five years). Not least for this reason, there are still profits to be made by land speculation: at the same time as one Arab shaikh has dissipated a considerable fortune (mainly of land obtained through marriage to an only-child Ajam girl) by a series of unfortunate transactions, Baba Ji's Ajam partner—who has the "knack"—could make windfall profits, for example, by buying a garden for 7,000 Rials and selling it two months later for 15,000 Rials.

The other main field of primary production, fishing, provides an arena for smaller operators but on an essentially similar pattern. Capital is generally owned by a manager and labor is hired on a day wage or share basis. But operations are mostly much smaller scaled and marketing is ad hoc through auctions, without large middlemen or important merchants. Small boats with crews varying from one to four men land their catch in the morning and offer it directly through the auction, where bidders buy for retail, or for small ventures of hiring transport and driving a load inland 30–100 km for immediate sale there. Profits in such operations are too variable and irregular for me to obtain any estimate of the incomes that can be earned this way, but

Auctioneer in the fish market

they are clearly not large, and the field is occupied by an unstable assemblage of failed merchants, temporary entrepreneurs, etc. The auctioneers likewise tend to be failed merchants, who make 1–2 Rials ($3–6) on a morning's work. Fishermen are generally full-time workers with fishing (and spells as sailors) as a dominant life career; their household economies are modest, somewhat better in the case of boat owners. Large land seines are also used, with a more marginal and ad hoc labor force to draw them, and modest and irregular income even for the net boss. The most substantial fishing operation is for sardines, from somewhat larger ships worth approximately 900 Rials and nets and other equipment adding up to a further 2,000 Rials—a total equivalent of nearly $10,000. A crew of ten men work for a three-month season and expect to catch around 6,000 Rials worth of fish. Of this, the ship takes 50 percent while the crew shares the rest, that is, 300 Rials to each crew member, or the equivalent of 3 Rials, or a $9–10, per day. Yet it is proving increasingly difficult for sardine vessel owners to recruit labor for such fishing—in part because the work is demanding and better wages can be made by labor migration, in part because catches are declining and the figures cited may be more characteristic of past years than of current operations. The explanations offered for these declining catches are the reduction of fish due to oil pollution and the dispersal of schools because of noise from engines, and traffic along the beach. Despite dissatisfaction with the trend, however, it is notable that the capital equipment in sardine fishing gives an annual return of about 100 percent (but maintenance/replacement of nets is also a major cost). The owner/captains of sardine vessels thereby obtain incomes so they can live comfortably all year from the returns of a three-month season; and the early inheritance of such a vessel was cited as the reason for one of the very few cases we came across of a youth's failing to leave Sohar for an extended period of labor migration.

Sardine catches are not sold directly at auctions, but generally are dried and handled by merchant middlemen in a special section of the *suq*. These middlemen are likewise in a contracting sector of business and are much less prosperous than traders in most other fields.

Thus, while some labor and capital linger on in the less expansive fields and sectors of the economy, because of the person's specialized knowledge and interest in a preestablished field of competance or style of work, the predominant picture is one of high and swift mobility in response to market changes, and adventurous entrepreneurship in pursuit of future profits. I was constantly taken aback by the diversity of experiences represented even in the quite short life histories of persons with whom I came into contact. Baba Ji's shop assistant had tried both labor and business in Zanzibar, worked for years as a sailor, married and established a family in Bombay (which he had subsequently lost through the death of both wife and children), then remarried in Sohar, and had a spell as auctioneer at the fish market before the present job. The long-time employee in the Sultan's customs department in Sohar on retirement invested his savings in one of Sohar's first taxis, only to lose his captial through bad management, accidents, and the problems of garage maintenance and spare parts at this early stage. Between August 1974 and December 1975, the three men with whom I was on the closest personal terms all changed their work: one went from working in the stores of an oil operation in inner Oman to serving as a bank clerk in Sohar: another changed from employment in road construction to running a carpenter's shop in

Mattrah employing six to eight Pakistani and Indian labor migrants; while the third had continuously but inconclusively been considering changing his employment while simultaneously launching a side venture employing two Pakistani tailors in a tailor's shop. The last is an innovation, since tailors' shops have not previously existed in Sohar, where all commercial sewing has been done privately by women. The importing of migrant labor is also a recent innovation that requires new forms of management (dealings with labor-recruiting agencies in Bombay or Karachi, obtaining license and work permits for the labor migrants in Muscat, etc.), though the competance to do so builds in part on preceding personal experience as labor migrants and more indirectly on practices associated with slave trade in the last century. Taking employment in a bank is likewise innovative in the sense that this is a town where the very first bank ever was established the previous year, and the man in question has no regular schooling, though he has reached a very high level of literacy by his own efforts.

As noted, only a few women participate marginally in the activity of the marketplace, and none to my knowledge takes employment for wages. But a majority are engaged in sewing, embroidery, and petty trade in their close neighborhood, and under pressure of necessity women will intensify these efforts and their imaginativeness in finding opportunities for earning income. The most striking case of innovation and resoluteness in this respect was that of the widow, mentioned before, who took over her deceased husband's vegetable booth.

These glimpses of some particular individuals, events, customs, and attitudes add up to a rather consistent picture of market behavior and how the market functions in the life of Soharis. Without pretense of systematic data, my purpose cannot be any kind of economic analysis of Sohar and its market: what I need to do is establish the general, qualitative features of the market which influence or predicate Sohari social behavior, particularly with respect to the social and cultural reproduction of pluralism which is the main focus of my analysis. To identify these and their particular entailments, we need to develop a model of the system on an aggregate level or macrolevel, but without losing anchorage in the activities and life situations of real people and thus doing violence to the linkages and interdependencies that obtain on this microlevel. By means of such a model I wish to explore the ways in which economic organization and the experiences that Soharis have of livelihood and wealth as components of man's fate affect the various social identities that compose Sohari pluralism.

The first requirement, then, is to turn the perspective around: so far I have sought to identify and distill general features from particular cases; now I must show how a number of widely distributed assumptions, attitudes, values, and skills cohere in an institutional complex that conditions and facilitates certain patterns of behavior in many individuals.

A key element in the Sohari market institution is the use of money in all trade and employment. It is interesting to note that this high degree of monetization has prevailed till recently without the existence of a local mint or any national regulation of a monetary medium. Since the accession of Sultan Qaboos in 1970, the Omani Rial has steadily been gaining ascendancy, and during the last years of Sultan Sa'id the Sa'id Rial was also of some importance. But the main currencies in the preceding decades and generations have been Indian Rupees and Maria Theresa dollars, and prices in the *suq* in 1974 were still frequently cited in Rupees, Dubai and Abu Dhabi Rials, and sometimes Saudi currency. More important than the form of currency, however, is the mode of its employment: for the evaluation and transfer of land and means of production just like all other goods; to facilitate swift competitive bidding in a variety of different forms of auction; to measure success in speculative ventures and to store value between such ventures; to compare the rewards of alternative employment; and so forth. And the values and priorities which govern men's decisions in this comprehensive market arena are most clearly revealed by the suspension of the rules of tactfulness and personal consideration that otherwise pervade all social interaction, and the striking fact that it is the merchant—rather than the landowner, the political leader, or the religious dignitary—who occupies the highest position in most men's ambition and represents the ideal vocation.

The effect of these orientations and facilities is to generate a very high degree of physical mobility, readiness to change work and acquire new skills, entrepreneurial adventurousness, and active capital management, as pervasive empirical characteristics of the male population of Sohar. Nor are such activities foreign to women, though segregation and strictures of modesty limit the scope of their realization. Consequently, there is a sensitive responsiveness of capital and labor allocations, in the population at large, to market changes.

However, Sohari consciousness has been shaped over the generations, not by the theoretical properties or potential of such a market organization but by the actual fluctuations that have eventuated and the experiences of (what they see as) the objective condition of the world which Soharis thereby have gained. It is therefore important to ascertain just what these market changes have been over the last generations, and what particular consequences for activities and life careers have eventuated. Of particular importance for the theme that concerns me are the patterns of circulation of wealth, and interlinkage of sectors of the economy.

With respect to the circulation of wealth, we have seen a set of institutional forms which favor capital over labor: it is not by hard toil but by the adroit management of capital that the great profits can be obtained in this society. The rewards of labor, though recently increased to a level that secures unprecedented welfare, still cannot add up to any considerable wealth. Traditionally, the same seems to have been true, even under the most exceptional circumstances. Thus, even the most adventurous forms of labor were still organized in relatively tight capitalist enterprises: the big profits from pearl fishing in the Gulf, in which Sohari labor participated, went to ship's captains and capitalist outfitters, and not to the divers; while as fighting men Soharis served as mercenaries only, and suffered from rather than participated in the piracy of the Gulf coast.

The rates of return on capital, on the other hand, show a very high level, barring catastrophes. Merchants in the *suq* today can obtain a return of 50–100 percent per annum on their capital. Entrepreneurial ventures show similar rates, and even traditional fishing operations with significant capital input give returns on the same order of magnitude. I can find no evidence that this is a recent artifact of rapid growth in the economy resulting from Oman's sudden oil revenues. Thus, life stories from very old people contained accounts of swift earnings in youth and rapid rise to wealth. Countless particular ventures twenty, thirty, and fifty years ago, which produced great earnings, were also recounted. In general, no surprise or amazement at present returns on captial (as opposed to wages) was expressed by Soharis, whereas they seemed untiring in their willingness to be amazed at the change in price levels. On the other hand, there is considerable direct and indirect evidence that sudden and great losses due to catastrophes were far more common: shipwrecks, looting by marauding bedouin tribes, and political upheavals are recounted from former times, and personal and secondhand biographies telling about the sudden loss of wealth are not infrequent. Thus, the general picture of former times is also of one of high rates of captial returns but greater danger that such wealth could suddenly be lost. The implication of this picture as far as social stratification is concerned is, self-evidently, one of great differences in wealth between capital owners and others, and also numerous swift career changes through successful rapid accumulation or sudden loss. The consistent experience of Soharis over remembered generations is that money proliferates if properly handled, but that wealth circulates quickly and very much depends on a person's innate talents, for better or for worse. Family histories would indicate that ascendancy has in fact been very unstable and short lived, measured in generations—perhaps because the profits that could be drawn from the primary production of land were, comparatively speaking, too low to favor a stable proprietory group, so the option of speculative ventures has served to draw also the landowners into the more swift and turbulent maelstrom of business. In this sense, Baba Ji's reservations against "putting his money in stones" derives some of its poignancy from his noncitizen minority status, but is representative of a broader and shared orientation among Soharis.

The other formative experience of economic forces which I see as having deeply affected Sohari consciousness of the relation of livelihood and identity is the close interlinkage of the sectors of the economy. This arises from a coincidence of ecological and geoeconomical conditions, transmuted by Sohar's market institutions.

First, one must recognize that the community of Sohar today, and I think any community of comparable size in the same location at any time in history so far, will depend on the twin foundations of local production and international trade. Perhaps one needs to have seen and lived in this stark environment to be sufficiently aware of the severe ecolgic limitations placed on local production: the distant, naked mountain range and the barren plain, the virtual absence of rainfall, the temperature regime, the exposed coastline—all combine to limit the extent to which a local population could sustain intself on what it locally produced, or pay for its consumption by means of local products. In agriculture, since artificial irrigation is a necessity for every kind of cultivation, any expansion of production requires heavy capital investments: either the construction of large-scale *falaj* (irrigation works) or the digging of numerous wells. Both these systems are also relatively capital intensive in their operation, since *falaj* maintenance requires continuous reconstruction by specialized, wage-paid labor, while lift irrigation requires additional energy expenditure in the form of draft animals (who must also produce their own fodder) or mechanical pumps.

On the other hand, it is precisely Sohar's geographical position— relative to seas, winds, and continents—that drove the sailing vessels of yesterday to offload cargoes on its barren shores and thus provide the basis for a supplementary, and at times primary, field of activity in international trading. This is likewise a very capital-intensive activity, since it entailed not mainly exports but transshipment and speculative exchange of merchandise of distant provenance which could not be held on credit. This is the trade which provides the historical context for the market orientation and the merchant motif in Sohar, as we have seen them reflected in the attitudes and practices described in this chapter.

But international trade in the Indian Ocean has for very long been highly susceptible to perturbations from political and economic causes, of which its virtual disappearance from the Batineh coast due to a new technology of shipping is only the last, though perhaps most dramatic, example. With each such perturbation, the relative productivity of capital and labor between trade and local production—and between the different alternatives within each of these sectors—would be changed. Thus, trade has suffered from depressions, periods of rampant piracy, or political hegemony elsewhere, or it has been buoyed by prosperity on the coasts of the Indian Ocean, relative peace, and excellent markets for particular products ranging from Oriental spices to African slaves to Arabian incense. Obversely, the attractiveness of investing scarce capital in primary production has waxed and waned. Given the monetization of labor and other means of production, and the facilities provided by Sohar's market institutions, the response of capital and labor has been one of swift movement between sectors—the more so with the more profit-conscious and speculatively inclined Soharis. (See figure 3.)

Both the changeable life stories in present and recent generations and the checkered history of trade and agriculture in Sohar (suggestively reconstructed in Williamson 1973) are evidence of the high degree of responsiveness to changing conditions which Soharis have shown.

I can now address the question of what implications these economic patterns may have for social organization in Sohar, especially for the articulation of identity and the conditions for the maintenance of plural cultural traditions. Their gross import would seem undeniable, and consistent with the picture of Sohari pluralism outlined in chapter 10.

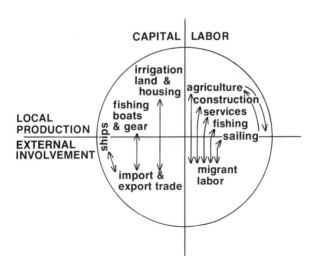

FIGURE 3. *Movements of labor and capital between major sectors of the economy.*

First, I should note that, given the market institutions that have characterized Sohar, a movement of capital between sectors of the economy will entail changes in the occupations of the capital owners almost as directly as do movements of labor. Because of the absence of banks (till 1974) and anything comparable to shares and a stock market, the only way one can effect capital movement is by purchasing private property in one sector and selling that which one has been holding in another. At the least, this will entail a major shift in the attentions and interests of even the most blasé owner, and normally it will involve discontinuing active management of one kind of asset and engaging in the management of another. Thus, the person who has had his capital in land will have been engaged in the management of agriculture, and if he moves his capital into a trade venture, he will have to function as his own trader unless he is prepared to work through a proxy and accept a considerable reduction in his profits. The vignette given above of the wealthy Ajam's sugar purchase (p. 152) can serve as an illustration of the close personal involvement that normally links capital and its owner in Sohar. In other words, flows of capital as well as flows of labor between sectors entail the movements of persons between the different "worlds" (see p. 59) of market, fish auction, orchard, sea, etc. In identifying economic circumstances that indicate the prevalence of such flows in the economic history of Sohar, I can therefore reasonably claim to have identified a dynamics that generates the active circulation of personnel between the different walks of life found in Sohar.

How might participation in such a world shape the person's conceptualization of self and others? Both the vertical movements between levels of wealth and the horizontal ones between sectors of the economy will no doubt be experienced by the individual as the result of objective and impersonal pushes and pulls, pressing him to change his occupation, often many times in the course of his life career. The emphatic themes in Sohari men's culture of the personal character of competence and each man's final responsibility for himself are a resigned acknowledgment of such a state of the world. At the same time, it is hardly possible in such a situation to see one's own identity, or that of others, as very intimately tied to any one particular occupational role. And the absence of such a linkage will, in turn, only reinforce the tendency to mobility. On the level of social classifications, this can only serve to weaken any conceptual schema that Soharis might attempt to use for seeing social differentiation in general as an ordered and unitary field. Indeed, the images most readily called forth are those of extreme variability: "Look how God made your hand: he gave you five fingers, but each a little bit different—one long, one short, one thick, one thin. People are the same way: every one of them different. Each has his own character."

Such a readiness to separate the essential identity of a person from his occupational role contrasts with conceptualizations that are prevalent in adjoining regions, both the Indian world and much of the Near and Middle East. It is also at odds with certain classifications within Sohar: the occupational caste character of the Banyan may be dismissed as a direct, Indian import, but the stigmatization of the Zatut (see p. 60) partakes of a similar idea. Likewise, of the whole set of identities tabulated in figure 3, a few other ascribed statuses do show categorical linkages with occupations in the sense that some combinations are *not* found; for example, Ajams (and Shiahs) are not soldiers, only Arabs are herders, bedouin are hardly ever merchants or fishermen. There are also some distinct statistical tendencies, acknowledged by Soharis themselves, such as a disproportion of Baluchis among soldiers and of Ajams among merchants. Thus, the market forces generating occupational circulation do not entirely overcome contrary tendencies, presumably arising from features within these separate cultural traditions, toward occupational specialization. It seems reasonable to see this situation in Sohar as a mixed result of homogenizing market processes—particularly intense in Sohar as compared to neighboring regions—and differentiating cultural and social processes similar to those found, with greater effect, elsewhere in the Middle East.

The most interesting questions, however, concern what might be the effects of this relatively open occupational structure on the content of the various other, coexisting cultural traditions. If we assume, as we reasonably may, that this high occupational mobility is not just a recent phenomenon but has coexisted with a pattern of stable, distinctive traditions in other domains of life, a number of intriguing questions arise. As a general culture historical perspective in anthropology, we are used to turning to ecology as a prime mover in cultural differentiation: the necessities and advantages entailed in different livelihoods are seen to shape different life styles and understandings and thus generate different cultural characteristics over time. In Sohar, on the contrary, we must imagine a broad variety of *common* experience in a whole range of occupations characterizing persons who nonetheless partake in *different* cultural traditions. Does this in any way affect the *kinds* of differences which are maintained in these coexisting traditions? Are they more similar in some respects that reflect their shared economic/occupational base? As a test case: women's and men's cultures constitute the only contrastive set in which members do not share this common experience and base. Are women's and men's cultural traditions different from each other in special ways, for this reason? In those cases where there are categorical or clear statistical correlations between certain cultural traditions and certain occupations, are these generated by objective competitive advantages and disadvantages that derive from particular, presumably small, cultural differences, or can they be traced to fundamental premises in the social classifications employed by Soharis? Presumably, hypotheses that try to address these questions can best be formulated and tested through the dynamic analysis of the changing relations of these cultural co-traditions, which I will attempt in part 4.

15

A Kaleidoscope of Persons

A Sohari's awareness of his own and every other person's singularity and uniqueness may be recognized as only one aspect of the morality of tact and responsibility outlined in chapter 11. It entails the necessity of each person's shaping his or her own behavior as appropriately as possible in *all* interpersonal relations, and being responsible for the results. Men see this responsibility as also embracing the behavior of the women for whom they are guardians (wives, unmarried daughters), whereas women see each adult as ultimately responsible for himself or herself. But for both sexes, this means that any one person's behavior cannot be understood in isolation, apart from his total life context, especially the priorities he pursues as a whole individual and the perfection and configuration of style and honor to which he aspires.

In my schematization of social organization for the purpose of analyzing the different cultural traditions, I have basically tried to distinguish the identity-entailing membership in each of these traditions, and have abstracted it from the flow of other life, so as to be able to conceptualize that other kind of flow—the traditions of knowledge and values (as Baluch, as woman, as Sunni, etc.)—as one of separate streams of culture. What I have thus separated is also joined: man and woman in their systematic interdependence in marriage and household, most other identities in their submergence to friendship and acquaintance in men's and women's networks, and nearly all in their random circulation between levels of wealth and occupational categories due to the effects of market processes. In addition, all these identities coalesce intimately in whole persons, who manage themselves and their affairs (and so their behavior in the capacities that I have sought to separate) in terms of an integrated concept of self and relatively unitary standards and priorities across these identities. In view of this, I must also raise the question of how such individual management, in its aggregate, may systematically affect the content and persistence of the several cultural traditions. That is, how may what a person wishes for and aspires to—as a whole person with temperament and gender and religious belief and all his other characteristics, knowing that he is shaping his own fate—how may all this affect his acts in any one particular of his capacities, for instance, as a Baluch? And will many such small and large decisions, made by many different persons who are Baluch, under the range of circumstances now obtaining in Sohar, impinge with systematic effect on what Baluchis by and large do, and what is entailed in being Baluch? And so on for each of the identities on which I focus.

Having tried to put the issue squarely, I must follow up by retreating from the formidable task of making a rigorous and complete analysis along such lines, and instead lower the level of my ambitions. I am not confident that I could develop the concepts and procedures actually to complete such an analysis; and within the scope of the material available to me and the format of this monograph I certainly do not have the occasion to explore this issue systematically. Yet we need to have some kind of picture of how individual persons and lives are shaped in Sohar, so as to judge what kind of relevance this may have for identity management. This I shall try to provide empirically by a quick series of personal biographies or portraits. Since Wikan (1982) gives extensive material of this kind on women, I shall concentrate mainly on supplementing it with portraits of men.

Let me make it quite clear, then, that what follows is not an attempt to adopt a methodology based on life histories; nor do I claim any special documentary validity for this material as compared to the other ethnographic data I have been providing. Rather, I see the portraits as alternative renderings of such data, which have the advantage of: (1) a certain immediacy that may make them more vivid to persons less familiar with sociological abstractions and/or Middle Eastern towns, and (2) an emphasis on how the identities I have been discussing coalesce in the person, and how Soharis choose to view themselves and present themselves—above all, as singular individuals trying to cope with exigencies and existential problems in a manner that will do them credit in their own eyes and in the eyes of others.

The portraits could have been multiplied, but the problem is already that the following twelve stories are rather too many. I have included so many to illustrate diverse memberships and diverse life situations. Inevitably, they include such persons as I, more or less fortuitously, came to know well. But while I was in the field I consciously tried to establish relations with the different categories of males of which Sohar is composed; so by the end of field work, my set of acquaintances could provide convenient examples for an approximate cross-section of society in this manner.

The verbatim materials that I provide are in part derived from early acquaintance (when such self-presentation constituted a natural part of getting acquainted), but are selected and supplemented in terms of later and deeper knowledge (when concentrated factual accounts of life and career were naturally less frequent in the conversations). Such texts are based on notes during the conversation and subsequent reconstruction immediately after the event, in part prepared cooperatively by my wife and me.

One salutary effect of introducing this perspective on the material is how it reveals what might otherwise be forgotten, given the focus of this monograph: that the management of the various memberships which I am discussing is not a uniform and explicit concern of actors. While some identities, such as gender, are ubiquitously relevant and explicit, others (such as ethnic categories) seem less conscious and more of the nature of self-evident facts of life; yet others (such as townspeople and bedouin) seem to emerge and persist almost as an inadvertent result of action designed in terms of other purposes—at least as far as most persons are concerned. The perspective also provokes me to suggest the crude but important generalization that the shape that Soharis give to most aspects of activity seems primarily adjusted to the considerations of obtaining wealth and maintaining appearances, and only secondarily to cultivating the particular identities entailing memberships in cultural traditions. But let this emerge from the portraits.

NIZWANI AHMED

Nizwani Ahmed retired in 1969 from a prominent post in the Omani civil service. He is a large and powerful man, with a black bristling beard and dark complexion. He lives in a large and well-built house with a separate *majlis* (reception/guest room) that is evidently rarely used. My first visit there was much disturbed by a crowd of neighborhood children who called and jeered in from the street through the narrow barred windows. Nizwani tried alternately to ignore their antics or have his family chase them away; once he went himself. When he has visitors, his nine-year-old son serves coffee, inexpertly but graciously.

"My tribe is Al Mulahi. My forefathers were prominent in Gwadar in Baluchistan, when the Sultan's son was there, long ago. They supported him and when he became Sultan they helped him unite Gwadar with Oman [in 1794]. So we became close and trusted supporters of the Al Bu Said, and have fought for them in all their struggles. In these battles the Al Mulahi have lost so many men, so though we are a very strong and famous tribe we are now a very small tribe: there are only seven houses left, and ten *xaddām*. The Al Mulahi are very strong persons; when we want something, we cannot be stopped.

"Five years ago I retired. I bought this land and built this house. I bought a Land Rover and made it into a taxi, hired a driver and did well. My pay in the customs had been very low: 25 Rupees a month, by the end it was 100 Rupees a month. I asked Sultan Said for a raise but he refused me, so I retired. But prices have risen so, and I have had troubles. Now the Land Rover just stands there; no one will repair it for me. I have run up debts with merchants in the *suq*, nearly 3,000 Rials, and now they want their money back. I own a share of land in [a village fifty miles from Muscat]. It is from my father—my share of the tribal grant when my ancestors first came from Gwadar. But the tenants went on strike and refused to water the trees. What could I do from here? If I moved to the village, what could I do there? Here there is fish in the *suq*, and my children can go to school; there I would have to travel to Mattrah to buy anything. So I made a settlement with those farmers: they water my trees, but take the whole crop.

"I have written to the Sultan Qaboos, asking for better severance bonus and a pension after my thirty-two years of service. People with much shorter service are now given thousands of Rials on retirement. Sultan Said gave me only 255 Rials, once and for all. Then next year, Sultan Qaboos came and everything changed. I have appealed to Sultan Qaboos for support, but my message never comes through to him. When you ask a deaf-mute to write your letter to a blind man, who will get your message? The Wazir-i-Diwan keeps my letter only as long as he who delivers it stands there, then throws in in the ocean. I have no shaikh to speak for me—our tribe is too small to have a shaikh. . . . No, my neighbor and brother-in-law cannot speak for me. He rarely sees the Sultan and is not liked by him. What is more, we have not been on speaking terms for ten years.

"I have just written again to the Sultan [he fetches his draft and reads out loud]: "Peace onto You, Sultan Qaboos of Oman, you are a small God to us and our protector in all hardships. Is there any opportunity and permission to speak to You and explain to You our situation, as You are the one set by God to be responsible for us and see to our needs? I assure You that we are thanking our God who brought You in the place of Your father to be responsible for us, so we are very happy and hope You have no difficulties or troubles in Your government of us, as we the population of Oman are not just Your subjects but truly Your slaves who wish You all well, and remember all Your acts and pray to God five times a day for Him to protect You from all dangers and difficulties. As God has mentioned in the Holy Koran: if the Sultan does something wrong against his people he will be remembered by God for what he has done, and likewise if he does something good for his people he will be remembered. There are many elsewhere who do bad things for their people, and we request of You to control Yourself and to be kind to the blind and the poor. Do not do as those others are doing whom I mentioned above. Just as the Prophet Daud was given the power over all animals and people, and even the seas and stars and sun and moon, so God has given You this position, and may You never lose it, and may God protect Your life and Your family as surely as we shall stand by You and are Your slaves and will fight for You against all who may try to make troubles for You."

"No one can criticize my behavior. I have no commerce with trouble makers or these uneducated neighbors. I go to the mosque, I go to the market, I say 'Good Day' - that's all. I know nothing about the common people here. . . . No, about the Ajams I know nothing at all. I have no connection with people like that, they are just here to make money and take it out of the country. They may know something about religion, that's all; otherwise they are totally uneducated, like animals. Arabs and Baluchis, some of them have breeding and education. As for Ajams, you should ask my brother-in-law about them. He knows them and has friends among them."

ABDUR RAHMAN ALI

Nizwani's half-sister's husband, Abdur Rahman Ali, is a small and meticulous man. Very reserved and quiet in manner he yet communicates an aura of authority and rank. As the Sultan's chief of intelligence in the area, he used to be much feared, but is much less so now under the young Sultan's benevolent and progressive rule.

Abdur Rahman was born in the extreme north of Oman, on the Mussandam peninsula, of Zidgali parents.

"My father had a small shop there, where he sold dried vegetables and rice. He died when I was twelve years old. I do not know where my father's father was from. We Zidgalis are scattered, a few here and a few there, of as many kinds as there are corners in a house—but it is all one house. All Zidgalis are Omanis: some live and die here, some travel abroad, but no other country is their homeland. The original ancestor of all Zidgalis was Uzd, who lived in Nejd. He had three sons: one went to Muscat (his descendants are the Al Bu Said), one went to interior Oman, and one went to Sindh (his descendants are Zidgali—"-gali" means "from"). So we are of the same family as the Al Bu Said.

"After Koran school I started working for the Wali of Mussandam, since I was good at writing. Then I worked for Wali Mudhaffar in Suwaik, who was himself illiterate. I was paid fifty Rupees a month in salary. When Mudhaffar was transferred to Sohar, I came here. When Mudhaffar's son was made Wali of Saham he sent me to help his son there; they raised my salary to sixty Rupees. I was there for thirteen months till Ali bin Mudhaffar was transferred to Shinaz, where I stayed with him for three more years till I came back to Sohar. I was tired of

working for ever for so low a salary and asked Sultan Said to transfer
me or, best of all, release me from service. The Sultan said no, but later
transferred me to the army. After fourteen years in the army, I
damaged my eyes from the backfire of a Brengun. I had to spend
fifty-one days in hospital in Dubai, and came out with reduced eyesight. I hăve now had forty-five years of service; thirty-one of those
years I have lived in Sohar."

[So here you have perhaps a small circle of close friends, with whom
you can spend your free time?]

"Not at all! I have *no* close friends. I go to the *suq*, I have friendly
relations with everyone there; I go to my house. That is enough.
Perhaps a few persons will come on ˁ*Eid*, or at the birth of a child, to
give their greetings only."

HUSSEIN MOHAMMED

In a small stall in a side passage of the *suq* is the herbal apothecary of
Hussein Mohammed, a stooped and modest figure, but earnest and
enthusiastic regarding his medicinal craft. He is a Shiah Arab, childless
and of modest means, an active and dedicated member of the Shiah
congregation.

"Our origin is from Bahrein, but my father and father's father were
born here in Sohar. I used to be a scribe for the Wali, but my eyes were
weak and I spoiled them working there. So I had to quit. Then I joined
as assistant and apprentice with Abdur Rahman Shatar, a Zidgali (and
Sunni) who owned the best herbal apothecary in Sohar. As I learned
the trade, I became his partner, but then after three years together he
became sick, and he retired and died after six months. Now I own and
run the shop. There are two thousand different medicines here. Some
herbs and other materials are collected in Oman, mostly supplied to me
by bedouin; most medicines are imported from abroad, largely
through dealers in Dubai. Iran is a great place for many things, and so
is Hejaz. Some of the medicines are mentioned in the Koran. There are
dried leaves for paste to set broken bones; leaves and seeds for con-
stipation, fever, children's stomach trouble; red almonds for women's
backache, rash, and itch; powder to mix with butterfat for headaches.
Here is a cloud substance from Egypt for failing eyesight, and Iranian
sour goat cheese for small children's stomach cramps, as well as several
varieties of *suqor* [opium extract] to make children sleep, and mercury
to drive away *jinns*.

"Some people come to me directly, and describe their symptoms, and
I must know all the medicines. Others come with prescriptions from a
basir [magician] and I compound the medicine. The two other shops in

the *suq* now come and consult me for difficult matters. But business is less than before, because the doctors at the new hospital do not believe in these medicines."

SULEIMAN ASHUR

Suleiman Ashur is forty-five years old, and runs a shop and soft drink stand just outside the *suq* area, close to the north gate of Higra. He is an Ajam and one of the leaders of the Shiah congregation; during Moharram in 1975–76 he read major parts of the ritual text.

"I was born in Bellah, farther south on the coast, as were my father's father and my father, who later moved to Kabura and died there. Our original ancestor came from Bandar Abbas, in Iran. My father and ancestors before him were weavers. They wove cloth for the headdresses used in Sur and the waistcloth used by the Sharkiya: these all used to be made by Ajams of the Batineh, but now hardly any do any more.

"I came to Sohar when I was fourteen years old. Then when I was eighteen I went to Kuwait, where I worked and saved for fourteen years. Then I came back and married my wife, who is from Sohar. Myself, I have no relatives here, but I have many in Bellah, where I often visit. When I first married, I rented the small house there across the street. All Ajams still lived close together here, inside the fortified wall then. There used to be much restlessness and warfare, and all the Ajams lived together inside the wall for protection against the Bedouin raiders. When the Bedouin attacked, the Ajam shaikh used to organize the defense; the Sultans also had to turn to him for help often.

"Most Ajams have orchards and cultivate, but many have shops too, and crafts. Ajams used to be the richest people in Sohar, but we fear God and will not take big profits. Whereas others sell next day for 150 Rials what they bought for 100 Rials, we take only 110 Rials, so the others have become more wealthy.

"I used to have a shop in the *suq*, but when it was destroyed by the big fire I built my house here, and opened one end of it for my shop. That way I can keep my shop open most of the time. When I am free, I have three or four friends whom I see regularly—we visit each other's houses. They are all Ajam. But I also had a very good friend who was not Ajam: Mān bin Abdallah, who was Wali of Kariyāt. He and his brother both had very good Ajam friends; finally they were both converted to the Shiah faith. Mān bin Abdallah ws my *wasta* and he was even chosen as shaikh of the Ajams of Kariyāt, though he was not Ajam himself.

"Our women wear the *burqa* [facemask] always. In size it is intermediate between the (small) Arab ones and the (bigger) Baluchi ones. Ajam women of Sohar also used to wear longer tunics, down to the lower calf, but now most of them have changed to the knee-length style.

"We have two Shiah mosques in Sohar: one old and one very old. Ajams have been in Sohar always: for a thousand years."

SAID SALEH

Said Saleh is a Baluch from the village of Sallan, neighboring Sohar on the north. He was born in 1938. Said is a meticulous and precise man with a birdlike face, immaculately clean, and gentle but impersonal in his manner.

"Sallan and the neighboring Zaffran were settled by about six hundred Baluchi refugees during the reign of Sultan Feisal [1883–1913; see below]. There were only two or three families living there then. They were fleeing from the ruler of Baluchistan, who sent ships to fetch them back, but the Wali of Sohar consulted the Sultan, who said they could stay. Both my parents are from Sallan. They both had been married before, and each had a son from their previous marriage. They settled in a *barasti* south of the mosque, and had three sons. I remember when I was very small, there was a famine in the village; only three houses had food left: the shaikh, and us, and one more. Everyone who came to those houses was fed, and we pulled through. But while I was still small, my father died. My mother declared she would never marry again, just work for her children and support herself and cherish the memory of her husband. We moved to a smaller *barasti* very close by the mosque, and she worked as a seamstress. But as soon as we children had grown up a little bit, her brother [the shaikh] made her remarry. She never had any children from that marriage.

"When I was ten, I was circumcised, together with six other boys, one of whom was my brother. They used to do it then on boys at the ages of six to twelve. Now they know better, and do it at birth, or a few days old, or before the boy is two or three years old.

"When I was eleven I left Sallan. I worked on a ship and came finally to Kuwait, where I started working on land. I worked all over the Gulf, but mostly in Qatar. Altogether I was out for ten years. I saved much money, and married, and then settled in Sallan. I married my cousin, the daughter of the shaikh. She is a very good woman: never gossips or repeats my words to anyone, not even to her own mother and father. I could never think of divorcing her, or taking a second wife. I have four children by her; my eldest daughter is eighteen and the smallest boy is two. We speak Baluchi at home—and Arabic, when we don't want the smaller ones to understand and so as to teach the older ones.

"From the money I had saved I bought garden land suitable for vegetables, and three cars—long ago, before there were many, at the time of the old Sultan. I hired drivers and ran them as taxis. But the drivers were careless since these were not their vehicles, and ruined them, so I lost them and the money, and I sold the garden to keep going and so lost that too. Those were all the profits I had saved from my work in Qatar. Now [1974] I work with the road contractor Strobag. The company pays well, but nowadays you need so much capital to start anything, about 3,000–4,000 Rials. I should like to start a shop for stoves, since fewer and fewer people now use wood fires for cooking.

"The house is recently constructed, in locally made brick. In the other house in this compound lives my wife's sister, but in a separate household. My daughter Khadiga was married about four years ago; she has a joint household with us but sleeps in a separate *barasti*. I shall build another room on the house for them. Her husband works in Abu Dhabi.... All the women here in Sallan wear the *burqa*: if you see anyone in Sohar who doesn't, it must be because they are not Sohari families, and come from Muscat or somewhere else south of Kabura.

"There are both Arabs and Baluch in this village. They intervisit and are friends. We all feel that we belong to one village, and hold together against outsiders. Baluchis and Arabs also sometimes intermarry, both ways. One of the Arab families here is Ibadhi, and one is Shiah. Ibadhis are almost like Sunnis, can pray together; but Shiah and Sunni cannot pray together. If a Sunni came into a Shiah mosque they would be very angry. Nor will they give a woman to a Sunni. The Shiahs are all descended from people from Iran, though some are Arabs.

[Why don't they change their religion?]

"Because why would the government tell them to do that? The government leaves them free to do as they like. Are they not all Moslems? You may change your school of law, though generally the child remains of the school of the father. But if you said you would change from Sunni to Shiah, everyone would try to dissuade you, but if you really insist, no one can stop you."

By Christmas 1975, Said had established a new enterprise in Muscat, stayed there in the week and came home every weekend.

"A carpenter friend advised me to start a small contracting firm and not give up even if it went poorly the first two or three months. Being away and living in shifting camps with the road-building company was a hardship, so I decided to try. I managed to lease a lot of forty by forty feet, and built a house for 2,000–3,000 Rials in materials and labor. This all becomes the landowner's after six years, and meanwhile I pay 100 Rials a month in rent. Perhaps after that I can keep it for another six years, at the rate of 200 Rials a month. I made three shops in it: one for a carpentry factory, one barbershop, and one to rent out (for 60 Rials a month). There are rooms in back for my Pakistani and Indian employees. I have four carpenters, one driver, one painter, one mason, and two barbers—nine persons altogether, and permits for five more: an electrician, a steel man, an engineer, and two masons. I prefer Indians. India is a poor country; they are happy to work hard and to earn money, whereas Pakistanis are better off, and demand more and work less.

"I had to buy 2,000 Rials the first month in carpenter's tools and machines, and 2,000 Rials for a truck. I take contracts for various buildings and deliveries—just now one thousand chairs for new government schools. It has worked out: I made 4,000 Rials net the first year; just now I earned 3,000 Rials minus materials in three months."

SHAIKH FEISAL

Shaikh Feisal is Said's mother's brother and his father-in-law, and was sheik of South Sallan until he handed it over to his son. He was born in A. D. 1894 and in 1974 was suffereing from approaching senility. A slender, handsome old man, he carries himself with great dignity and wears immaculate white clothes, but is a modest man and can be seen occasionally in the market driving or riding his small donkey.

"My father's father came here from Makran when he was fifteen, from the village of Shiráhin. He had to leave Baluchistan because of difficulties with the Shah's government at the time. He married three wives and had four sons. His descendants today are so many—no one knows them all. My father was Karam [that is, Abdul Karim], his Muridsan. He was made shaikh of Sallan under Sultan Feisal bin Turki. He had two sons and two daughters; I am the eldest. I succeeded my father as Shaikh. Later I divided Sallan in two, kept the southern part, and nominated a new shaikh for the northern part. I have been shaikh under three Sultans.

"I have married four wives: first the two who are the mothers of my three sons and six daughters. The third one I divorced. The fourth one I married recently. My first two wives live together in the main house; my new wife lives elsewhere, near her brother's son. She has no father or mother, and was previously married but has no issue. All four are Baluchi, and of my own family: that is best because then you know about them, that they are good. Otherwise, they might start trouble between the families. My six daughters have all gone to family: three to their cousins, two to second cousins, and one to a distant relative."

Shaikh Feisal's son-in-law tells how the old man used to be a very brave and strong person and a good shaikh.

"No one dared to speak or act against him. These Arabs would come; if they did not act correctly he would punish them. Once four men came who owed money to a man in Sallan. They refused to pay him back and threatened him. The shaikh caught them singlehandedly and tied them up, then took them to the Wali at his leisure.

"The bedouin used to raid the area for slaves. They would catch and steal the slaves of Sallan people, and even our own children, and take them to Buremi and sell them. The worst ones were the Awamir tribe. When they came, everyone used to seek refuge in the fort of Sohar— and have their houses and gardens looted by the bedouin. But Shaikh Feisal built a fort of sandbags in Sallan, against the wall of the mosque, and fought them off with sword and rifle.

Shaikh Feisal goes to fetch his sword, a long, narrow curved sword in a sheath.

"It was made in Iran. My father took it along on Haj. On the way some Arabs came and asked to buy it. But he knew that then they would use it to rob him, so he refused. They threatened to take it by force if he did not give it to them. Then, while he read the *fateh* prayer, it came out of its sheath and went into the river. Those bedouin searched and searched but could not find it! The handle was spoiled by the water. My father tried several times unsuccessfully to repair it, till in a dream he saw how he must do it in ivory. Ever since it has remained strong.

"I myself have made Haj four times."

"[Why so many?]"

"I had the money, and four must be better than three, three better than two! I got the money from my gardens, from dates and *barasti*, etc. I also got forty-five Rials for being shaikh. Now they give me thirty Rials as pension, after I let my youngest son, who is clever with the government, take over."

"Shaikh Feisal had eleven slaves. Eight of these were alive around 1960, when they were freed: of the four who chose to remain in Sallan, three were old and are now dead, while the fourth, a woman of middle age has later moved permanently to the Gulf areas of labor migration.

SHAIKH ISMAIL

Shaikh Ismail is a tall, modest, and reserved man. He steps down from his donkey some distance from any house he is approaching, as a sign of respect for his host, and lives in an unassuming *barasti* house in the "bedouin" zone of settlement on the inside of the orchard belt. But his house has a TV antenna (though no electrical generator) and a plywood *majlis*.

"I am not myself of the tribe of this ward. My own tribe is Shirawi, a small tribe, perhaps from the mountains, perhaps from the Abu Dhabi side—the old people never told me. My father's father was a big landowner; he made an alliance with the Ajams in Higra. Then in connection with some fighting between tribes he transferred to here. During my father's time, the shaikh of this ward became incapable; when compensation was to be paid, my father had to pay it for the people; when they were in jail, he would speak for them. For a while my father tried letting the old shaikh and an assistant alternate every other year, but much of the time he was shaikh himself."

Shaikh Ismail's father became a very prominent landowner; he married four wives and had one son by each. Ismail has also been married four times, but has largely lost the property he obtained as his patrimony.

"When my father and the original shaikh both died, there was no one to have authority here. The Wazir came on inspection. Since he found no shaikh here he called a meeting to ask the people who should be their shaikh. They chose me.

"My rival was Mahmud. He is not of the local tribe, as he claims to be; he is Maghrebi [from Saudi Arabia]. He has not become shaikh in the correct way: his father was simply the doorkeeper at the fort, got some good connections that way."

SHAIKH MAHMUD

Shaikh Mahmud is a confident and busy person. He speaks swiftly and precisely, has detailed information at his fingertips, often serves as imam at the Friday mosque besides his political and administrative duties.

"My father was captain of the guard in the fort since the time of Sultan Feisal. He was responsible for leading them in battle, and he reported on them to the Sultan in Muscat. When the Sultan visited, my father led the guard of honor outside the fort. He was also shaikh of this ward.

"Now I am shaikh. I have full authority here. No one can sit, stand, or sleep without my permission, or get a passport, or anything. No, there is no control on an outsider buying property and settling in our ward, if he is Omani. . . . The qualities required of a shaikh are personal. Most important, he must show interest and responsibility. If someone is arrested and taken to Muscat jail direct without anyone being informed, the shaikh should not wait till that person's family inquires, he should *discover* that the person has disappeared, trace him, and go to

Muscat. He should be as a father is to a child; if someone needs money for fine, bail, etc. the shaikh should pay. That way, if he is only number three shaikh in the ward, the people will like him and respect him, and raise him up to the first position.. . .

"The ward is composed of several peoples, of different tribes. There are about 1,800 persons, counting children. Of these, I have made 23 children and children's children; including my brothers and their descendants, we are 50–55 persons!

[What about the situation now, with two shaikhs in one ward?]

"If people go some to one shaikh, some to the other, that is OK as long as the two shaikhs cooperate. Shaikh Ismail used to have most of the people; I had less. But shaikh Ismail lives far out, people have to pay two or two and a half Rials for a taxi to him. He cannot read or write, which means: (1) he is wrong more often than he is right, and (2) he cannot write letters, statements, and so on for the people. Things are not done only by speaking. And what is more, to speak well you must be educated to have the correct grammar and pronunciation. So now, most people have changed to me as their shaikh."

KATITI

Katiti is a tall, black ex-slave in her forties. She lives alone, since her husband moved permanently to Kuwait, where he has taken a second wife.

"I was born in Muscat, and was the slave of the Sultan's wazir. In the summer we used to go to Nakhl, where it is cooler. There is a natural spring there, where the water wells forth from the mountain, hot in the winter and cold in the summer, and all the gardens are watered from it.

"I married Mudhaffar's slave, and moved here in marriage. [Mudhaffar (see p. 32) was himself the trusted slave of Sultan Feisal, who made him Wali of Sohar.] We were not ordinary servant slaves; we were special slaves. Inside the fort, we had our own house and cooked our own food. My husband was in charge of the Wali's stores: food stores and issuing rations, that is. I supervised all the female slaves. There were about thirty or forty slaves in the fort, counting the children. All the working slaves were from Dhofar. The soldiers, on the other hand, were Beni Omar Arabs, then as now. Because it is a big tribe found in many places, so people are afraid of them and respect them. They are strong and brave, fight well, and are not afraid to die. We could not go outside the fort. If we had important errands or wanted to visit someone outside the fort, we had to ask Mudhaffar's permission. All the time, we were kept inside the fort.

"Mudhaffar was very severe, but a good Wali. He was made Wali of the whole Batineh coast four times, because in between the Sultan sent him to Sur, Inner Oman, and Gwadar. But whenever other Walis came here, there would be so much unrest [*harb*] between the tribes: not just among the bedouin, also all the others. If 2 men met and quarreled, in a moment 200 would be there, lined up on each side and fighting. What Mudhaffar did was to catch all the shaikhs of all the main tribes and keep them as hostages in the fort to hold the area quiet.

"Before Mudhaffar, his brother Salem was Wali. He was married to my father's sister. He was a very cruel man. If people came to him for mediation, he would kick them and abuse them. It is our custom that in the morning, the wife will wish her husband good morning and good health when he wakes up. Salem never bothered to answer such greetings from my aunt, he just moved his foot slightly [threatening to kick]. . . . Our tribe is the Al Bu Said." ("No, they are not of the Al Bu Said: they *belong* to the Al Bu Said [*maṣa* Al Bu Said]," others corrected indignantly at a later occasion.)

ALI YUSUF

Ali Yusuf, a fluent English speaker, was no doubt my closest friend in Sohar. He is a small and neat Arab, with the regular features and slight build so characteristic of Omanis. He was twenty-eight years old when I first met him.

"I was born in Sohar of poor parents who both came from Kabura, farther south on the Batineh coast. My mother died when I was quite small, but our neighbor Mohammed and his wife were very kind to me; she was like a mother to me and sewed my clothes and took care of me. Then my father remarried, and my stepmother made troubles for me. See how tactical they are, those women: in front of my father she was friendly and kind, but behind his back she scolded me and spanked me and gave me second-rate food. So I ran away when I was eleven years old to seek an education. I came to Bombay, where I worked in a café in the daytime and went to school at night, and after that I was in many other places, getting schooling wherever I could and special training when I had oil company jobs. When I came back I was twenty-two years old, and nobody recognized me!

"My first marriage was shortly after I came back to Oman. I knew nobody and my father arranged it all. But my wife quarreled and from the very beginning would not obey, so I had to leave her. . . . My first wife did nothing bad herself, but I discovered that the mother strayed, so I divorced my wife, because she might become like that.

"After that, I decided I must do things for myself. So *I* found Fatima. She is my relative, so I saw her when I came visiting for *Eid*. I talked to her, told her I would ask her father, and made her agree, all before I went, myself, and asked for her from her father. . . . It is great trouble for me that she is so uneducated. I must teach her everything—what is nice, what is the right way—but even so it is better that way than to marry an educated woman from another family. I do not want her to wear the *burqa*; it is a bad custom."

Ali was employed away from Sohar, so he needed an arrangement whereby he could leave his wife under reliable supervision. He had left his father's house because of his stepmother's treatment, so he would not place Fatima there. Consequently, he left her with her own parents, although he was bitter because his father-in-law had kept the whole bride price and given no gold jewelry to the bride.

"The second and third month we were married I was away in Mattrah. I sent forty and forty-five Rials to Fatima's father, and he spent it all for his whole family. When I came back for a visit, I wanted to take Fatima with me to Mattrah, but her parents said no. I had no money, was a new man in a weak situation. I could not complain about the bride price and the money for food. But Fatima was my wife, and I wanted to take her with me. They refused and complained to the Wali!

"The Wali asked: 'What is your complaint?'

"I said: 'I have no complaint, it is those people who complain.'

"The Wali asked them: 'What is it that is wrong?'

"My father-in-law said: 'This man is taking our daughter from us.'

"When the Wali was told that we were married, he said: 'How can you say that? If they were not married, it would mean that he is stealing your daughter; when they are married, he must be responsible for her.'

"'But we made a special agreement at marriage that she should remain in the house.'

"The Wali said: 'This is a very serious charge; you must go to Muscat if you want to make it.' When my father-in-law refused, the Wali scolded him: 'How can you live in this country if you do not accept my ruling? I say you or I or even the Sultan cannot keep a man from taking his wife with him. That is my ruling, and if you do not accept my ruling, how can you stay here?'

"So the Wali ordered me to remove my wife. . . . I got a taxi and called Fatima out. Her mother followed; she climbed onto the taxi, but I caught her by the leg and pulled her down, and we went off. We lived six months in Mattrah. When I was transferred to Fahud [Inner Oman], I left Fatima with her parents again. My father was very angry with me, and refused to visit us."

The cross-pressures that must be reconciled to form one's role in this society can be illustrated by Ali's dilemmas, and solution, regarding the issue of residence during May–June 1974.* The showdown was brought about by his return on sick leave. ("I sensed that something was wrong the moment I entered the house," Ali says.) But Fatima would not enlighten him until his fever and convalescence were fin-- ished, and he had recovered. Then she asked him to build a house for her, still refusing to tell him why life with her own parents had become insufferable to her.

Ali had already, sometime previously, secured a housesite for future use. It was located (advantageously) close to the main road, but in an area with a temporary ban on cement buildings because the final course of the road had not yet been decided. Only a thatch house could be erected there, and Ali argued strongly against it, pointing out the loss involved in putting up a temporary building. Yet Fatima insisted, and forced the issue by taking Ali before his own father and demanding a house of her own, threatening otherwise to take her case to the Wali (see chapter 11). The main considerations that impinged on his decision seem to be as follows.

1. The impossibility of leaving a wife alone in the house while the husband is absent on labor migration. "If a woman has three or four children, if she has sons who are thirteen or fourteen years old and understand things, then the husband can leave her, but not otherwise. Someone must be responsible for her; she must not be left alone. . . . If someone climbed over the fence, came in and Fatima was alone, could she fight him? He could steal and take away anything he wished." "Unfaithfulness by the wife is a great shame for the husband. It happens because he is stupid.He is responsible, he should think. . . . If he is away, then he must set another person to watch over her; he must make reliable arrangements. [But is not the shame greatest for her?] "No, it comes from lack of education. How can she know the right from the wrong when her parents, her husband do not show her and look after her?"

2. The balance of sanctions between spouses. On the one hand, Ali scolded Fatima for not understanding the economy of the matter— only to regret his harsh tongue when she cried. Furthermore, "I complained that Fatima [by involving him with his affines] causes me so much trouble that I have been thinking I must divorce her. But when I say this, she cries." On the other hand, there is a strong fear that a dissatisfied wife will cause irreparable shame to her husband: "The wife becomes angry, and goes and does a bad thing. I do not involve myself in such things, but many men are looking for an opportunity. . . . Women should be spoiled."

---

*A detailed account of this case is found in Wikan 1982, chap. 12.

3. The loss of income by working in Sohar rather than as a labor migrant. Jobs are fewer and salaries are lower in Sohar. Ali envisaged alternative solutions: asking for six month's compassionate leave from his job, and taking a much more poorly paid job as a clerk in the local hospital; procrastinating on completing the house, so Fatima would not be able to or no longer wish to move. In the end he secured a steady, fairly well paid job in the new bank.

4. Fear of the authorities and compliance with regulations. "The Shariat commits a husband to give his wife a house *separate* from his father or her father.... The Wali will support her demand." I do not think Ali seriously entertained such an interpretation of the law, but he was clearly afraid of being called to account for himself before the Wali—probably because of the precedent of his last case against his parents-in-law, when the Wali supported him by "ordering" him to remove her.

5. Relations to affines. Ali was on very poor terms with them because of their long history of disagreements (above), though both sides tried to remain polite to each other. When he did proceed to build his *barasti* house, while living with them, he made no mention of the fact to them nor they to him. Finally, when the house was ready and he wanted to move his furniture, he said to his father-in-law: "Are you free to drive my furniture for me tomorrow morning?" " 'Yes,' said my father-in-law, 'I'm free.' Later he said: 'Ali, it is better to wait till the evening,' but I answered, 'No'. Then he said he wanted to see my father about my plans to move. I said: 'Go and see him, but it is for me to tell him that I am moving!' So finally, he did drive me, as I asked." On the third trip, when he moved Fatima, her little sister also came along to spend the first night there in the new house. "My mother-in-law is better; my father-in-law is worst. Being a relative, he should not behave like this: he is my father's cousin and his sister is married to another cousin of my father."

6. Relations to his own father. "My father is angry with me for not having Fatima live in his house. Now, he asked me: 'Do you remember what I have said?' 'Yes,' I answered, 'but not exactly, so please repeat it.' And my father said: 'I told you that you would get trouble from leaving Fatima in her father's house.' The day after we moved in here, my father came visiting—once in the morning and then again in the evening. He never came to the other place.... He is old and un-educated, sometimes sick, and says that I am responsible for him. But how can a son be responsible for the father? It must be the other way around! But my father fed me when I was small; now I must feed him. I give him twenty-five to thirty Rials a month" (while he was working in Inner Oman).

7. Public opinion. "When I came home on sick leave, one of the old

women in the neighborhood said to me: 'Ali, are you a man?' I said, 'Yes, I am a man.' She said, 'Think about my words.' So I thought about it that night, spoke to Fatima about it. It was then I decided to move her to a separate house."

8. Self-respect. "Every person must be responsible for himself.... Now I have worked, taken care of my life, no one can say a bad word against me. I want to protect that reputation."

So Ali built a *barasti* house, quit his well-paid job away from home, took his wife out of the uxorilocal extended family arrangement, and settled in Sohar as a bank clerk. "When I get my month's salary, I show it to Fatima and say 'Do you know why it is so little, so much less than before?' She answers: 'It is not the money I want; I want *you* to be with me.' " "No, my father does not come here; he is still angry—not with me, but with Fatima's family. I visit him sometimes, and give him money—fifteen Rials every month, since he is an old man."—"Fatima's parents are angry—and my heart is still black for what they did before. But I hide it, and just agree with everything they say, do not listen to them, and have nothing to do with them." "I insist that Fatima visit her mother every Friday, after having cleaned up the breakfast, for three or four hours. It is right that she should visit them, according to religion. But I cannot forget how they acted, and do not see them much myself. When I work overtime at the bank, I tell Fatima to go to her mother after evening classes and wait for me there. I drop by when I am finished, but stay only a moment and then take her home."

ABDULLAH KHALFAN

Abdullah Khalfan is about forty years old, of middle stature and light brown skin. He counts himself as pure Arab, though there are indications that his lineage may derive from Persian Baluchis. He is a reflective and widely acquainted and informed person (numerous fragments of viewpoints and opinions have been cited from him in the previous chapters). His domestic relations, particularly events surrounding the marriage of his eldest daughter, are closely portrayed in Wikan 1982, chapter 11 of this book, and elsewhere.

"I was born and grew up here in Sohar. My father died when I was six or eight years old, my mother when I was twelve, so I was brought up by my [agnatic] uncles.... I was really much closer to my mother's brothers than to my father's brothers, who were legally responsible for me after my father's death. There was not one particular of them responsible, they all shared. But it was my mother's mother who really looked after me. My mother received no support; she remarried and died shortly. My father left very little property.... My uncles did not respect me; they made me work hard without recognition. I decided that the only way to make them respect me was to succeed independently—then they would associate themselves with me. Now they say:

"'Yes, Abdullah, who works in the hospital, who works in agricultural extension, he is our brother, he is our family!'

"I worked very hard, educated myself, including a correspondence course in English. Then I went to Kuwait and worked in the main generating plant there. I received various training in the various departments. Finally I became responsible in the main control room.

"After I had been two years in Kuwait, I came back for a visit with the money I had saved. I owned part of a garden together with twenty relatives (sisters, uncles, etc.). It is no good with so many: one wants water here, one there; plant mango here, no, have road here, etc. So I sold my part, and bought a separate garden with only date trees. Many of them have been destroyed by storms. But my main interest is in planting new, diversified fruits and vegetables besides dates.

"I continued to work in Kuwait for ten years altogether. I married [his mother's sister's daughter] and brought my wife to Kuwait; several of our children were born there. Then I came back to Oman: first I worked in agricultural extension, and was stationed in Sib, but later I started here in the hospital. We live in the house in town only in the winter. We use the *barasti* house in the garden in the summer; it is much cooler. Now I am improving the garden house; we shall live here all year. [He then improved the town house, and started letting it to expatriate Jordanian and Sudanese schoolteachers.) Here in the garden, you are better than a king: you can do as you like, no one tells you what to do, and though you are king you have nothing to worry about, no bodyguards and no fear of poisoned food.... When my wife cooks, she goes first in the garden and takes what she needs: peppers, chilies, fruits, etc....We have free *barasti* for baking bread; in the town it would be much trouble to fetch, or cost one-half Rial to buy. We have wood for cooking from felling six date trees a year, in town we would have to buy."

Abdullah has six children ages two to fourteen, about whose upbringing he is very concerned. Though he fusses considerably and commands them much, he does not react to the fact that they do not obey him readily. Nor does he insist on respect, whereas he very strongly emphasizes the ideology of *teaching* them and instructing them in the right way to do things. Yet he muses:

"Now my children are small, they want to be with their parents always, and do as we do. But when they go to school and study, they will learn that they can eat separately, sleep separately; they will become modern. Each way is good for those who practice it: so motorcycles and air travel are right for the future. Young people now choose convenience and take little pleasure in what requires work. . . . My children will probably not want to live here. Nowadays everyone wants to be a clerk, have a motorbike and radio, not work in a garden."

Abdullah is secretary for cultural and educational activities in the club in Sohar.

"For National Day I made a play, called 'Old and New,' how a very sick boy is taken to a mullah. I played the mullah, with a big beard, who read in books, wrote a *tawiz* [Koranic amulet], and warned him to be careful of so many superstitious things. Then there was the contrast of taking the boy to a modern doctor. It was a very good and educational play."

Through most of our acquaintance, Abdullah vacillated about changing his job from the hospital to the new bank, or something else. Access to free medicines and distilled water at the hospital were important considerations that held him back. He also took temporary tasks, such as assisting an Indian consultant company in running a trial census.

"But I wish I had stayed in agricultural extension. They gave me good training, and put me in charge of Sib. By now I would have had a very good job."

MIKI

Miki is a dark-skinned, powerfully built, extroverted man about forty years old.

"I was born here in Sohar; my tribe is Maghrebi. My father was crippled in his hands and feet, very poor, needed money and assistance from his brother, who had gone to Dubai for pearl diving. He set out with me, eight years old, because I was his favorite child, to find his brother. We traveled to Dubai, but could not find my father's brother. Some bedouin of the Al Bumher tribe came, and said they knew where my father's brother was, and that they could take me to him, but not my father since he was weak. So he sent me with them. They took me back to Bureimi, and meanwhile instructed me not to say who I was or that I was looking for anyone—or else other bedouin might kidnap me. At night, when we came to Bureimi, they put me in a house where many people came and looked at me. I asked why all these people came. The bedouin said:

'They have not seen a boy from Sohar before. They want to greet you.'

"I waited and waited, then some people came and took me to another hamlet of Bureimi. They said:

"'Talk no more about looking for your father's brother. Now you are our slave and we have bought you, and you must do everything as we say and work for us or we shall kill you.'

"First they set me to herd the sheep and the camels in the desert. They gave me no food for four days at a time, between watering the camels; I had only the milk from the camel cows. I also was set to do all kinds of other work and they were very harsh with me. They had so many slaves, and did not work themselves. Many of the slaves, both boys and girls, were from Sohar. I worked very hard, did everything as they said, so they would not mistreat me. When I was thirteen, they sent me to the coast by Dubai to dive for pearls. Whatever I found, they took—they just gave me simple food, simple clothes. At night, I never slept deeply, always on guard; sometimes I would hear how they said to each other:

"'We must watch him so he does not try to escape. Kill him if he tries.'

"The people who owned me were a rich and powerful family in Bureimi, not Bedouin people but townspeople. As the years went by they trusted me more, and were very satisfied with me. Often people wanted to buy me. They would not sell. I saw a man offer 1500 Rupees for me. My owners said no.

"About this time the British established an army post in Sharjah. A friend of mine said I should get a job there, then I would get education for myself and that would be better. The people who owned me said OK, so I went to work there. I did not tell the British I was a slave. Every month the people who owned me took my whole salary.

[Why didn't you tell the British officer, and become free?]

"I trusted no one, did not think what I could do, was afraid those people would kill me if I made trouble.

"After eight years in the army, there was a war in Hawaza between two tribes, and the British army was sent to make peace. For the settlement two Walis had a meeting in the fort. We were there to watch the meeting. One of those Walis had a slave who had heard from my mother about me. When I did not come back, she had inquired and inquired about me, told everyone to look for me everywhere. She had told this slave about me, about my name, about how I had a birthmark on my forehead. That slave heard one of the soldiers call my name "Miki"; he looked and saw the birthmark on my forehead. So he had someone call me out of the room to speak to me. I was suspicious and asked one of my companions to cover me from inside, in case this was a trap. I went out, and the slave said,

"You are Miki and I have a message from your mother. She is inquiring about you and wants you to come home."

"I did not believe him, and said, 'What is my mother's name?' He said her name, and I said, 'Who are my brothers and sisters?' He said their names. So I knew he was telling the truth. I said I could not leave my post now. 'Let me write to her.' So I wrote her a letter.

"From that moment I had no peace. I thought of my mother day and night. For one month I waited for a reply from my letter. I put money aside so I could escape, but told no one. Finally I went to the captain, and said I must have ten days leave immediately. He said impossible. I said then I must resign my post, leave my uniform, and go. He said,

" 'Let me think about it till lunch.' After lunch he said, 'OK. You have ten days, plus five days for travel.'

"I got on an army transport to Sharika army post in Bureimi. There, I got off, went to the *suq*, and said,

" 'I want to go to the coast.' A man with a Bedford truck said, 'I am going just now. I shall take you for fifteen Rupees.'

"So I drove with him. He drove directly to the *suq* here in Sohar; but I did not know the place (I was only eight years old when I left). I got off and went into the restaurant. There I asked a man if he could show me the house of Abdallah and Fatima. He said he did not know them, but another man, who was listening, said

" 'I know them. They are my neighbors. Come with me.'

"So he took me home.

"When I came home, I met my brothers and sister only. My father had died after I was stolen, and my mother was away in Muscat. I waited two days for my mother, then she came. I went up to her to greet her. She started crying, clung to me, and would not let me go. Then she fainted, stopped breathing; she was unconscious for one full hour.

"After I disappeared, she had gone half mad, was very sick all the time until I came back. After one full hour, she woke up again, then we could sit down together and talk.

"I stayed ten days with her, then went back to Bureimi. I went to those people who had bought me from the Bedouins: they asked me where I had been. I told them that I had been and seen my mother and brothers, that I wanted to be free. I offered them what they had paid for me (250 Rupees). They said,

" 'No, you have paid us that back many times with the work you have done for us and the salary you have handed over to us. You are free now, and you are always welcome in our house and must visit us whenever you can.'

"So I continued my job in the army. I went to visit my mother and I worked with Major Hirst. When he left for England, I quit my job there. Eight years I worked in the army and gave those people my salary, two years I kept it for myself. Altogether it was eighteen years from when those bedouin stole me till I saw my mother again.

"She said to me:

'Make yourself a *barasti* here, get married.'

"So I did and settled here. My mother went to Muscat to distant relatives to arrange a marriage for my brother. They said,

" 'No, he is hunchbacked.' So she said:

'I have a strong son who was taken by the bedouin and held slave, but has now returned.'

"They said that was OK, they did not mind that. My wife did not want to move so far away, yet they gave her in marriage. But now she likes living here. She has had two boys, who died, and three daughters, one of them a twin with one of the boys. Now she has her little son Yusuf; she has been very afraid to lose him.

"I worked as a driver, in the Gulf area and in Oman. I worked eighteen months for the petroleum company, in Muscat, just before Qaboos became Sultan. After Qaboos, I built this house—borrowed money for the materials. Now, I have this truck with a partner—I borrowed 200 Rials to buy it, now I am trying to buy him out. I have succeeded in my life through force and strength. Often I dream about those years; they haunt me, and in the daytime I think about them."

Part 4

The Reproduction of Cultural Diversity

16

Cultural Dynamics
and Its Context

Both to forestall misinterpretation and to be capable of coherent analysis, it may now be necessary for me to clarify the concept of "culture" which I employ in this study. Indeed, no material is more challenging to the anthropologist's conceptualizations of culture than that from plural situations in complex civilizations, if his material covers any of the larger domains of life and captures everyday events in the contexts where they occur. As I see it, there are three major issues. How do we conceive of the boundaries of "a culture," its extent in time and place? What are the necessary relations of similarity and/or interdependence between individuals who share/partake in a common culture? And what do we suppose to be the structure of a culture; that is, how can we best conceive of its parts, and the kinds of interrelations which obtain between them? I do not think I can answer these ontological questions with sufficient accuracy and general validity, but I must confront them, since the suppositions that might be offered as answers in fact provide necessary premises for my epistemology and mode of analyses.

I shall address myself first to the last of the three questions formulated above. When I have referred to the various syndromes of connected cultural features as "cultural traditions" and "cultures" I have clearly had in mind an ideational concept of culture (see Keesing 1974). Each culture of which I am speaking is not a set of behaviors, or patterns of behavior, but a set of ideas *behind* such behavior which, together with other factors, shape the events of behavior and cause patterns. Those other factors I see mainly as physical factors (resources, environment), strategic factors (constraints and pressures on the actor which are interactionally predicated, but in turn may arise *inter alia* from the ideas entertained by others), and contextual factors (in the weak sense of referring to constraints on what can be practiced in the concrete context). But saying something is ideational clearly leaves open a wide range of senses, as Keesing (1974) proceeds to illustrate. I understand the "ideas" of a culture to be both thought and enacted. They are thought in the broad sense of being in part coldly

191

reasoned with and in part emotionally felt and succumbed to; that is, they are variously ordered by processes that may be logical or psychological. They are also ordered, related to each other, by being enacted: they are both spoken and used to interpret and to act on the world. Different current "schools" of anthropology seem to focus rather exclusively on one or another of these sources of order, and to treat that which they select as if it were the main wellspring of all pattern or structure in a culture. I would argue that we must admit the operation of all these sources of determination on a culture. The weakness inherent in a narrow focus on only one, or some, becomes particularly clear if we return to the broad ontological questions raised in the preceding paragraph.

By narrowing the focus, what might we be committing ourselves to in the way of assumptions about (1) how a culture is bounded in time and space, and (2) the degree of sharing and interdependence that obtains between individuals who partake in the culture? For example, the "shift to meaning" in the analysis of culture which in different variants is found in contemporary anthropology is highly attractive in that it captures many of the basic ideational aspects of speech and other behavior. But how much meaning must be conveyed between them for us to be able to regard two persons as participating in the same culture? Or, obversely, how little shared meaning should there be for us to be justified in saying that two persons participate in different cultures? Most behavior (other than speech acts) is never entirely "meaningless," even to an observer from what we would be used to regarding as an entirely different culture. How full of meaning must the acts of another be; and must the meanings be identical with those entertained by the other, or need they be only compatible; or can they indeed be contradictory and still justify the view that the two persons "share a culture"? Concretely, in Sohar men and women have similar ideas about many standards and rules that apply to the behavior of, say, women; but there are distinct differences. And if one looks into the premises or basic ideas of personhood, identity, and responsibility, one finds quite marked and consistent differences (see chapters 9 and 20). It is the kinds of ideas shared between women, contrasted to those embraced by men, which I see as the main justification for distinguishing a man's and a woman's culture—although the behavior and expression of the one gender are quite meaningful to, and indeed not particularly misunderstood by, the other gender. It is the same between townspeople and bedouin, only here the differences on the level of overt rules and proprieties are great and many, whereas the basic ideals and conceptions are more similar. The differences are full of meaning on both sides, but differently evaluated. We should be careful not to collapse the mere capacity to recognize a significance in a

symbolic act and embracing a particular value position regarding the
act both under our omnibus concept of meaning, since the two can be
very unequally distributed. In a situation of pluralism, most particularly, we must surely be prepared to find persons with great facility
and experience in interpreting the symbolic significance of acts in
others which they would categorically repudiate as possible acts for
themselves.

Soharis have a range of concepts and named identities whereby they
order and anticipate the distribution of these ideas (*in casu* man,
woman, and the ambiguous *xanith*; townsman, bedouin, etc.). Persons
with these named identities largely embrace the ideas, enact them, and
(selectively) enroll others to share in them by recruiting some of those
others to join their own social category and identity and by instilling
their own ideas in them.

Thus, in the sense that I use the term *culture* here, to participate in a
culture is to embrace (most of) its distinctive evaluations, not just to be
able to "read" the meaning of behavior as an "enacted document"
(Geertz 1973:10), and thus to be able to interpret/understand the acts
of another. Each of the cultural traditions I have identified is constituted as a special set of ideas* regarding significances and values
which is shared, embraced, and transmitted by persons with a common
social identity. To my mind, this view of what is a culture also directs
attention in the most fruitful direction: toward what brings about the
production and reproduction of a culture, namely, that it is part of the
person, not just what others think; it is valued, believed in, and
embraced by some persons, and therefore enacted, not just com-
prehended.

My aim in the following part of the monograph is to analyze the
processes that bring about continuity and change in the component
cultural traditions in Sohar—that is, the processes of cultural repro-

---

*The concept of "ideas," on the other hand, of which cultures are composed, is
rather an omnibus concept in this usage. It can refer to a wide range of levels:
from deep, underlying, and only diffusely articulated premises about personhood, existence, goodness, and evil to particular skills, attitudes, or styles of
behavior that are practiced with pride or resignation. To attempt to isolate a
more coherent level of basic components of culture so as to build a model
similar to those whereby linguists seek to generate sentences in a language
from a basic set of rules is to my mind to do violence to the facts that we can
observe: that consciousness of significance and value attaches to very discrepant levels of generality and specificity. I would suggest that this is probably so
because culture indeed lacks the coherence of speech, because it not only is a
communicative vehicle but also serves to order activities, and so is influenced
by a diversity of pragmatics (cf. Barth 1981. 81 f.)

duction. With the view of culture that I have adopted, it becomes important to be alert to changes over time in the *other* factors that shape behavior, which constitute, one might say, parameters for any particular expression of culture in behavior. My point is, that people with the same ideas—the same culture—living under the differing conditions of, say, 1950 and today, would in fact shape somewhat different lives for themselves and exhibit somewhat divergent behavior patterns, even if they did embrace the same ideas at these two different points of time. In our concrete discussion, we must be able to identify the changes that have taken place in these other factors, so as not mistakenly to construe the changes in behavior patterns caused by them to be direct reflections of changes in the meanings and values that constitute the cultural traditions.

But changes in external factors, and in the overt shape of life, enter into my analysis in an even more profound way: I see them over time as affecting the cultures themselves. The "ideas" that compose a culture do not exist, and are not transmitted, as abstract, discrete, and immutable units; they are affected by the experience of the people who hold them. The traditional anthropological definition of culture has taught us to emphasize its *learned* character. If we wish to develop a dynamic analysis of cultural reproduction, we must use a realistic model of how culture—that is, meanings, understandings, evaluations—is indeed learned. To avoid a too narrow prototype of what these processes are like (our thoughts are too readily directed through a concept of socialization to the instructing activities of parents and teachers), I would urge us to embrace a program of analyzing culture as an "experience-induced tradition." The meanings, understandings, and values that we hold have developed and assumed their nuances in experienced contexts. The "meaning" of the *burqa* (facemask) and the content of the idea of female modesty (*yistihi*: "she feels embarrassment"; see Wikan [1982], chapter 4), when the *burqa* has been used for some years as a device to control and manipulate withdrawal/exposure in the total range of a woman's social relationships, take on a cloud of associations and evocations which *is* the *burqa's* meaning to the woman. It seems to me impossible to imagine that any person could be taught to recognize *and embrace* these ideas, in the same form, by any other means than by using the *burqa*. (For a brief discussion of men's and women's overt understandings of the *burqa*, p. 237.) This implies that the ideas that compose a culture must develop in each separate person as a precipitate of continuing experience through life. When such ideas are shared, it must reflect a parallelism or identity of experiences between persons—not least in the form of conversations and interactions about these experiences, through which they are worked over symbolically and further interpreted. The relationship between external events and the ideas held by a person must clearly be dialectical: reality is grasped or experienced only by means of the ideas that a culture provides, that is, it is socially and culturally constructed. But ideas cannot arbitrarily and imperiously shape the course of events, so "experience" will be affected by other factors as well as by the ideas that propelled persons to act. And the precipitate of these events, in the form of such produced and constructed experiences, affects and in due course constitutes the equipment with which new events—and also new ideas—are interpreted.

Such a view of processes allows a marginalist analysis of cultural dynamics and change: How will small—marginal—changes in events and behavior patterns affect the ideas that compose a shared cultural tradition, *through* the experiences that they induce in some or many of the participants in that culture—and the future processes of inter-action, interpretation, value judgment, and sanction which are thereby set in motion.*

This view does not deny—on the contrary, it should serve to uncover—such structures as obtain in a culture. Quite obviously, for example, some pairs of ideas are interconnected in binary fashion, and more complex structures of logical interrelation of many ideas are also found. There is no assumption that all variation in form will prove to be continuous (Barth 1981: 65); identification of discontinuous, and linked, variations serves as the best—perhaps the only method-ologically compelling—demonstration of the presence of structural interconnection.

Finally, one other aspect of this perspective should be placed in focus. It entails that it is the experiences of yesterday which determine the content of a culture today. Thus, where accumulated experiences differ qualitatively from the experiences that can be reaped today, there is a source of cultural change. Novel events will, of course, be interpreted in terms of the concepts and meanings available to people from the culture that they command, but they will not thereby repro-duce in identical form the experiences reaped in earlier contexts from different events. And so, ideas will be affected. This is not to say that new understandings will arise as objectively valid and accurate re-flections of the import of new events. We know that people react variously with rejection, rationalization, comprehensive dis-illusionment, etc., under different circumstances, reflecting differing

---

*Such a marginalist perspective does not address the problem of how a supposedly *tabula rasa* infant is enrolled into a cultural tradition; it asks how an ongoing shared cultural tradition persists and changes. But it can, I believe, be accommodated to several alternative theories of child development, par-ticularly those that do not axiomatically stipulate *tabula rasa*.

degrees of embracement and valuation, and different linkages, of different ideas. But it seems a logical entailment of the basic position I have adopted that novel events (unless they do not even impinge on the senses of the members of a culture) will have some kind of effect on some component of that culture. Thus, to acknowledge that people place a social and cultural construction on reality provides no basis for arguing that they will be impervious to the changing state of the world. Nor, on the other hand, does it entail the bowdlerized thesis that the "statistical norms of one era become the jural rules of the next," as formulated and rejected by Kelly (1977:280). Whatever connections may exist cannot be short-circuited in such fasion, but can only be mapped and understood in terms of a model of the complex processes that are involved, especially those entailed in individuated experience and social interaction and interpretation.

The viewpoints presented so far are crude and rather self-evident insights familiar from life experience in a rapidly changing world. The difficulty is to transform them into a coherent methodological and analytical position for the description and study of the dynamics of unfamiliar cultures and life situations. Some steps in that direction are best made in conjunction with a substantive discussion of changing parameters, and changing features of the cultural traditions, in Sohar over the last generation or two. The first will be provided in the next chapter; the latter will be presented in chapters 18–20.

17 The Changing Historical Circumstances

The most important changing parameters of life in Sohar in the present century comprise technology and economy, education, security, and cultural orientation. Each of these factors has changed in a way to transform major preconditions for life and activity.

Changes in means of transport have gravely reduced the town's very basis for existence. With the introduction of steam in shipping, Sohar lost its advantages in terms of geographical location, and became a backwater. This aggravated an economic decline already brought about by external political factors: the reduction and final elimination of slave trade due to British intervention through the nineteenth century, the separation of Zanzibar as a country independent of Oman in 1856, and the elimination of the arms trade (via Oman, particularly Sohar, from Europe to Baluchistan and Afghanistan) due to British pressure in 1912. But shipping of some local and regional importance continued; a large and imposing new custom house was built in Sohar around 1930 (of local materials: ancient, used and reused baked bricks, and mortar of lime burned from seashells), which is now decaying; and customs records show up to thirty ships a day calling on Sohar as late as 1960. Recently, however, the development of roads for land transport has spelled the definitive end to Sohar as a port. Whereas the main track along the Batineh coast was reported to be nearly impassable in 1958, even for Land Rovers (Philips 1971:39), rapid improvements have been made, particularly since 1970, so today nearly all transport is overland by truck, from either Muscat/Mattrah harbor or Dubai. This change has in large part been implemented by Soharis themselves, who have engaged in small transport enterprises, as exemplified by Miki (chapter 15). In these cases, it does not seem to be capital from the declining shipping sector which was transferred directly into motor transport, but rather savings accumulated by Sohari townsmen from a variety of other activities that were invested in land transport equipment and activity.

The development of motorized land transport has eclipsed the previously flourishing camel transport activity. Till the middle 1960s

Modern storage buildings and disappearing forms of transport.

the bedouin surrounding Sohar provided essential services with, and derived a considerable income from, their camel flocks by engaging in transport. Standard contracts allowed either the simple hire of a certain number of camels or a contract of delivery where the bedouin also provided camelteers and security, for double the price. Because of the decline in demand for camel transport, very few camels are now owned by the settled bedouin around Sohar; and former camel owners have not been particularly active in developing motor traffic. These technological and economic changes have thus been important in differentially affecting the circumstances of different component groups and traditions in Sohar.

A second major field of technical change is in the means of irrigation, where mechanical pumps have replaced the labor-intensive lift systems. Philips described the traditional system in 1958 briefly: "A rope, one end of which is attached to a large leather bucket [*dalu*] and the other to either a bullock or other animal, passes over a wooden pulley wheel held high above the well by a derrick of three or four straight tree limbs. As the beast walks away from the well, usually down a steeply inclined plane to make his job easier, the bucket comes up; as the beast returns, the bucket goes down, while all the time the wooden pulley wheel, called a *manjur*, sends an eerie creaking wail through the quiet groves. This laboring groan is a sound one can never forget, and conjures up al-Batinah in the mind's eye more readily than any other sound or scent" (Philips 1971:41–42). In 1974 we were able to locate only one such device in the environs of Sohar, while all other cultivation was dependent on diesel pumps. This change has been brought about entirely through local, individual initiative, largely antedating any form of agricultural extension service, and without any credit facilities.

One might have expected the resultant significant reduction of labor demands in cultivation to depress the local level of unskilled wages. In fact, the change has been the opposite (see the development of daily wages, chapter 14), due to another and overshadowing exogenous factor. From about 1950, opportunities for migrant labor started burgeoning in the oil production areas of the Gulf. This employment opportunity no doubt affected the local labor market; it also entailed that most young Soharis could succeed in saving up some capital and return to Sohar with prospects of some kind of self-employment rather than offering themselves on the day labor market. It also led to the sending home of remittances. Beginning in August 1967, Oman's own oil revenues started, and the local boom in practically all activities gave further impetus to this trend. The result has been a staggering increase in welfare and prosperity. Soharis see it as if all the legitimate material needs of everyone are being satisfied; new consumer goods are constantly appearing and new forms of consumption are developing. In other words, the observations on which this whole description is based were made at a moment of unprecedented material improvement and plenty; and it is difficult to judge how this affects the quality of social relationships and the general tenor of values and attitudes. Soharis themselves, however, do not express the view that prosperity has changed them or their society qualitatively (yet), and seem to respond to these circumstances in a way suggesting that they regard them as rather external and not terribly important, though highly welcome.

A second field of major change is education. The traditional pattern was one where Koran schools taught limited literacy to preteenage children; any further education depended on the initiative of the individual (male) and had to be obtained elsewhere. From what I can ascertain, Sultan Sa'id pursued a consistent policy of preventing the development of any form of modern, Western education. There were three elementary schools in Oman in 1969, and a total school population of 900 pupils ("Oman," p. 54), none of them in Sohar. The Sultan further discouraged foreign education by refusing reentry into Oman to persons who had obtained secondary school training. As a consequence, formal education could not serve as a criterion for any appointment to any position or profession for Omanis, though it did so for expatriates: particularly in the medical service, a number of Pakistani and Indian doctors, and Indian nurses, were recruited. With the accession of Sultan Qaboos, this policy was fundamentally changed. An ambitious program of school building and recruiting of teachers (especially from Egypt and Jordan) was launched. Omanis with education, living abroad, were encouraged to return home, and Zanzibaris of Omani descent were recruited (very few of these to Sohar, however). By 1975 there was a school population of 49,229 pupils (Statistical Year Book). The ideals of education seem to be wholeheartedly and completely embraced by Soharis, so there is a massive opinion encouraging everyone to make use of the new facilities, and universal acceptance of the values and ideals entailed. Thus, husbands press their wives to attend adult literacy classes, and parents are highly committed to their children's schooling and concerned about their performance. The Imam of the main Sunni mosque summarized the position: "Oman used to be closed and dark; now it is light. Education is provided to everyone. Foreigners can come, and companies make activity and prosperity. Oman needs imports, and can obtain them only by developing."

The immediate result has been that young boys now remain home, living as "children" and attending school, rather than departing on labor migration and "becoming adult" through the pursuit of adventure, training, and income of their own. Another more insidious effect is an indirect attack on Omani self-pride and the identification of children with their own traditions. This comes about through the communication of quite negative attitudes toward everything local and traditional, and thus Omani, by expatriate schoolteachers of rather limited perspective. Sohari schoolchildren are particularly vulnerable to such influences: they are attuned to the tactful and tolerant stance of their own culture, and must interpret the criticism as serious and authoritative. The authority of schoolteachers is further strengthened by the stress among parents on the extraordinary value of modern education, and the importance of assimilating its messages and catching up with the world. The fact that many experienced adults may regard these teachers as both crude and ridiculous figures has little effect when such judgments are not clearly communicated to the child. The first overt effects of this situation can be seen in changes in dress and adornment, where girls in school were instructed as to what is pretty and what is old-fashioned and were eager to comply—leading also by 1975 to some slight experimentation along the same lines among young women. Long-term effects, whether leading to change or increasing resistance, are difficult to predict. (Certain apects of this question will be taken up in chapter 20.)

A third field of change in the preconditions of life, leading to changes in patterns of social mobilization and the exercise of authority, arises from the changing circumstances of security. The last thirty years have seen a deep transformation in this respect. Until 1954 and for most key areas even until 1958–59, the interior of Oman was autonomous, and the Imam who served as figurehead of the constellation of tribes and leaders there went so far toward international recognition of independence as to apply for membership in the Arab League. A formal peace treaty in 1920 between Sultan Taimur and a council of leaders from the interior formally confirmed the autonomy of the interior tribes and towns, stating that the people of the interior "shall be at peace with the Sultan, and shall not attack the coastal towns, where they shall have full right of movement and security. People from the coast may enter (inner) Oman on lawful business and for commercial purposes. The government of the Sultan shall not interfere in tribal affairs. Claims against 'the people of Oman' by merchants and others were to be decided according to the law of Islam" ("Oman," p. 41).

But the territorial limits of the Sultan's writ were not specified clearly and generally seem to have extended only some ten miles inland from Sohar, and the terms of the agreement do not seem to have been very carefully observed by either side. The townspeople of Sohar apparently saw themselves, with considerable justification, as an isolated island of "civilization" surrounded by a wilderness of anarchy, left in the daily defense of their life style and existence, largely to their own devices. This was reflected in their vulnerability to bedouin attack, but also in the institutions for internal security.

There used to be feuds between families: they killed one of you, you killed one of them. Because the government was weak, they could act this way. If a tribe could muster 2,000 men and the government had only 200 soldiers, how could the government settle everything? But now, the government has cannons, tanks, airplanes. Tribes mean nothing, and no one will pursue feuds. These feuds used to take place inside Sohar town too. Here are so many different tribes, there could be so much trouble. But now, because of the power of the government, tribes mean nothing.

In that situation of some decades ago, Soharis also see the perpetuation of any form of sultanate as the major, and problematic, purpose of the central government: "The old Sultan was so strong. With only rifles and an old-fashioned army, he ruled this country and made everybody afraid of him, whereas Qaboos has all this new military equipment that puts overwhelming force behind him. The old Sultan Sa'id must have been a very intelligent man to manage—even the British did as he said." This indicates the outlines of a set of balances which must have sustained Sa'id and his predecessors: whereas the main power of the country was organized in large Arab tribal descent groups, these were divided both by the cultural difference between bedouin and townsmen and by the rivalry between the Hinawi and Ghafari factions. Against this divided force, the Sultan could pit his own army, disproportionately manned by Baluch mercenaries. On the regional level, on the other hand, an arrangement had to be found whereby the Sultan's central authority could devolve upon or be delegated to his local deputies without dissipating the power in the center or creating local challenges to it. Thus, it was essential that the Wali of Sohar serve as the Sultan's deputy without thereby fragmenting the centralized unity of the state. For this purpose, slave collateral lines of the dynasty—like the Walis Salem and Mudhaffar mentioned above—were particularly suitable, since they were both very closely identified with the Sultan and could not turn against him as rival pretenders. The force with which they could confront the tribally and ethnically divided citizens was in turn made up of mercenary outsiders: the Beni Omar mountaineers, who neither could be used to strike upward against the Sultan's Baluch army nor had locally divided loyalties vis-à-vis the resident Baluchis. Thus, besides the positive need of individual Sohari residents at this time to secure their interests through clear membership in a larger collectivity, there are also structural indications that the perpetuation of centralized authority depended directly on a balancing of such sectional and communal divisions, and so might actively serve to reinforce them.

The present regime, on the contrary, stands for a determined and explicit ideology of unity, and devolution of every kind of sectional or communal common interest group. The position was declared in the change of the nation's name with the accession of Sultan Qaboos, from "Muscat and Oman" to "Oman." Soharis are very aware of this, and seem to embrace the program with conviction: they emphasize to each other, as well as to the anthropologist, that the important distinction is between Omani and non-Omani, not language or culture group; that all schools of Islam are the same; that "he, the Sultan, has said that all are equal, that there are no slaves, no lords, only Omanis, and that he is a brother of all." Nor did the South Yemeni-supported rebellion in Dhofar seem to concern or interest Soharis in any way: it was interpreted in the perspective of all previous unrest in the interior, only much farther away. Any kind of revolutionary orientation appears to have been absent even as a covert undercurrent in Sohar in 1974 and 1975.

This emphasis on a new identity as Omani nationals is compatible with what may be regarded as a shift in a fourth and final parameter of Sohar's constitution: the major cultural orientation. Today, there seems to be a concurrence among Soharis, the Omani authorities, and the outside world to regard Oman unequivocally as belonging in the Arab, Islamic, and oil-rich Near East. It takes a major mental effort to recreate the cultural, political, and economic landscape that obtained before 1914 and that seems to have determined Omani orientations well into the 1950s: Arabic-speaking peoples were politically impotent and, indeed, apart from the questionable case of Egypt, ruled themselves nowhere except in Oman; Turkey and India were the great centers of Islam; and the Arabian homeland was emphatically poor in material resources. Looking out from Sohar, across the Indian Ocean, the great city of Bombay had a glittering allure that could be matched only by that of New York in certain parts and periods of European fantasy. The scene was dominated by the imperial British presence; and apart from Indian harbors, Basrah, Bandar Abbas, and Zanzibar were the enticing ports of call.

The orientation of the Sultans in Muscat in this situation is readily documented. To start in the middle of the nineteenth century, Sultan Sa'id bin Sultan had his sons variously by an Abyssinian wife, a Malabar concubine, and a Georgian wife (Miles 1919:346). Sultan Feisal bin Turki (1888–1913) is scorned by the main historian of the epoch (Kelly, in Hopwood 1972:118) for preferring the Gujerati language to Arabic. Sultan Taimur bin Feisal (1913–1932), on his abdication in 1932, moved to Bombay, where he resided under the name of Mr. T.F.T. al-Said (Philips 1971:17). Before this, he had sent his son and successor, Sa'id, to five years' schooling at Mayo College at Ajmer, in Rajputana, India, followed by a year in Baghdad (then a British mandate territory) for studies in Arabic literature and history (ibid pp. 17–18).

Sohari consciousness in 1910 or 1930 is far more difficult to judge or document, but I hear echoes of the same orientation in the travel goals and reminiscences of the days before oil development in the Gulf. Quite clearly, with Ottoman Turkey as the model of an Islamic state and British India as the epitome of wealth and civilization, the conditions of cultural diversity and persistence of plural traditions would be conceptually very different from those that obtain in the present frame of Arab nationalism. If so, one may expect this, together with the other changing parameters, to be reflected in changing forms of cultural expression and coexistence.

18

The Dynamics of Ethnic Groups and Congregations

The reproduction of cultural diversity in Sohar depends both on the replenishment of the distinctive groups and categories in terms of membership and on the transmission or adoption of distinct cultural features by those members. The processes involved and the ensuing patterns of contemporary persistence and change differ considerably between the differently constituted cultural traditions. I may usefully begin my review of this with a discussion of the component ethnic groups of Sohar. The minority groups are perhaps most easy to conceptualize in these terms, since their persistence is more obviously precarious.

Baluch in Sohari awareness conforms very closely to what one would associate in English usuage with an ethnic label. The Baluchis are seen as having their own separate language and their own characteristic cultural traditions. Yet it makes sense to Soharis to speak of Baluchis who no longer practice their distinctive customs, and Baluchis who no longer know the Baluchi language. To be called Baluch for any other reason than that one is born of Baluchi parents is not part of Sohari thinking—though the possibility is clearly implied in the statement that at the time of the spread of Islam, some Arab families were sent by the Prophet to Baluchistan to "become Baluch" and teach the true religion by example (see pp. 45f.). On occasion, this account is also used to validate a claim that some Baluch tribes are of truly good (meaning Arab) blood. In cases of mixed marriages in Sohar, it is recognized that the issue of the marriage will be part Baluch and part Arab, regardless of whether the Baluch parent is the mother or the father. But the question of whether the essential cause is physical inheritance or cultural influence in the home is not conceptually resolved: "blood" and behavior are connected in that the former to large extent predicates the latter, but it does so in terms of a broad conception of parental influence rather than a narrow conception of genetic determination.

It should be emphasized that "Baluch" in Sohar is purely a social category, not a corporate group for any purpose. There is no unified organization beyond the level of the vilage shaikhs found in most of

A Baluchi senior man, third-generation Sohari.

those village communities where Baluchis predominate. Thus, there exists a situation where a Baluchi cultural tradition is identified, but practiced more fully or in reduced versions by different persons and neighborhoods; where the Baluchi language is spoken (with varying competence) by a number of persons some of whom are by common agreement *not* themselves Baluch while some who are Baluch do not speak the language; and where the widest sense of the term *Baluch* comprises a category of men, women, and children whose ancestors hailed from Baluchistan and who supposedly can always be distinguished by their "face" (see p. 37)—again in the mixed sense of physical features and demeanor reflecting their parentage. These diffuse and multivalent boundary phenomena clearly reflect empirical processes of change that have been and are taking place within Sohar. An understanding of the dynamics of reproduction of a Baluchi cultural traditions in Sohar requires that I identify and understand these processes.

To do so successfully, I argue that we cannot proceed directly with analytical and exteriorist questions regarding "patterns" of "recruitment" and "transmission." I must ask how Baluchi identity is embraced and practiced in Sohar. In other words, I need to look at how different persons integrate a Baluch identity into their life and career (what it gives them and what it costs them), and I need to look at how Baluch identity is practiced in the community (where it is in focus as part of the definition of situation in interaction, and where it is only indirectly or covertly relevant). Only then can I demonstrate how new persons may be enrolled in the identity, and what it is that they thereby will be enrolled into.

I shall first focus on the overt cultural expressions of Baluch identity (see chapter 4). It is striking that, apart from language, the distinguishing items cluster in the female domain: women's dress, marriage customs, women's domestic skills. For a boy or man to embrace his Baluch identity, all he has to do overtly is to speak Baluchi in situations where other Baluchi speakers do so, and (questionably) marry a Baluch girl. A woman's whole presentation of self, on the other hand, is constantly colored by a Baluch identity: her face mask and particularly her dress stand out as strikingly distinctive; her domestic activities recurrently assert her identity. If one looks more subjectively on the level of meaning (how the actors themselves seem to interpret and evaluate their acts and identities), the contrast between the sexes may be less sharp but still significant. Men would proudly announce to me their Baluch identity, give accounts of their ancestry and place of origin if known, and enumerate distinctive Baluchi customs. But these matters were never presented as relevant to any particular relationships between men, nor were they compared, even implicitly, to customs practiced by other ethnic groups (with the exception noted below). The attitudes held by women were indicated on the very first occasion when the topic was brought up in a circle of six or eight women to which my wife was in the process of gaining entrance. In response to my wife's question of what precisely *is* the difference between Baluch and Arab dress, the one Baluch woman in the circle got up, swept out her arms to show off her dress to the best effect, and walked a few steps to model the outfit. The Arab women in the circle seemed ambivalent, clearly feeling that the dress was more outré but perhaps also more beautiful than their own. The differences in the cut of the face mask were also judged and discussed. A recurring feature of the Baluch woman's information on Baluchi custom was her emphasis on the greater recognition and respect for women which they implied (notably, direct gift of gold from the groom to the bride, rather than—as Arab custom has it—the groom's giving a gift of money to the bride's father, who purchases gold at his own discretion for the daughter; sexual abstinence during latter months of pregnancy and for forty days after birth, etc.). The one exception to the male abstention from invidious comparison of customs likewise concerned the relations between the sexes: a Baluch friend of mine in a private conversation pointed out the implication of the absence of public proof of virginity at marriage among Baluchis: "We think that is a private matter for the two persons concerned." In view of the central importance of the expression of mutual respect between spouses for the quality of the marital relationship in Sohar (see Wikan 1977:316, 1982:290), it is reasonable to regard these customs and attitudes as very significant, particularly for the woman.

Uniquely among the major ethnic identities embraced in Sohar (that is, apart from the Zidgali remnants), Baluch is the only one that does not entail membership in a separate Great Tradition or civilization. While Arab, Iranian, and Indian can confront each other conceptually as complete alternative schemes of existence, replete with institutions and traditions beyond the ken of a common man, Baluch is an identity implying only such behavior as common men practice. There is no state, no government, no religion, and no historical/literary/cultural heritage elsewhere to which one is connected, only a geographical original homeland; and there is no potential conflict that must be resolved in being Baluch and being a member of the town of Sohar and the state of Oman.

The place of Baluchi culture in Sohar thus seems so far assured and stable: it is embraced with positive commitment by both men and women and is seen by women as particularly valuable and advantageous to their self-realization while at the same time, as a domestically centered tradition, particularly dependent on them for its transmission. It was only the progressive accumulation of data on variation in time and space that led me to modify this initial assessment. The kinds of information that gradually emerged may be exemplified by some items:

a. In the large village of Magis, north of Sohar, there is a considerable community of Baluchis who no longer speak Baluchi among themselves.

b. The Baluchis in the northern ward of Sallan village have increasingly and now largely adopted Arab dress, while those in South Sallan with whom we had most contact practice the full range of Baluchi dress and custom.

c. In a census of Sobara we were informed that one of the prominent men there was Baluchi. "No," said my wife's friend Latifa with a shocked expression when she heard this. "He is our mother's brother; he is Arab." But Latifa's paternal uncle Hamid explained that, by origin, he is indeed Baluch, but "now they speak Arabic, are married to Arabs—so now they are Arabs." Indeed, Latifa's own family, it later emerged from the same source, are also descended from Baluchis, but they long ago stopped speaking Baluchi or practicing Baluchi customs, so now they have become completely Arab.

d.   While Abdullah (chapter 15) conceives of himself as "pure Arab," his paternal grandfather turned up in the accounts of (the Baluch) Shaikh Feisal of South Sallan (chapter 15) as having been shaikh of North Sallan at the time of Shaikh Feisal's father. "He did not speak Baluchi, but was originally of Baluch descent." This view seemed new to Abdullah when I reported it to him, and he dismissed it as incorrect. But after some discussion, he ended up closing the whole exchange with exasperation: "Yes, *long ago* perhaps they came from Baluchistan. From where else would the people of this coast have come—out of the empty desert?"

There should be sufficient indications of the existence of a historical trend, among at least some Baluch families and communities, of progressive erosion of cultural distinctness and ultimate assimilation into Arab identity. What may be the set of processes involved, and what are the resulting conditions of persistence of a Baluchi cultural tradition?

We may identify three factors of vitalization or reinforcement of Baluchi culture in the recent past which no longer obtain. First, there was a flow of immigrants from Baluchistan. I met persons among Sohari Baluch who were themselves born in Baluchistan; and until Gwadar was sold in 1958 there would indeed have been no way for Omani authorities to prevent such entry. Thus, the Baluch category was constantly being replenished by new, culturally unadulterated members. Second, under the former conditions of insecurity there was a strong awareness of the importance of deep and primary group loyalties in improving the chances of survival. Other ethnic groups also emphasize their corporate role in defense at that time; and the villagers in Sallan cite their identity as Baluch as the crucial identity being mobilized when they stood up against marauding bedouin behind the sandbags in the Sallan mosque (see p. 175). In the pragmatic context of self-defense, persons could thus experience their identity as "Baluch" being contrasted not to other ethnic groups but to bedouin tribes, and constituting their main asset for survival. Third, with India (and secondarily imperial Iran, Ottoman Turkey, and colonial East Africa) as the major destinations for labor migration, young Baluch men would experience ethnically composite societies as the universal pattern, and thereby have a sectorial Baluch identity reinforced. Some older people—of both sexes—have paid visits to Baluchistan and to kinsmen there. With the present preponderance of Arab states as destinations for labor migrations, and the strong emphasis on Arab nationhood and the differentiation of Arab and non-Arab labor migrants, many young men may now be tempted to cover their Baluch identity behind their Omani passports, and certainly will not have Baluch identity reinforced by the experience of labor migration.

Even under the reinforcing conditions that formerly obtained, Baluchi traditions seem to have been liable to erosion over time, though no doubt less so than now, or else the cases of assimilation reported above (such as Sobara, or for Abdullah's family line) would probably not have taken place. What might be the major forces effecting this trend? Soharis themselves see them as intermarriage and intermingling. By both Arab and Baluch it is Baluchi culture that is regarded as representing the deviant, specialized competence. Thus, when an Arab man marries a Baluch woman, the *killeh* (marriage tent) is set up in *his* compound, as he cannot be expected to compromise on his Arab and male customary rights. The woman in such marriages almost invariably comes to assume Arab dress and the children, though recognized as being of mixed descent, take the paternal side as their categorical identity. If a Baluchi man marries an Arab woman, on the other hand, he cannot expect his Arab in-laws to assume the Baluchi custom of setting up the *killeh* with them, so again, Arab custom prevails. The spouses will speak Arabic in the home, the woman will retain Arabic dress, and she is not expected to learn and adopt the distinctive skills and activities of a Baluch woman. Thus, the explanation offered by informants for the more prevalent adoption of Arab dress and custom in North Sallan than in South Sallan is in terms of a greater admixture with Arabs through intermarriage in the northern ward. It is likewise in the case of language: Baluchi is preferred between Baluchi speakers, but the presence of an Arab redefines the situation as one where—out of elementary politeness—Arabic should be spoken. Members of small Baluchi neighborhoods explained the disuse of Baluchi in these terms: "The neighborhood is so small, there is almost always an Arab among us when we meet, so we speak Arabic between ourselves, and Baluchi only inside the home."

A prerequisite for withstanding acculturation to Arabic language and custom thus seems to be the maintenance of a minimal level of separation of Baluchis from non-Baluchis—either spatially or at least in regard to some essential social situations. It is striking that although Baluch identity is embrace with assurance and pride by the individual, no individual efforts seem to be made to secure these conditions for its maintenance. There is no categorical view, and no recognizable practice, of endogamy within the ethnic category, and the factors that encourage men to seek "strangers"—which would generally imply Arabs—as marriage partners are as operative among Baluch as among

Arab youths. My wife's closest Baluchi friend may serve as an example: proud as she is of her Baluchi dress, custom, and identity, she yet chooses to associate with a circle of women from the closest surrounding houses—all Arab—rather than go 15–20 yards farther to join the immediately adjoining Baluchi cluster (see figure 2) or walk less than 100 yards to join her closest kinswomen.

The other major force at work reducing the practice of distinctively Baluchi culture and custom is the force of change. While many of the cultural items that at present constitute the Baluchi tradition no doubt have some antiquity, there are no grounds for assuming them all to be ancient or to regard their objective antiquity as a particularly significant aspect as far as contemporary practitioners are concerned. We may expect Baluch culture to be quite as dynamic through time as the other cultural traditions in Sohar; the significant question in regard to cultural pluralism is whether the balance of changes increases or decreases the distinctness of Baluch from other contrasted ethnic traditions in the locality. Rather than address the very difficult theoretical and methodological issue of how one might seek to quantify such a measure, I shall look concretely at the processes apparently at work at the moment. Those that stand out most clearly are changing fashions, and all the phenomena bracketed under the omnibus term *modernization*. Male Sohari dress is uniform in that variations in clothing do not express ethnic identity—without any implication that Baluch men are wearing "Arab dress." Current government emphasis is against the adoption of Western dress and for the use, among government employees, of an "Omani" dress very close to that prevalent in Sohar. But there is also a new style encroaching on Sohar from the Gulf, carried by labor migrants who work there and return wearing the looser, flowing robe and headdress of that area—a distinctively Arab style. Under the influence of this style, there is no evidence of a symbolic Baluchi retrenchment around any distinctive Baluchi style or elements, but rather an apparent readiness to participate in the "Arabization." Among women, fashions these days likewise seem to emanate from the Gulf, notably Abu Dhabi. Fashions in gold jewelry change year by year and Baluch women participate in this, though a few of their distinguishing traits are retained (nose ring, and a necklace incorporating a British Indian gold sovereign). *Burqa* (face masks) are becoming ever narrower and more diminutive—a trend in which Baluchi women participate, though somewhat more reluctantly than Arab women, and with retention of the slightly more heart-shaped cut of main cloth. The trend in the gown is most interesting: Arab women, used to a certain marking of the waistline, are moving toward a closer-fitted bodice and waist like that found in most Western dresses, whereas Baluchis with their extremely wide and square cut, have no way of modifying their dress in this fashionable direction. But the outcome of this seems to be that Baluchi women become stranded as "old-fashioned" rather than assertively "Baluch." In no current response to fashion is there any evidence of either the intent or the effect of dichotomization, that is, changing in such a way as to signal difference more clearly and emphatically. I judge the opposite character of some Arab and Baluchi marriage customs (noted in chapter 4) to be the result of processes encouraging the development of such dichotomizing symbols or emblems in former times. Today they cannot be observed to operate.

The same is true in the broad field of "modernization." Baluch and Arab are subject to the same influences, from the same external sources, and do not seem to adopt any items with a view to expressing their local differences. Thus, step by step, as autochthonous customs and practices are abandoned and new ones adopted, the substantive differences in content between the Baluch and Arab traditions are reduced. Here again, distinctly Baluchi traits become "old-fashioned" whereas cosmopolitan, new traits become by implication "Arabic."

Where do Soharis stand with respect to the deeper premises and conceptions that sustain a cultural tradition? Without a study in depth of the symbols and structures of Baluch and Arab cultures in Sohar, it is indeed difficult to say. My material offers no sound basis on which to identify the ideas, or cognitive and emotional structures, that lie behind distinctly Baluch behavior or preferences (for example, Baluch men's more positive orientation to physical activity, danger, and martial occupations, or Baluch women's stronger involvement and creativity in design, color, and other esthetic expression). When these cultural wellsprings have not been identified, any representation of the nature of change in them is obviously out of reach. But the *trend* seems undeniable, and its extrapolated result apparent to all Soharis: "In due course, all the people on this coast will change to Arabic and become Arabs." Such a conclusion would prejudge the question of what possible future relevance the ethnic labels may obtain as a basis for mobilizing interest groups within the society; but as far as the cultural distinctness of a Baluchi tradition in terms of its content goes, it seems a reasonable prediction.

The situation of the Ajam ethnic group in Sohar is rather different, in several respects, from that of the Baluchis. As a first step in analysis, it is important to be aware of variables located outside the Sohar context, so we do not fallaciously try to explain features that derive from them in terms of processes internal to Sohar. A valid interpretation of the label "Ajam" is "Iranian"; in other words, it embraces a large and culturally diverse category of people deriving from Iran or Persia. The immigrants who, over the centuries, have given rise to Sohar's Ajams do not actually represent this whole range, but yet show

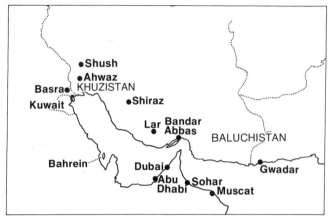

MAP 2. *Some towns and regions surrounding the Arabian Gulf.*

diversity. They were largely urban, or nontribal village people, and seem to have come overwhelmingly from the areas of Khuzistan, the Gulf coast eastward to Bandar Abbas, or the interior regions around Lar. It should be remembered, incidentally, that for periods during the eighteenth and nineteenth centuries, some of these areas were indeed administered by Oman under lease or mandate from the Shah (Kelly 1968:13, 1972:166). Khuzistan and the Gulf coast of Iran contain populations that are both Persian and Arabic in language, culture, and declared identity. Only the Persian-speaking immigrants from this coast to Sohar will have been regarded as "Ajam" subsequent to their immigration; but some of these were Sunni, while others were Shiah by religious persuasion. The population around Lar from which immigrants were drawn were all Shiah, but spoke a different dialect of Persian from the immigrants from Khuzistan—differences that still obtain between different subgroups of Sohari Ajam. (See map 2.)

The core of the Ajam community in Sohar seems to derive from Lar and to be based on immigration five to eight generations ago, although others have joined them later. Two other ambiguous groups on the margins of the Ajam category may be noted. One is known as Awadh-iyya. Undisputably Persian speaking and hailing from Iran, there is apparent doubt among most people in Sohar as to whether the Awadh-iyyas should properly be counted as Ajam, since they are not Shiah but Sunni. By their own account, they are a composite group based on locality of origin rather than common descent (see chapter 5): the grandfathers or great-grandfathers of the present senior generation migrated from the city of Ahwaz in Khuzistan to Bandar Abbas (and thus their name, Awadhiyya, meaning "Ahwazis"). From there the first Awadhiyya arrived in Sohar about 1920; others followed shortly after, and today they reportedly number eighty persons in Sohar. As Sunnis they are assimilated into the Arab and Baluch congregations in their neighborhood of residence; they have also intermarried with Arabs and many individuals have consequently discontinued the use of Persian language. They themselves are ambivalent about a status as "Ajam," since they do not want to be associated with a Shiah identity, and outsiders are divided as to how they should be classified.

The other case concerns the main population of the whole ward of Shizaw, an admittedly compound population that, according to some, is in the process of "becoming a tribe (qabila)." The Arab majority of the ward carries a diversity of lineage names, numerically prominent among them being the descent group of Al Farsi, meaning, literally, "Persian." While many claim that this and the name of the ward itself are "just names," reputedly knowledgeable persons give the following account. The name Shizawi derives from the name Shuza (or Shush in modern standard Persian), the classical city of Susa. From there the Al Farsi and others arrived about 150 years ago, much as the Awadhiyya arrived a century later. As Sunnis, they swiftly mixed with Arabs and took on Arab identity, so today they have become Arabs. A special historical complication arises in that there is also a small group of Ajam Shizawis. These, however, reflect a different story. About 80 years ago, a lineage of Shiah Ajams was involved in a killing and unable to defend itself or pay compensation. The Shizawi shaikh, as a purely political move, paid the compensation for them in return for their political support or clientage; they thus became part of the Shizawi political unit but were not incorporated on an equal basis as (descent) group members. They now live dispersed, and they are not a remnant or indication of true Shizawi origins.

With these complicated preliminaries in mind, I may now review the question of the reproduction and change of the Ajam cultural tradition. In contrast to the case of Baluchis, the constitution of a major portion of the Ajams as an essentially separate congregation is of critical importance. It provides the body of Ajams with a corporate organization in their congregational Shiah institutions, more hierarchical and coordinated than those of Sunnis. It entails the presence of potentially powerful means of internal collective sanctions by which discipline in the group can be maintained and common policy and practice imposed. It also entails that the main identity that distinguishes most Ajams from other Soharis, and unites them among themselves, is one that is ideologically antagonistical to that of the Sunni-Ibazhi plurality. It allows others categorically to confound membership in the Ajam cultural tradition with the distinctive identity as Shiahs, ignoring the perhaps 5 percent Shiah non-Ajams and about equal number Ajam non-Shiahs; and even for most Ajams it allows them emotionally to fuse Ajam identity with the powerful religious membership and thus enhance its force.

With respect to the cultural items that have composed an Ajam cultural tradition, rapid changes seem to be taking place in them, and in the whole tradition's conditions of persistence. The picture was aptly sketched by a senior member of the Awadhiyya group, in answer to my question of whether his father had done right in moving from Bandar Abbas to Sohar in the early 1920s.

He did very wisely. In those days, Reza Shah Pahlavi had just seized power, and he wanted to change people by force, and make everyone into Europeans. Anyone who had a son, he was forced to send his son into the army; anyone who had a daughter, that daughter would be forced to take some work outside the home. Here in Sohar, we were allowed to pursue our own customs. Our customs were already very much like those of the Arabs in Sohar while we lived in Bandar Abbas: we dressed in a similar way, our women used the *burqa* [facemask], etc. That is precisely why we moved: Pahlavi banned *burqas*, beards, turbans, etc.; we wanted to keep such things. But now, some of our young boys want to leave it all. They go about bareheaded instead of wearing the turban. Yet that is different: it is voluntary, with changing times, it is not by force.

Persian language is likewise disappearing. While perhaps three out of four of the total Ajam population are able to speak it, only one in ten uses it consistently in daily life, and many of the small children no longer learn it. Fashions in dress have nearly merged with those of Sohari Arabs, and features of domestic custom have become optional and ideosyncratic. The twin pressures of modernization and Arabization are thus rapidly reducing the range and distinctness of an Ajam cultural tradition without, in the case of the Shiah majority, eliminating the social category.

This reduction of cultural distinctness is traced to several contributing causes by Soharis. In the case of the non-Shiah Ajam minority, intermarriage with Arabs is cited as the major cause. While the Shiah Ajams have few Arab coreligionists with whom they can intermarry, other causes of increased intermingling are cited in their case. Residentially, Ajams and Arabs have become much more intermixed: the Ajam sector of Higra (that is, their settlement inside the old city walls) has been about 50 percent abandoned over the last twenty years (because of the ban on building in combination with a number of practical considerations; cf. pp. 64 ff.), leading to a dispersal of the former residents into mixed neighborhoods. Increasing security and changing patterns of administration have reduced the number of occasions for collective action. Thus, while the Ajam shaikh of a generation ago would lead the Ajam contingent in defense of the town and was a key figure to whom the Sultans had to turn simply to maintain their control of Sohar, the present Shaikh, Abdullah b. Ali, emphasized his role as an intermediary on the individual level only, and is credited with always having tried to reduce the differences and counteract all secular distinctions between the groups. Indeed, whereas the traditional expectation has been for each ethnic group to keep largely to itself, and thus keep its language and customs intact, the Ajam leadership today underplays every difference, emphasizes the shared identity as Omanis, stresses the obligation of all to mix and treat each other equally, and even questions the moral necessity of endogamy: "Some say we are all Moslem, we may intermarry, while others say Sunni should marry Sunni and Jaffari [that is, Shiah] should marry Jaffari."

Trying to judge the force and value for the individual of his embracement of ethnic identity in Sohar today, I would emphasize some marked contrasts between Ajams and Baluchis. To the men, the assertion of Ajam identity is fraught with two dangers or costs that are not entailed in Baluch identity: identification with an antagonistic sect or congregation, and identification with a foreign and powerful nation and state. Both these potential disadvantages are best handled by muting the assertion of identity and underplaying the existence of differences in a way that is quite unnecessary for Baluchis. Those Ajams who do not in fact embrace Shiah beliefs are thus particularly susceptible to Arab assimilation. Those who are Shiah may experience their double distinctness as being *more* precious than do Baluchis; but they will be encouraged to emphasize the comparative irrelevance of their Shiah identity for most everyday activities, their tolerance of change—and thus cultural assimilation—in all nonreligious domains, and their individual submergence in the shared, secular society of Sohar. Whatever their deepest feelings may be, this is not a praxis that will strengthen the retention and transmission of a distinctly Ajam cultural tradition. For women, these political and wider social considerations will have much less force; on the other hand, there do not seem to be any clear advantages for a woman in retaining an Ajam domestic culture—as there are for Baluch women—except those that derive from Shiah law and the somewhat greater community involvement and assertion entailed in the *matam* collective activities of Shiah women.

ZIDGALI AND BANYAN

The other two traditional ethnic categories, Zidgali and Banyan, are so much smaller as to be subject to a different set of conditions for persistence. They seem to occupy opposite extremes. Zidgalis have had a distinctive language and distinctive cultural traditions (though these latter are supposed to be similar in many ways to Baluchi customs, despite the only very distant linguistic relationship to Baluchi), but they lack a distinct homeland and any replenishment by immigration, and have no concentrated settlements, no common occupational orientation, and no religious distinctness. Processes that would contribute to the reproduction of Zidgali identity and shared cultural tradition cannot be identified or observed in the contemporary setting; both language and customs are expected to die with the present adult generation, in the estimates of both Zidgali and non-Zidgali. Banyans, on the other hand, look to India for most aspects of their identity; they are almost universally born, educated, and married there and will in due course die and be cremated there. In Sohar they live in a compact neighborhood of adjoining houses and meet with the Banyans of neighboring towns for occasional Friday picnics and outings, they are uniformly merchants, and they share a religion that places them entirely outside the pale of theological or matrimonial acceptance in the eyes of all other residents. My impression is indeed that their identity as a categorically distinct group has been strengthened, rather than reduced, over the last generation, in part through their choice of Indian rather than Omani citizenship once their status as British subjects could no longer be retained. Recent Omani restrictions on the business activities of noncitizens (the requirement of Omani partnership in all companies) have served only to increase an estrangement that has deeper and more diffuse sources.

RELIGIOUS GROUPS

The dynamics of religious and congregational groups can be much more briefly and easily summarized. Persons are born into a congregation and their membership is, for all practical purposes, unalterable. With almost no intermarriage between congregations (except for the less strict Sunni-Ibazhi distinction), each category is replenished and maintained as an integral consequence of normal population processes. Sunni, Ibazhi, Shiah, and Hindu thus seem to constitute relatively stable categories over time, and there is no indication that this will change in the near future. The only reservation concerns the theoretical possibility of a sudden expulsion or exodus of the Hindu Banyan community.

The cultural *content* that characterizes each sect tradition is also no doubt more stable than is that of ethnic groups. The congregations each have their sacred texts that fix a major source of ideas in immutable form. The social organization of congregations is likewise one that militates against local diversification and change. Whereas ethnic traditions are mostly asserted and communicated in domestic situations where two persons go about coping with the exigencies of daily living, religious knowledge is communicated in formal teaching situations, to adults as well as children, by a specialist enrolled in a hierarchical system of orthodoxy. And though learning is lifelong and many persons accumulate a considerable body of theological knowledge, most members of a congregation continue as laypersons to be dependent on the guidance and authority of their imam. Thus, their status is defined as one of ignorance, and they are committed to positions and understandings that are dictated to them and cannot be modified by them. We do not need to conclude from this that the values embraced by the members of a congregation are static. Soharis suggest, for example, that the interpretation of what constitutes women's rights has recently been modified among Sunnis and Shiahs (cf. p. 129). But these are, religiously speaking, modifications of detail, and it is difficult to imagine that they could be consistently cumulative, considering the anchoring of the whole tradition in the sacred texts.

19

The Changing Place of Bedouin and Ex-Slaves

No doubt the greatest contrast in overt life style between members of any of the coexisting cultural traditions in Sohar has been that between bedouin and townspeople. The contrasts could hardly be more dramatic and pervasive: the civilized and protected urban life versus the stark exposure and hardship of life in the open; the discreet and tactful, and often devious ways of the town versus the rough, outspoken, and courageous style of the bedouin; the solid houses of ancient brick behind the massive walls of Higra versus the tentless campsites under scattered acacias at the desert's edge; the delicate gold filigree of the townswomen's jewelry versus the rough silver of the bedouin women's; the sophisticated miniature *burqa* of the town versus the full face mask of the bedouin.*

These two ways of life have coexisted in close proximity and interdependence for centuries and probably millennia, retaining such sharp contrasts. Yet the evidence of publicly acknowledged tradition, and of personal careers and memories, indicates that a significant component of the present Arab population of Sohar is descended from goat- and sheep-herding shawawi bedouin, and that the whole present belt of settlement in what I have called the inner zone between the irrigated gardens and the interior plain is largely composed of a population that less than fifty years ago practiced a fully traditional shawawi life style. A closer description of the dynamics of reproduction and change of the bedouin cultural tradition should thus involve two distinct analyses: (1) the changing manner in which a distinctive social category of bedouin is reproduced within the social system of Sohar, and (2) the changing content of the cultural tradition associated with this category. In the inner-zone periphery of Sohar there are a number of bedouin groups that collectively and persistently seek to maintain

*My materials on bedouin are entirely derived from conversations with men only, since my wife's circles of friends and acquaintances did not include any bedouin women.

218

their identity and distinctiveness, while at the same time a massive change is taking place, transforming their life style and assimilating them to more urban patterns. My discussion will focus mainly on this zone of settlement between the irrigated area and the interior plain, where most of the Sohari population that is today identified as bedouin are located. Data from other groups will be brought in only to highlight features and test hypotheses relating to the processes in this zone.

The zone of bedouin settlement in Sohar is composed, from south to north, mainly of members of the Makabil, Shiblu, and Ghethy tribes. It is a zone of stable and traditional residence, with a continuity of population from the houseless shawawi days. Each of the groups has a history of small moves and resettlements in the region, and traces common descent relations to other, collateral branches elsewhere; but settlement on their present sites was variously claimed to extend from eighty to several hundred years back for the different groups.

According to older people, their style of life started to change about the time of the accession of Sultan Taimur (1913). Before that, their life was indistinguishable from that of shawawi groups in more marginal areas of today: they had neither houses nor tents, and very little material property. Times were very unsettled: they had to be always prepared to hide or move, and they felt that if they owned anything they would only lose it anyway. Contact with townspeople was rather limited—"Townspeople used to sit along the seashore and not come in here." Members of the effective tribal segment of 60–100 men *had* to stay together for mutual protection—"If one had to go anywhere, they all went with him; if one was threatened, they all fought for him." People had a mixed economy, combining goat and sheep herding, and camel keeping, with agriculture partly on their own land but mainly as contract labor or sharecroppers.

As security increased and the technology and economy changed, this life was gradually transformed, and today the bedouin of this zone pursue a very much modified life style. Camels are practically non-existent, and bedouin involvement in land transport is essentially discontinued. Animals are still kept in considerable numbers, and agriculture is pursued by those who own land and by a certain number of laborers, but mainly the bedouin have entered fully into the open labor market and pursue a wide range of occupations and employment, a great number as labor migrants. All settlement is in *barasti* (datefrond) houses of town construction, but distinctively without the compound wall that is a most essential part of a town home: among the bedouin, the several huts of a residential unit may be grouped so as to produce a quasi-secluded inner court area, but the courtyard will be exposed to outside view in some directions and mainly depend on distance for a degree of privacy. Bedouin houses also contain a considerable amount of domestic equipment today, not qualitatively different from what one finds among townspeople. Almost all bedouin women have changed to the diminutive Sohari *burqa*, and in other aspects of female dress they appear indistinguishable from, though on an average less sumptuous than, town Arabs.

Other traditional features tend to persist with greater force. There is still a notable difference in dialect between the Arabic spoken at home among bedouin and that spoken in town homes. Domestic customs, food preparation and dishes, and other details of everyday life remain distinctive. Bedouin men generally stand out quite clearly in their manner of self-presentation: there is less attention to immaculateness and cleanliness, circumspection, and constraint than among towns-men, and more emphasis on self-assertion, allowing a bedouin man to appear more outspoken and direct, argumentative, humorous, and generally flamboyant in his role play. Most distinctive are the emphasis placed on tribe and descent, the political importance of tribal shaikhs and agnatic solidarity, and the high frequency of agnatic cousin marri-age and patrilocal residence. Many of these features are, somewhat ambivalently, regarded by other Sohari men as constituting traditional and honorable virtues, though others are clearly devalued, as noted above (see chapter 8). The bedouin themselves are aware of these urban attitudes, and of the mixture of admiration, fear, and contempt which they entail. As a consequence, they are themselves ambivalent and defensive, both proud and aware that they are stigmatized. One of the shaikhs thus told me how, two years previously, he had been called with a number of other bedouin shaikhs to Muscat to consult with the minister of interior.

When I arrived, I was recognized by a Zangibari, and while I waited to see the minister he started abusing me. He said: "You always come here, make trouble and demands, and cost the government time and money!"
"No," I answered, "You are the one who is costing the Sultan money. His hand is in your mouth, but your hands are over his eyes! As for us, we have been *called* to Muscat, so we must come!"
The Zangibari was very angry, but someone advised him just to keep quiet and show respect for us: "They look after the Sultan's subjects. They solve problems for the government, they don't make them."

In their history of progressive acculturation, these tribes of the inner settled zone do not appear to be unique. The small Shirawi group from which one of the shaikhs of Shizawi comes (see chapter 15) is of bed-ouin descent, though strongly assimilated to Sohari town life style and mores. Other neighborhoods and whole wards in the coastal zone itself, such as Gheyl (see p. 146), are likewise reported to be of bedouin descent. The minor distinctive customs of Gheyl, indeed, are all such as could be explained as remnants of bedouin customs; thus, the freer relations between the sexes within the neighborhood also characterize bedouin life because of both a tighter kinship network in neighborhoods and a greater trust in traditional virtues and integrity. Their emphasis on collective entertainment of guests is consistent with the greater collective solidarity of bedouin communities and their more assertive style of self-presentation, including more emphatic hospitality. Finally, their "old-fashionedness" in details of clothing and jewelry is consistent with a bedouin background. The result, in the case of Gheyl and, I believe, in similar cases elsewhere, is a lingering stigma in the eyes of others that they are not true people of the city, but "just"-settled bedouin. But the almost complete assimilation of such groups to urban life indicates that the onset of this history of acculturation probably came significantly earlier in Gheyl than in the inner zone. I conclude that the factors responsible for the acculturation cannot be found in gross external changes—modernization, the impact of central administration since Sultan Taimur, etc.—but must be traced to the particular situation of each group in a composite context of circumstances.

Despite the stigmatization that bedouin custom entails, and despite the speed with which these customs have been discontinued in a number of neighborhoods, the social identity of a person as a member of a bedouin tribe is actively embraced. Indeed, almost uniquely among the component cultural traditions of Sohar (the Shiah congregation being the other partial exception; see pp. 213f.), tribal segments of the bedouin make collective and consistent efforts to protect and maintain their identity and (though to a less degree) distinctive life style and culture. The efforts that are made in this respect, and their results insofar as they can be identified, can provide valuable insight into the preconditions of cultural persistence in this social environment.

The retrenchment of bedouin identity centers on marriage and landownership: it depends, according to bedouin men, on tribal endogamy, and compact and exclusive residence. While they are emphatic that a bedouin "may marry whoever he wishes" (that is, bedouin are not a stigmatized endogamous group), they confirm the statistical pattern illustrated by the census of one such group (p. 145) that about nineteen of twenty marriages are within the local tribe. The explicit justifications of this pattern are threefold: it prevents mixture, it forestalls political difficulties, and it prevents the encroachment of strangers into the local community. Purity of blood itself is desirable, and since a child is held to receive its blood from both parents, tribal endogamy is preferable. Secondly, it was explained to me that the present time is one of peace and security, but intertribal anarchy may swiftly and suddenly return. If this were to happen, and one had let one's children intermarry with members of other tribes, one would find oneself in a position where one's own descendants would be living among potential enemies. It is much better to keep one's family (in this case, daughters) inside the tribe, where one can protect them and never be divided from them. Third, if you intermarry with persons of other tribes, they become your relations in the next generation. They then may want to move in with you, claim land as their mother's inheritance or demand the right to purchase land, and so infiltrate the tribal territory.

This eventuality is regarded as perhaps the greatest threat to tribal identity, one against which all members of the tribe as a collectivity are much concerned to maintain a united front. Thus, the local branch of Shiblu settled around the site on which the new hospital had recently been constructed have been unable to monopolize their territory and are swiftly being penetrated and interspersed with townspeople who are awarded grants by the government for house construction. This is considered to spell the end of the Shiblu as a social reality. The Makabil, on the other hand, point with clear satisfaction to the fact that only *one* property has been sold out of the tribe, and that this was an unforeseen result of a sequence of transactions where the property in question passed quickly from hand to hand, suddenly to end up outside the tribal membership. After this accident, the Makabil declare that they will be even more attentive and careful: any person from outside who tried to buy would be turned away, and any Makbali who might be prepared to sell would be prevented from this through the exercise of his neighbors' first option to buy, if necessary by putting collective pressure on him.

Identity in these cases is thus being maintained through conscious and successful collective efforts to maintain a segregated, encapsulated kinship network and a homogeneous, closed neighborhood. In the preceding chapter, I adopted the Soharis' own contention that cross-ethnic marriages and residential intermixture are the main factors responsible for the disappearance of non-Arab ethnic traditions and the assimilation of non-Arab to Arab identity. Yet in the case of the bedouin, endogamy and residential exclusiveness have failed to secure the reproduction of the main body of distinctive customs and practices of the bedouin, who instead present a picture of sweeping and pro-found change in most aspects of life style. Does this in fact falsify the view presented before, and is there instead a wholesale and rapid acculturation process proceeding in precisely the situation that was claimed to provide the strongest protection against such a process?

There is no denying that the settled bedouin of the inner zone have assumed a number of material objects and adopted patterns of be-

havior like those of townspeople. It is true that many of these concrete
features have also been changing among townspeople in the same time
interval, and were not developed as original innovations within that
cultural tradition; but both sides clearly hold the view (and I agree with
them) that it is the bedouin population that has changed more swiftly,
and in the course of that change has become less and less distinguishable from the townspeople. The impetus for such a change,
however, cannot be represented as a new and sudden familiarity with
town ways on the part of the bedouin—we must assume that they have
for very long had sufficeint contact so the bedouin were quite familiar
with these other options even when they did not adopt them. This
might suggest an alternative formulation, that what we are observing is
not so much an acculturation as an adaptation, whereby a previously
shifting population upon sedentarization develops a number of new
features of life style which, quite incidentally, make them more similar
to neighboring, sedentary people. Other features, such as localized
unilineal descent groups and parallel cousin marriage, are not at odds
with the new adaptation, and so are retained.

I would suggest that the changes among those bedouin who settle
and are drawn closer into the motley life of the town of Sohar are best
viewed neither as a acculturation situation or nor as a case of cultural
adaption. Rather, I need to analyze their case from the perspective
outlined in chapter 16. Most of the changes in people's behavioral
patterns can be shown to be induced by the change of the *context* in
which the now-settled bedouin individual makes his choices, cultivates
his self-presentation, and designs his allocations and strategies. In the
short run we need not assume any major changes in bedouin culture,
conceived of as an ideational system, but only observe the implications
of the changed circumstances under which these ideas will serve to
guide and propel him. Let us, therefore, on the contrary, assume an
initially stable and unaltered set of values and priorities and explore
the implications of the changed context for choice. Indeed, I would
suggest that one single major difference, from which can be derived
most of the changes in patterns between traditional bedouin life and
the life of contemporary bedouin in Sohar, can be identified in the one
crucial parameter of security.

I shall consider the contrasts briefly. Traditional bedouin life un-
folded outside the town's and sultanate's direct administration. Personal security and honor had to be defended by each adult male for
himself and his closest dependent family; there was no Wali to whom
one could turn to escape the onerous tasks of asserting oneself and
sanctioning others. No matter how highly the morality of restraint and
respect for others may be valued, these polite virtues that could be
cultivated in town and gave such esteem there were simply not prac-

ticable under the anarchic and acephalous conditions of bedouin life. An unwillingness to defend oneself by overt and bellicose techniques of fighting and threatening others would there only lead to humiliating abdication and stigmatization as Zatut (pariah), rather than recognition as a civilized gentleman. In the context of Sohar, on the other hand, then as now, such belligerence would swiftly bring down on its practitioner the massive and destructive sanctions of the state apparatus—no matter how highly bravery and self-pride might be valued by him and others. The rudeness and directness of nomads and the restrained and beautiful manners of townsmen may thus be generated from fundamental differences in their opportunity situation rather than differences in their standards of excellence in judging persons and realizing themselves as persons.

I have also indicated how collective security among traditional shawawi bedouin was furthered by minimizing material possessions—thereby both enhancing mobility and escape and reducing one's attraction as an object of plunder. Bedouin were thus precluded from developing all the small habits and interests connected with material possessions which could be cultivated in town, and their life style thus lacked a number of features of town life—by force of circumstance, not from an ideational difference in values and appetites. Adopting town life, these opportunities suddenly presented themselves, and it is as plausible to regard the consequent elaboration of practices and conveniences as the realization of previously frustrated desires and ambitions, as to see them as the adoption of a new culture of the townsman. The same applies to the traditional bedouin emphasis on hospitality: the lower, and perhaps even negative marginal utility of wealth and the great importance of friends and allies in an anarchic regime would favor a strategy of hospitality rather than accumulation, and thus encourage very different uses of surplus among migratory bedouin and in town, with pervasive consequences for overt life style. There is no necessity to postulate that whereas nomadic bedouin admire hospitable persons more and wealthy persons less than do townsmen, upon settling they quickly changed their minds under the influence of town culture. On the contrary, whatever their relative priorities may be, they should be able to see that, under the changed circumstances, former practices are no longer optimal, and saving and husbanding wealth entail far greater advantages and far fewer risks than before.

Indeed, a similar argument may be developed for features that at present distinguish settled bedouin patterns from those of townsfolk, as in their marriage and residence practices. Agnatic loyalty, parallel cousin marriage, and patrilocal residence are emphasized as explicit ideals among townspeople as well as bedouin. Thus, it cannot be in the presence of these ideals that we find the explanation of their high frequency of observance among the settled bedouin, but rather in distinctive features of the contexts of choice that obtain among the bedouin. If we formulate these from the viewpoint of a young adult male, his situation of choice is notably affected by the initial fact of his tribe's localized and politically corporate character. In this situation, agnatic loyalty secures the support of a constituted, solidary group, and not merely, as among townsmen, a more nebulous membership enhancing the father's authority. Patrilocal residence provides a free house site for the marrying couple and assistance in house construction, not just propinquity to the father. Finally and perhaps most importantly, tribal endogamy secures this residence right as well as greatly facilitating marriage negotiations, since it assures the tribal exclusiveness positively valued by all tribal members. None of these advantages is entailed in the normal town context, so even if the same ideals were embraced with equal strength, one would surely expect lower frequencies of such choices in the nonbedouin population.

However, it would be as premature to affirm that there has been no change of culture accompanying sedentarization, or indeed no significant difference in values between traditional bedouin and townsmen, as to see every overt change of behavior as evidence of acculturation. Values are not immutable, and there is every reason to expect them to reflect accumulated experience (see chapter 16). Thus, in a life situation where certain qualities in persons prove to be advantageous to them and those linked or allied to them, while other qualities work to their detriment, this cannot but act back on people's evaluations of how desirable these qualities are, in oneself and others.

Let me try to reconstitute the argument I have been building as a schematic model to depict the dynamic connections that I am positing. We must recognize that bedouin and town populations have been in significant intercommunication, so the example represented by town life and the stigmatization of bedouin customs by townspeople cannot be represented as novel factors for the settling bedouin, though the intensity of these factors was doubtless enhanced. It is also necessary to recognize that both populations have participated in a community of language and religion—they share categories and concepts with which to constitute and evaluate their representations of mankind and the world. These shared concepts are such as to give positive value to a broad range of qualities in the person: there is no doubt about the positive evaluation by all of honesty, politeness, bravery, cleverness, etc., but there is less clarity as to the conceptual priority these qualities should be given in the compromises and exigencies of real life. In terms of the context of this life, on the other hand—the tasks, dangers, and experiences that characterize it—there obtains a consistent contrast between traditional bedouin and townspeople. The consistent experience of bedouins, shared among them and exemplified by the role models most closely available to them, will favor the practice of priorities and role solutions consistently at variance with those of townspeople. Salient differences will be the emphasis on honesty over politeness, bravery over cleverness, self-assertion over noninvolvement, and hospitality over the accumulation of wealth. These features, then, may be identified as valuations most likely to emerge in a bedouin cultural tradition. What is more, this greater allowance for self-assertion, bravery, and directness of expression entails a considerably enhanced leeway for young men's individual expression of themselves as adults and men. Most significantly, in the presence of senior agnates there is less need to suppress such activities under the constraints of politeness and respect that so severely inhibit the son's expression of self before his father and seniors in the town context. Whereas the junior generation among townsmen are in a kind of double-bind situation that can most simply be resolved by escape from the proximity of senior agnates—and the various patterns of early labor migration, extended absence, marriage with "strangers," and neolocal residence on return—the bedouin emphases with respect to male virtues will allow such youths to enhance both their own position and their father's and agnate's honor simultaneously. They are thereby free also to practice the virtues and reap the benefits of close family endogamy and patrilocal residence, thereby contributing to a pattern of social organization based more pervasively on patrilineal descent groups. We can thus see emerging a set of interconnected premises, consistent with the main thrust of experience in the traditional bedouin context and reinforced by alignments and localizations that result from the actors' favored decisions. The model thereby generates features characteristic of bedouin patterns as a coherent, variant Arabic subculture.

In the situation of sedentarization, centralized administration, and new occupations, these value positions will be less systemtically reinforced by current experiences, but they continue to be embraced insofar as they are seen as constitutive of the bedouin man's cherished identity. The keeping of material equipment at a minimum and the practice of hospitality are no longer opportune in the new situation, and both tend to be discontinued although the theoretical ideal may be retained and signaled in a greater carelessness about the quality and condition of clothes and houses, and a mild code of obligations to hospitality. The basic ideals of manliness and quality of the person, on the other hand, have been retained and are pursued, even at some cost vis-á-vis the wider society, while the innumerable overt features of traditional Bedouin life ways (such as house type, diet, dependence on herding, prestige value of camels, the use of silver jewelry and large facemasks) have been discarded in favor of patterns borrowed from the town. No doubt the increased exposure to stigmatization in encounters with nonbedouin has increased the pressure on persons to modify their bedouin practices, but so far this has led to neither an abandonment of cental values nor a retrenchment of identity around select emblems from bedouin life style, say, in a manner analogous to that of Baluchi female dress. This relative imperviousness I would trace to two sources.

First, the situation of increased contact has not led to an increased conceptual polarization of bedouin and townspeople. A major factor seems to be that the bedouin's cherished ideals—both the masculine qualities and the agnatic solidarity and tribal pedigrees— are indeed valued also in town culture, though less clearly achieved there. Perhaps an apposite analogy would be the cowboy in American consciousness: while hardly acceptable among successful urbanites and businessmen, he yet embodies ideals in terms of which more genteel and prestigious persons fall short. My wife's material would suggest that bedouin identity is more unambiguously stigmatizing among women than among men in town, as one might expect from their lower ranking of such masculine ideals.

Secondly, it is highly relevant that the immediate focus of organization for the bedouin is not bedouin but a particular tribal identity that only incidently entails "being" a bedouin. It will therefore be of no particular importance to signal one's membership in this wider group—it is one's identity as Makbali, or member of another tribe, *in contrast to* all other tribes as well as townsmen which is at issue. This is the identity that gives the tangible advantages and community membership, and it cannot be signaled by idioms taken from a life style that is shared by the immediately contrasting groups of those other tribes.

Thus the superficial picture of wholesale cultural change and assimilation of settled bedouin to town life is deceptive, and masks far more diffentiated processes of persistence and change in the bedouin cultural tradition.

The contemporary features of *xaddam* (ex-slave) identity and behavior contrast markedly with those described for the bedouin. Like them, they may be characterized as a stigmatized category. But paradoxically, while this identity seems to be basically repudiated, the cultural elements that compose the distinctive tradition are embraced and practiced in such a way as to reaffirm a *xadim* identity. In the following, I shall analyze the current picture of change and reproduction, arguing that such a paradox is only apparent, and that the behavioral patterns adopted by contemporary ex-slaves in Sohar are to large extent strategically predicated by their opportunity situation.

As I have noted manumission for most of the remaining slaves seems to have taken place around 1955–60, and for quite a while before that there had existed in Sohar a population of freed slaves and their descendants. The insinuation of slave admixture can also be made against persons and family lines without implying (patrilineal) descent from identifiable slaves, but based simply on African somatic features. Thus, as a social category, *xaddam* is diffusely bounded. It is also logically inherent in its origin in the definition of slave that it is a category by virtue of the member's relationship to nonmembers and not to each other: one is a slave to one's own owners, and not by virtue of relations to other slaves. As an identity on the basis of which to embrace shared group membership and shared cultural values, it thus has a peculiar character. Indeed, the very concept has been abolished and banned by recent decree of the Sultan, according to Soharis: "Now they are free people, just as good as anybody else. No one can say these people are bad, these are good. . . . The Wali can punish any man who calls another *xadim*, and they should no more say *Habib* to others."

The response of ex-slaves to this changed situation has been a relatively massive repudiation of the former identity, expressed in a wholesale emigration by a considerable sector of the population with manumission, and a discontinuation of relationships to the former owners' tribe, neighborhood, or house. Only some few older, economically weak persons continue to acknowledge and cultivate such ties, and they do it, according to their former owners, in such a way as to maximize their economic benefits in return for very limited services and tokens of respect.

When the category of *xadim* persists in general Sohari consciousness, one would expect it to do so mainly through ascription by others, and to be sustained through differential treatment of ex-slaves rather than active embracement by them. With a style of social interaction as graceful and tolerant as that of Sohar, such discrimination is not easiliy visible, but reveals itself on certain critical issues. Thus, when the son of the shaikh of a ward of Sohar wanted to marry a *xadim* (as his second wife), there was a certain amount of general indignation and his own parents were against it, but this could not prevent the marriage from taking place. Likewise, in a recent case brought before a *qadhi*, members of a family protested a man's right to marry his daughter to a *xadim*. The *qadhi*, however, after assuring himself that the girl was aware of the future groom's identity and yet consented to the marriage, then allowed the marriage to take place. Despite legal and ideological efforts on the part of Omani authorities, there can thus be no doubt that the identity of ex-slaves is maintained and imposed as a disability by the not-so-disabled rest of the population.

In the Sohari view, however, the source of *xadim* identity is not in the attitudes of others but carried within the ex-slaves themselves, that is, in their "blood." It is thus conceived of as a somatic, racial property of the person rather than a cultural property or a social ascription. Clearly, Sohari conceptions of the determination of somatic characteristics do not correspond to those of scientific genetics (or modern Western folk versions of genetics), and so the ideas cannot be equated with any particular variant of Western racism. But roughly, I understand the Sohari view to be that fundamental features of a person's character and moral qualities are somatically based, and transmitted from parents—both father and mother—to children, though in the mechanisms of this transmission no categorical dichotomy is made between genetics and other forms of parental influence (see p. 43). This somatic basis holds true for all descent-based groups, particularly ethnic groups, whose members can supposedly always be recognized by their "face" (see chapter 4). But the emphasis on "blood" in the case of the *xaddam* is more strongly on the inherent and ineradicable source of identity in the body of the person, and so reproduces an abolished legal disability as an inherent personal failing. This view seems less clearly or categorically to be held by women. For example, they feel free to discuss a person's physical features with the detached tactlessness with which they treat prices and monetary values (see Wikan 1982: 135)—as if these were external matters that do not touch the owner's person. I see no evidence, however, that ex-slave men have at their command an alternative, distinctive model of personhood that would absolve them from the stigma entailed by the mainstream view.

What implications might such a view of the construction of self have on a person's comportment, on the strategies by which he can defend and enhance his social position? It is essential to remember that Sohari male society is thoroughly dominated by ideals of tactfulness, manners, and grace (see chapter 11), as an eternal tournament of perfection. What might be the effect of entering this tournament with a stigma based on blood and inherent qualities? Since the stigma is viewed as inherent, it can (conceptually) never be overcome. Nor is it possible, surrounded by tact and politeness, to confront it, forcing others to live up to their rules of tolerance and declare its irrelevance: to create the confrontation necessary to enforce such agreement would be grossly to break the rules of politeness, tact, and noninterference with others. Yet without such clarification, the stigma will always be with you as a potential threat, unspecified in magnitude and relevance, always capable of spoiling in the eyes of others whatever degree of perfection has been achieved in any and every performance.

If this is how the ex-slaves' position in society is currently constructed, the only attractive strategy would be to pursue a somewhat different course from that of the nonstigmatized townsmen. There *are* prizes other than grace and perfection that are valued in Sohari life, some of them tangible in ways that make them less conditional on other people's acceptance and judgment. The most salient are those of wealth and power. I have noted that the code of politeness that rules Sohari society and constrains the majority of men does not seem to interfere with their effectiveness in their struggle to obtain wealth (see p. 148). It does, however, severely limit them in the ways in which they can exhibit the fruits of this struggle to the public, and it puts severe restrictions on the ways in which they can pursue and exercise power. If ex-slaves refrain from involving themselves too deeply in the polite tournament of perfection, they gain a greater freedom to show off their wealth and thus benefit socially from it, and to pursue and exercise power over others. This also is consistent with the experience of slavehood: largely tied to influential and powerful citizens, they were used to act as the trusted agents of such persons and thus exercise a power by means of which they could extract a respect from commoners which might not otherwise be granted (see chapter 5). By adopting a strategy of directy pursuing these tangible rewards, ex-slaves can capitalize on the stigma that places them outside polite society and compete with enhanced effectiveness against those others who are hampered by those sensibilities. Indeed, this is a strategy often adopted by members of stigmatized minorities. What is perhaps relatively singular is that the style of behavior that it entails is one that strongly reaffirms a prejudicial identity that they would seem otherwise in a favorable position to escape. Men tend to be highly assertive, brusque in their exercise of whatever influence or privilege they hold, and unsubtle in drawing attention to whatever wealth or income they command. They do not particularly disguise their pragmatic view of social relations, and are direct in drawing attention to the "connections" they have. Likewise, they are less circumspect in showing their eagerness for and enjoyment of even minor positions of authority, and their entrepreneurship. All these are modes of behavior that others may read as revealing crudeness, ruthlessness, lack of culture, and brutality, conjuring up memories of former harsh Walis' wicked slave retainers and prison guards. But in the contemporary situation they do facilitate a man's efforts swiftly to build up a self-image, and a claim to respect, based on these more tangible achievements in an increasingly open and pragmatic society.

The behavioral style of ex-slave women seems not to be notably modified in the direction of that of other townswomen but to retain its distinctive *xadim* features. As in the case of the men, this may be interpreted to express not a commitment to a *xadim* identity so much as a valuation of those particular features of behavior and the advantages they entail. Essentially, ex-slave women are allowed greater freedom without shame: compared to other women, they have enhanced mobility; greater leeway for conversation, laughter, and assertiveness in public; freedom to dress without the *burqa* and *abba* (cloak); freedom to perform as singers at weddings; etc. Perhaps these are freedoms that many of them would give up to attain the enhanced respectability of the more cloistered townswomen, but since the stigma of blood precludes the successful achievement of such respectability, little would be gained by abandoning these privlileges. To the extent that *xadim* women need to construct a model of the self in the permissive context of women's society, they can also represent their modes of behavior as more modern and cosmopolitan, and thus valuable. For both sexes, I would therefore suggest that what we see in the retention of behavior patterns associated with a slave identity is not the embracement and signaling of that identity but the result of a pragmatic strategy reflecting a situation of lingering stigma. This would indicate that the contemporary pattern is only a phase in a longer-term assimilation and homogenization of the two populations as detribalized, town Arabs.

20 Gender Cultures

Gender cultures are of particular analytic interest, since their differences cannot be traced back to different geographical and historical points of origin elsewhere, but must, somehow, be primarily related to each other and to the social circumstances under which they are expressed and reproduced. In this chapter I shall reconsider men's and women's cultures in Sohar from this perspective.

I have argued (in Chapter 9) that major organizational conditions for the reproduction of men's and women's cultures in Sohar are found in the pervasive pattern of segregation of the sexes and in the modesty-derived patterns of constraint on the movement and public appearance of women. These patterns counterbalance the pair bonding of spouses, and result in the conditions under which fundamental differences in experience and consciousness emerge between men and women despite quite comprehensive mutual knowledge of the other gender's conditions of life, standards of worth and excellence, and so forth.

I have listed elsewhere the outer forms whereby the differences between the genders are signaled. There is an obvious and direct connection between the veiling and masking aspects of dress and the seclusion and constraints imposed on women, and likewise a connection between the avoidance of overt, tangible decorations among men and their avoidance of ostentation. Otherwise, the particular embellishments and extensions of the person whereby gender identity is expressed seem to be fairly arbitrarily assigned to men and women.

Not so the general standards of value and excellence that apply to men and women, respectively: these seem very closely connected with, or dependent on, the distinctive contexts of men's and women's lives. The most salient are the differences in the organization and scale of men's and women's networks. The relative seclusion of women implants them in a small world comprised mainly of close neighbors, while men participate in and are tested in the large-scale world of public and in part impersonal institutions and forces. These difference are reflected in the overt symbolism observed by the sexes as they pass between the private and public spheres. Women's rituals mainly take place at the *exit* from domestic compounds (masks, headcloths, and *abbas* are donned and adjusted), whereas those of men mark their *entrance* into a compound (knocking, hesitation, warning shouts, etc.; see chapter 12). This reflects the respective worlds to which they are adapted. How, then, does it affect their activities, their experiences, and the concepts they use to interpret themselves and others?

The cherished activities of men (other than leisure) take place in various public fora. What propels them, and provides the criteria of excellence of performance and value of person, are the pursuit of wealth and the exercise of manners. Success in the former is pragmatically and objectively demonstrated in profits, and the accumulation of money and property. As noted, economic relationships often take on the character of contests, where success in bargaining seems to be a central prize. Thus, success in the pursuit of wealth seems to serve for men as an important index of personal value, a source of pride and self-esteem, as well as a standard for judging others; and it is in its achievement, not in its display or use, that wealth has this special significance.

But even more important, or at least more pervasive, are the activities of exhibiting good manners. Beautiful manners among men seem to be regarded as the essence of civilization and refinement among townspeople (contrasted conceptually with the wild state/ crudeness of bedouin nontownsmen), and by both townspeople and bedouin as an index of personal honor and integrity. I have discussed the special emphasis on politeness, tact, and tolerance in this code simultaneously as a measure of one's own value and self-esteem and as a measure of the value of others. It does not seem at all fanciful to see men's life in Sohar as a perpetual tournament of manners in a large, public arena, where the judges are both oneself and an impersonal public of strangers. The qualities that men are encouraged to develop and emulate in such a situation are elegance, swiftness, subtlety, foresight, and the integrity of being a "whole" person with a stable, reliable morality. But inevitably, in such a large and public arena with its ever-shifting encounters and frequently very incomplete mutual information among contestants and judges, skill in impression management is also rewarded and the test is often whether one can bring off a series of performances by suppleness, bluff, and even deception rather than by naïve honesty and transparency.

The cherished activity of women, on the other hand, is clearly *visiting* in the secluded, private fora of domestic compounds, mainly during the periods of the day when all men are absent (Wikan 1982:114 ff.). Such intervisiting is by definition personal, mutual, and recurrent; it involves the person in the give and take of reciprocal hospitality and conviviality. In this cherished and dominant activity of women there is no conspicuous jury, since it involves the *ascribed* status of neighbor—a woman is undeniably part of the neighborhood and the neighbors cannot disown her. The self-confidence shown by women in this situation is thus *not* painfully achieved, precarious, and critically judged as among men; it reflects a security that is automatically granted. Generosity in the hospitality of intervisiting likewise does not become ambivalent for giver or receiver; there is no virtue in a moderation like that practiced among men. On the contrary, women are free to enjoy what is served up with extravagance: it entails an exchange of compliments, where the guests are honored and the generosity of the hostess is acknowledged in the act of consumption. This is so at odds with the experience of men that men seem unable to interpret its import correctly, and the women's practice of hospitality in intervisiting is perhaps the classical theme of conflicts between spouses (ibid., p. 126f.).

A very significant aspect of the cherished activity of women is its nondiscriminatory quality. Wikan (1982:120 ff., 164 ff.) points to the striking difference between women, whose circles of intimates are composed of neighbors (*giran*), and of men who have friends (singular = *sadiq*). As noted above, the character of a man's friends is used by others as an indicator of his own character: friendship entails an evaluation of persons, with the risk of finding and being found wanting, and its content is built on a privileged trust from which others are excluded. Neighborliness does not depend on personal evaluation and does not exclude anyone; thus it also precludes any conception of guilt by association. This circumstance of women's life context allows women the untroubled practice and realization of the basic Sohari virtue of tolerance, of an undiscriminating grant of value and tact to others. Where men must compromise this virtue by constantly (though discreetly) judging, and are exposed to the potential insult of being judged and found wanting, and thus must enter as competitors in a subtle sociometric contest or withdraw in the haughty security of distance and isolation, women are left free to socialize without risk. Where men hope at best to be able to say "Nobody can say a bad word against me" (see p. 182), if a woman says a bad word against anyone, it immediately recoils, as it should by Sohari ideology, on the speaker herself. Because their worlds differ so in social scale and organization, the critical issues and existential problems of men and women become very different, even when they pursue the same goals. In practice, therefore, the standards by which their performances are judged become different by virtue of the fact that what is difficult, and critical, in their performances is different. Furthermore, the wisdom about society and life which can be distilled and accumulated from men's and women's lives, the pictures that they build up to conceptualize society, and the human condition, and the critical skills and ethics of living must inevitably become very different. In this particular aspect, men, unlike women, will inhabit a world full of cases and chances of failures, defeats, and embarrassments; they will be forced to acknowledge the precariousness of their own value as persons despite its formal assertion in the tact and good manners of others. They must develop and make use of concepts to handle the paradox of tact and discrimination, tolerance and avoidance, and the complexity of society and other persons,—indeed, the basic deviousness of others.

Is there then nothing that is precarious in the life of women, no breaches of standards and no losses of honor and value? Of course, women can commit acts that reduce their personal value in their own eyes and in the eyes of others; and Wikan, in an extended discussion (1982: chap. 7), argues forcefully and convincingly that concepts of honor, esteem, and self-realization are highly applicable and significant in the analysis of the behavior of Sohari women. But the moral and ideological classification of breaches and other acts must be linked with the pragmatics of the consequences of such acts for the actor; Wikan develops a highly significant distinction between the near and the distant public (ibid., pp. 147 f., 163 ff.). Briefly, the significant public that observes and may respond to the acts of a woman is by virtue of her network position a *near* public of persons who know her and know much about her. The interpretation that a distant public of strangers might place on her acts is of very secondary and marginal concern to her, and then mainly in terms of the repercussions it might have for her husband, concerned as he is for his reputation in the wider Sohar—that anonymous sea of a "distant public."

In other words, two significant aspects emerge. First, there are profound differences in the structure, and so the mode of response, of the relevant public for men and women, and thereby in the consequences of their acts. Women are oriented to a "near" public, who know them and are not deceived by surface appearances. Men must consider a "distant" public, who are ill-informed and consequently looking for clues. Thus, the rules of behavior by which the genders must seek to safeguard their reputations will be different. Second, the very concepts of reputation and honor will differ in their salient aspects.

Women may conceive of a person's honor as a considered, averaged-out judgment of that whole person, her good and less good qualities. Such an "honor" is not liable to be destroyed by one fault or one breach. Nor is it likely, in the humdrum lives of women, that they entertain a dramatic, glorious, or tragic view of honor as the hidden true fiber of the person, liable to be tried and revealed in one critical, climactic moment of life. Men, on the other hand, are in a position where their value in the eyes of others, a distant public, may be thought of in more dramatic terms: honor as a conceptualization of being without blemish, without clues of any weakness—a condition that may be suddenly and utterly destroyed by a calamitous event or act, a failure at a critical time of testing (see Wikan's discussion, 1982:153). Even the supposedly ultimate transgression that may be committed by a woman—unchastity or unfaithfulness—was differently conceived and spoken of by men and women. The women of my wife's circle would have no reservations about condemning the disgracefulness of the act, but would not do so of the person; in the particular case of a person in their own circle they defended her against even the most moderate sanctions by my wife with the argument: "What bad has she done *you*?" Men, on the other hand, were prepared to declare (in general terms) the transgressions of wives and daughters as acts that would destroy the honor of their men.

There can be little doubt as to the existence of differences in the meaning of the *concept* of honor as it is sustained in women's and men's cultures. But it should be observed that the *relevance* of the more absolute aspects of men's concept of honor was considerably restricted, in real life, by their practice of a tactful unwillingness to gossip about particular cases or to sanction particular persons, and, on the particular issues of unvirtuous women, by their preference for discreet disengagement (see Ali's reaction to his first wife, chapter 15: 178) or immaculate pretense (Wikan 1982:162: "*Zogti, mafi hash!*" [My wife, there is nothing the matter with her]) rather than accusations and sanctions.

In other important respects, there are likewise fundamental differences between the ideas embraced in men's and women's cultures. One concerns their respective conceptions of individual responsibility. Both men and women acknowledge the legal framework of whatever school of Islamic law to which they belong, and recognize the legal role of men as guardians of women for certain purposes. But men generalize this guardianship as one that entails full moral responsibility by the male for his female ward: her acts rebound on him, not on herself. As Ali formulated it, "It comes from lack of education: how can she know the right from wrong when her parents and her husband do not show her and look after her?" Or, a woman's bad acts happen "because her husband is stupid. He is responsible; he should think. He must stop her from doing such things. If he is away, he must set another person to watch over her, make reliable arrangements."

Women on the other hand see themselves as autonomous and morally responsible persons, involved as equals with their husbands in a relationship that both sides shape. "You should have seen Shaikha before—how good she was! . . . Whereas he was impossible to make content, he scolded her and beat her, for no good reason. . . . But now that he has become good, she has turned bad" (Wikan 1982: 272). But when they consider the characters both of men and women, women turn to a different source for their explanation of the person's qualities. It is not (failure in) knowledge, education, or knowing what is right that lies at the root of misdemeanor: it is the person's nature or inherent characteristics, his/her "way" (*roh*) or "nature" (*sumr*). And in resigning themselves to such imperfections in persons and the world, women seem likewise to carry a basic value of tolerance and non-interference a distinct step farther than their men succeed in doing.

I should emphasize that men and women not only differ in the concepts they use to analyze the same situations, but the differences in their cultures go deeper, or more covertly, in that key concepts and symbols that are overtly shared may have quite profoundly different meanings in men's and women's culture. I have already suggested this for the concept of honor. It can be driven home with a brief exploration of the meanings associated in men's and women's cultures with that key symbol, the *burqa* (facemask). (The topic is extensively discussed in Wikan, 1982: chap. 5.)

For men, the *burqa* is a veiling device. This does not mean that there is homogeneity and agreement among men as to its value and precise meaning. To Ali (whose deceased mother came from the southernmost part of the Batineh and perhaps did not wear it, or wore it more reluctantly), "it is based on a misunderstanding of the circumstances of the Prophet's daughter Fatima's *burqa*. She wore it to go to school so nobody should know who she was, because the Prophet's enemies would want to kill her. The Prophet does *not* say you should cover the face, only arms, legs, body, and hair. But these uneducated women do not know this, and think the *burqa* is like clothing, a blouse or something, and feel ashamed to show themselves without it." To Said, on the other hand, "the *burqa* is a good thing. It is used because of Muslim modesty, and also because it keeps the woman's face from becoming black from the sun. If you see two women, one wearing the *burqa* and one without, you will see that the one without has turned dark from exposure." According to Suleiman Ashur, "Even a girl's own parents cannot recognize her when she wears a *burqa*. I once passed my own daughter on her way out, right here in the lane, and as I entered my house I asked my wife: 'Where is our daughter?' This is a sterotyped, recurring anecdote among Sohari fathers, and captures perhaps most succinctly men's view of what the *burqa* means and how it functions.

Women, clearly entertain rather different ideas. They early asked my wife to try on a *burqa*, and shrieked with delight at how it beautified her. They lovingly attend to the cut and color of a *burqa*, adjusting it to their own facial form and discussing the fit they achieve. They manipulate it in all-woman and intimate company, removing it and reassuming it in an individualized, apparently sensitive response to changing moods; some women appear to wear it almost always, even when they are alone. Contrary to the male view, they clearly do not feel that it anonymizes, but rather that it accentuates individuality, and that it does not cover up the face, but beautifies it.

I have already shown or hinted that a number of other basic behaviors have highly discrepant meanings for women and men. Hospitality is an expression of respect and generosity among women, but ambivalently one of superiority and ostentation among men. Silence instead of conversation is a sign of contentment and confidence between women, but of unease and boorishness among men. Humor and teasing are friendly and warm among women, but unseemly and threatening among men. There is a wide range of concepts, symbols, ·and idioms of which the import and meaning in women's and men's cultures are different and sometimes highly at variance.

The coexistence and reproduction of two such traditions, two such streams of culture, within one undeniably intermarrying population raise a number of interesting questions. First, I should note the surface agreement: men and women repeatedly refer to "our" customs as a joint body of culture, and their conversations and conceptualizations was cast in the "same" language, the same words, the same material symbols. Quite apart from their conversations with initially undiscriminating anthropologists, men and women in Sohar are engaged in a perpetual conversation with each other—indeed in the life of most individuals, with a person of the other sex as the most important and most intimate alter.

Do not the differences that I have pointed out lead to recurring differences in interpretation, and so to constant misunderstandings between men and women? If so, should not the misunderstandings produce an awareness of confusion and a struggle for clarification which presumably through time would generate a standardization of meanings? I read the literature on Western urban families to contain some suggestions that can help us to think about these questions. In terms of Bott's (1957) classic investigation of families and social networks in London, conjugal role relations will vary with the social networks in which they are situated: more joint in the more loosely knit networks. Berger and Kellner (1964) indicate that the process involved in creating such joint conjugal roles, and the shared view of life and the world which they entail, is found in the character of marriage as "a long conversation." In the Sohar case, gender differences in network scale and the pervasive rules of segregation of sexes (affecting frequency and content of *interaction* much more than existence/nonexistence of *relationships* across the gender dichotomy) make a direct comparison more difficult. I have claimed that men's networks are quite loosely knit and open, and that even the smaller-scale networks of women show a degree of looseness. The significant factor in reducing the jointness of conjugal roles, and the building of shared views and premises, must then lie in the interactional independence *enforced* on spouses by the observation of sexual segregation. I see opposed processes at work: both a growing intimacy in many, successful marriages drawing the spouses together toward a shared world view, and a categorical distinctness in the other parts of their activities and relationships, reaffirming the differences of their worlds. In Sohar, the scales are weighted in favor of differences (involving nearly *all* others) over sharing (arising from only the one, albeit often most valued, cross-gender relationship between spouses).*

If those are the organizational preconditions for the reproduction of difference, what then are the wellsprings of the differences themselves that are thus reproduced? These wellsprings must be different, or generative of differences, between men and women. The easy answer is that they are "traditional" and arbitrary—any difference that might have appeared, under other conditions or by chance, between the cultural heritages of men and of women will subsequently be passed on to persons ascribed to these identities and thereby recruited to serve as carriers of the respective traditions. On the other extreme, one might search for processes, active in the life of each person, whereby the gender-characteristic meanings are somehow generated or revitalized for each new individual who embraces that identity.

I have built my description and analysis on the view that there is at least a major force indicated in the latter alternative (see my program to analyze culture as an experience-induced tradition, chapter 16). In line with this, I have sought to identify and describe that particular set of circumstances that provides a contrastive context for the experience of the superficially "same" items by members of the two genders. Note, for example, the difference between the two genders' experience of the *burqa*. For the man (whatever it may have been to him as a child), it entails subscribing to the view that his wife—who is supremely valuable to him but also potentially shatteringly destructive of his honor if she is unfaithful—should assume the mask before all male strangers, and remove it only before himself and God (see Wikan 1982:101). For the woman it is something assumed on adulthood, when she becomes mistress of her own house, and subsequently is used as an extension of herself and symbol of her social personhood. It seems compellingly

*I acknowledge the direct impetus of Hannerz 1980, esp. pp. 221 ff., for this discussion.

obvious that for her, the *burqa* must, through the experience of use, take on a cloud of associations and evocations that *is* the *burqa's* meaning to her, whereas for the husband it remains the veiling and shielding device, symbolic of her virtue and his privilege of intimacy.

Likewise, I find the argument compelling that a concept of personal responsibility will mean different things if its context of relevance is seen primarily as the domestic scene of cooperation and confrontation—as I find it plausible that the women do—or else as the Shariah law texts and the Wali's court—as the men explicitly do. I am also prepared to argue that "teasing" will be interpreted as associated with very different emotions if one's repeated experience of it is located in the social context of a small, stable audience of intimates—as it will be for women (and children)—or else on a public arena where the main scenario is an exacting tournament of manners—as it will be for men.

In this vein, I would argue for the existence of persisting wellsprings of "meaning" in the experienced context of events that will differ, perhaps profoundly, according to the person's position in a social organization, and that these meanings will continue to develop as a precipitate of continuing experience through life. When such ideas are *shared*, and thus constituted as a cultural tradition, I would trace this to three sources, which I would provisionally hypothesize are all broadly necessary conditions: (1) those who share the culture are initially equipped with the same or very similar concepts for interpreting events, that is, classifying and retaining their experiences; (2) the events and contexts of events in their lives are sufficiently parallel or identical to produce, in combination with point 1, essentially similar precipitates of experience; and (3) the persons engage in conversations and other interactions *about* these experiences with others, through which the experiences are externalized, worked over symbolically, and further interpreted, elaborated, and standardized. I would suggest that, in men's and women's cultures in Sohar, we are observing a case where there is no significant difference under point 1: mothers are the trainers and educators of all small children, and though they no doubt project somewhat different standards and interpretations on little girls and little boys, there is no reason to believe that these differences are large enough to predispose the direction or slant of the child's experience by establishing truly different interpretative schemata. It is in this sense that one may speak, as I did above, of men and women speaking the "same" language, using the same words, and referring to the same material symbols. But gender role opportunities and the pattern of segregation introduce dichotomous conditions under points 2 and 3, so all the major differences between men's and women's cultures can plausibly be generated from them. Thus, I am prepared to argue that men's and women's cultures, in contrast to the other cultural streams I have discussed, primarily depend on contextual wellsprings for their reproduction, rather than dichotomized cultural heritages. They thus constitute "streams" and "traditions," not so much by virtue of being passed on from generation to generation as by virtue of being externalized and reinforced in the synchronic contexts of men's and women's distinct circles and networks.

One further set of questions arises from this material and discussion: are there not differences and inequalities between these two cultural streams with respect to the adequacy with which members of each culture interpret themselves to themselves and to each other? The query I raise concerns two distinct aspects. One may wonder what is the adequacy of the particular concepts and symbols that participants in a culture employ: their capacity as vehicles to externalize salient aspects of the particular experiences that such participants are having. Are significant features of women's and men's situations and experiences captured and communicated through concepts such as "her nature/way" or "being responsible for oneself"? On the other hand, one may observe the fora and encounters in which questions of standards and identities are raised, and ask what their potential is for generating insight, under the particular circumstances of the social situations where such conversations are pursued.

Striking qualitative contrasts obtain between communications of this kind in the men's cultural stream and those in the women's. Men are exposed to and served by, a number of specialized traditions and specialist roles. The Wali, *qadhis* and shaikhs, imams and other pious persons, each with an extensive corpus of training and accumulated literary instructions and insights—all are capable or obligated to give guidance and guidelines for behavior and perception. A fairly widespread basic male literacy makes a modest, but surprisingly varied selection of books and journals accessible locally through friends or acquaintances, or somewhat randomly and intermittently by purchase. The common experience of labor migration exposes men to numerous other sources of insight and self-awareness. The art of serious, responsible public speaking and instruction is valued and cultivated. And most basically and ubiquitously, ideals of conversation and social interaction encourage articulate, thoughtful discussions on the topics of morality, religion, worldly wisdom, and life's trials and problems.

Women are in a very different situation. To the extent that they are served by the specialists noted above, what is articulated for them is the *men's* concepts and reflections, not those that make up the women's culture. Women's concepts and reflections are limited to women's circles only, to the social informality of conviviality and visiting, to a pragmatic commentary—very drastically truncated by the avoidance of criticism, gossip, and scandal—on occasional personal relations and problems, and to the rare occurrence of special, privileged communication of accumulated wisdom and advice between especially trusted women. The conditions for externalization, abstraction, and generalization are thus very much poorer in the tradition of women's culture than in that of men.

The inequality in the social organization of the two traditions is also greatly exacerbated by the difference in their overt valuation, where all authority and legitimacy are given to the culture of the men. It comprises the universally superior variant, deriving from the holy law on which the structure of society is based and the true godhead from which the very existence of mankind and the world derive. To the extent that the ideas of women differ from this, the difference arises by definition from ignorance: "We are like donkeys." The effect is that men's culture is constantly resupplying women with concepts, symbols, and authoritative statements that, according to the argument developed here, will *mis*represent their world. Such a situation would represent a classic case of what has been termed *symbolic violence* (Bourdieu and Passeron 1977), that is, the power of imposing arbitrary meanings as legitimate while concealing the power relations that are the basis of their force. This power is, of course, not invalidated—though its violence is no doubt softened—by the prevalent and often exquisite tact and tolerance that obtains between persons of the two genders.

In such a situation, the collectivity of women who embrace women's culture will be in a very poor position to articulate their own experiences and develop their own conceptual and symbolic apparatus, with the consequence that such concepts and symbols as they have are probably fairly inadequate for the purpose of representing themselves successfully to themselves and to each other. On the other hand, there is also some basis for an argument that a local population of women in such a situation at least escapes that set of distortions that arise from incorporation in a tradition with a much larger scale of organization, over which a local population can exercise little or no control. In such terms, one might represent men as having abdicated before a central state and Muscat, a world religion and Mecca, and various other distant and disguised sources of influence on that very tradition that they embrace. Quite apart from these highly speculative perspectives on freedom and conceptual adequacy, however, the difference between the organization and conceptual sources of the two traditions is highly instructive.

Finally, I should add a note on contemporary change in the conditions and forms of men's and women's cultures in Sohar. According to women there, "The present times are women's times. Even when the man *has* the right, the woman is *given* the right." Besides such a change in the climate of interpretation, specific reforms and rules are introduced, and new facilities are being made available. Perhaps most important, in terms of roles and social participation as much as the new skills acquired, are public schools for girls as well as boys, and adult literacy classes attended by a large number of women. With modern viewpoints being so wholeheartedly embraced, and the support of traditional Omani virtues of tolerance of other and new patterns, the potential for rapid change is no doubt present. What is more, if the present analysis is correct in locating the main sources of the distinction between men's and women's cultures in the person's own experience and praxis, rather than in the transmission of an extensive and potentially tenacious heritage, one would expect quite drastic cultural changes to follow very quickly on the adoption of a truly new praxis.

21 The Organization of Diversity

One major step on the way toward giving an account of the dynamics of cultural pluralism in Sohar must be to construct a representation of the main structure of this society, so as to be able to show how it, as a context, impinges on the particular processes of cultural reproduction. I have met this requirement mainly by offering a sketch of the rules that govern interpersonal action in Sohar (chapter 11 and elsewhere): briefly, by describing the requirements of tact and grace and the constraints that spring from them on how embraced identities are handled, confronted, and enacted. Before pursuing the main analytical theme further, it may be useful to dwell somewhat on this mode of depicting "the social structure of Sohar." My purpose in investigating Sohar has not been to resolve anthropological (and anthropologist-produced) problems in the ethnography of the Middle East, but the materials discussed here may yet have some lessons of regional relevance.

"Social structure" in the dominant British tradition is (and may in a basic, common-sense reading reasonably be) taken to refer to the way in which the component parts of a society are connected or put together. Quite naturally, then, one looks for the major component groups of which society is composed: are they, for example, descent-based corporate groups, classes, or, in the Middle East as in many other plural situations, perhaps "peoples" or ethnic groups? To decide which of these kinds of grouping is most primary, and just how it underlies and affects much or most other relationships and phenomena, has been a vexing problem in the anthropological literature on Middle Eastern towns and complex societies. I have tried to show for Sohar how descent, important though it is in a number of ways, provides a thoroughly inadequate model of the social system of the town (and, to the extent that it is used in certain kinds of conversations by Soharis, both a tertiary and a "false" consciousness). Most social life is certainly *not* organized around groups based on descent; indeed, such groups have hardly any corporate characteristics and the branching, segmentary schematism of descent is *not* exploited for the conceptual ordering of collective relations. This same seems to be true also in other parts of Middle Eastern civilization. (For a recent statement from Morocco, see Geertz, Geertz, and Rosen 1979, especially C. Geertz, p. 235 and H. Geertz, p. 355.)

Nor does class provide a very compelling template for the basic divisions or components of Sohari society. For one thing, one cannot but be impressed with the impermanence of the possible bases for a class organization of the population of Sohar. Wealth is insecure in a context where primary production is secondary and marginal, and where speculative and farflung trade and labor migration provide the main sources of income in the community. Family relations are such that there is little continuity in wealth, occupation, and social identity between parents and children, and affinal relations are optional and very secondary at best, so wider family circles and networks do not provide the underpinnings for person or activity. Nor are the possible forms of expression of hierarchy much in evidence. Ideals of moderation and a broad unity of life style provide poor idioms of differentiation, and suitable public or collective fora for broadcasting equality and inequality are few—all circumstances that must limit the articulation of public information and consensus on class position, and consequently its salience for the organization of social relations. Indeed, the very segregation and separation of the social circles and worlds of spouses seem to strike at the roots of the development of class consciousness and identification. Finally, there is in Sohar no pervasive struggle for control of collective political institutions and decisions which might galvanize an "establishment" and the emergence of a unified hierarchy. This is so both because, in harmony with the literal meaning of Islam as "submission," administration is seen as the execution of preordained divine rules rather than the privileged exercise of control and because Sohar is merely a provincial town in a highly centralized sultanate, and so is a very insignificant arena for politics.

Such factors as these are present, with varying force, in other traditional Middle Eastern urban centers—though the infrastructure of differentiating productive activities is usually far stronger—and have generally been judged to make class unrevealing as a central concept for analysis. Brown (1976) discusses the issue perceptively in his study of the Moroccan city of Salé, and depicts a division of the citizens between elite and masses where these conform more closely to Weberian status group concepts, only slowly and incompletely emerging as classes over the last hundred years (ibid., pp. 213–18). I fail to identify such a trend in Sohar.

The third kind of grouping mentioned, which has served in the anthropological literature to conceptualize the basic parts of which traditional Middle Eastern societies are composed, is that of peoples or ethnic groups. I have tried to document through the preceding chapters how the organization of Sohar cannot be satisfactorily depicted in such terms. How representative of, or aberrant from, other traditional Middle Eastern towns is Sohar in this respect? Coon (1951) has given the most compelling formulation of Middle Eastern society as an ordered mosaic of ethnic groups in his brillant portrayal of unity and diversity in the region. Most recently, Geertz (in Geertz, Geertz, and Rosen 1979: 140 ff.) has restated an essentially similar view of Moroccan society in his focus on the *nisba* groups (the "kinds" of people that townsmen name, entailing a kinship and subcultural unity of the group) as the primary units of social organization.* Many of the same features that have emerged from the present materials on Sohar are also found in the community of Sefrou, from which his data derive. There is a diversity of crossing identifications and identities of persons (ibid., p. 241 n 34), a variable and often poor fit of *nisba* categories to various ordered social activities, etc. Such irregularities are handled by devices such as a concept of "*nisba* compactness" with respect to occupation (varying from high correlation among blacksmiths to lowest among grocers) (ibid., p. 145 and table 3), and the irregularities are such as to require the construction of a set of "socioethnic" sociological categories to replace *nisbas* for the homogenizing of the vast statistical materials at the team's command (ibid., appendix, pp. 338 ff.). The enterprise is not altogether successful: there does not seem to be any way to partition the Sefrou community into one coherent set of categories which can be represented as an encompassing structure and context for other identities and organized activities.

So also elsewhere in the Middle East: while ethnic disjunction and interdependence is often conspicuous, a segmentation along such lines can rarely be given primacy, and the picture would most places be more clearly and simply revealed by a cross-tabulation such as that summarized for Sohar in table 1. It is, of course, always possible to subdivide the population of an ethnic composite community into a series of ethnic groups that orders and embraces all the personnel. The crucial questions to determine the salience of such a division as a social structure must be: (a) how well do the categories serve to reveal *pattern* in various major fields of activity? and (b) how *necessary* are the categories for each other, as parts of a joint whole, that is, how compelling

---

*Geertz's wider purpose is a "cultural" analysis, in which he employs metaphors derived from the bazaar and from information search under conditions of imperfect communication to characterize the society as a whole. It is in his specific handling of social organization that I discern this focus on *nisba* groups as the basic component groups or parts of society.

is the structure that they compose? In Sohar, as in so many communities in the Middle East, it is not merely that ethnic identity does
not predicate other statuses and activities with any appreciable rigor;
there does not even seem to be any obvious interdependence or pattern
in the constellation of coexisting ethnic groups. Throughout the sub-
regions of the Middle East, one will find that whereas some ethnic
groups may be ubiquituous in an area, others are variably present or
absent without apparent consequences for the other groups or for the
social system as a whole. In Sohar it would not seem to make any
difference to the way that town functions whether Zidgalis, or even
Baluchis or Ajams, were present or absent; indeed, Khoja Ismailis have
disappeared since 1950 and Jews since 1900 without apparently changing the structure of the town in any notable way. To represent any
particular mosaic as *the* basic structure of the society must therefore
clearly be vacuous: Sohar, and other Middle Eastern communities,
must be depicted as built on a structure that allows peoples, religious
communities, occupations, and other gross groups and categories to
come and go, as in fact they do, without dismantling the basic structure
of society.

Where then can I look for the basic constraints, the persisting
structure, if there is such, that governs the coexistence of cultural
traditions and the intermingling of persons—or are there no such
constraints? Is any and every mixture organizationally viable as a
community? I would maintain, as I have for a long time (for example,
Barth 1959, 1964), that it is the traditional structural-functional position that social structure should refer to an axiomatic system of enduring social *groups* which serves us so poorly in analyzing and understanding the complex societies of the Middle East. It is necessary to go
down to the level of individual actors as the analytical "parts" of these
societies, and to search for social "structure" in some enduring factors
in their patterns of relationships.

This is a view that has recently been espoused by anthropologists
working in Moroccan society. Brown (1976: 213) finds the social
structure of Salé in "networks, or coalitions formed around relatively
powerful individuals" and Rosen (1979:19, in Geertz, Geertz, and
Rosen) argues for Sefrou that one must begin "not with resultant
groupings, but with some of the concepts through which individuals
establish their own and each others' social attachment." I concur, but
would press the analysis further. It is not the shape of social networks
but the factors that *generate* such shapes by making persons fashion
such networks which should be identified as the enduring "structure"
in such societies. Likewise, it is not sufficient to report how individuals
conceptualize social attachments; we should uncover the forces that
propel or constrain them to *embrace* identities, to *construct* whatever

social persons they become. Only then can we claim to have identified the enduring foundations of social form.

To accomodate the historical and contemporary fact of ever-new peoples arriving and intermingling and disappearing, new occupations and life ways emerging and others being forgotten, new groups forming and others dissolving, the structure we seek must be found not on the substantive level of how groups are recruited or indeed networks and relations are established but on a metalevel composed of guidelines on how to mingle, how to choose among changing options, how to judge the merits of alternative memberships and commitments. Therefore, the image of a mosaic is misleading: if one were to stay with it, one would have to see the search as not of looking for how the pieces are shaped so as to fit together in a particular pattern—which they don't—but of identifying the connecting putty in which they are set, the stuff capable of connecting them in some kind of edifice despite their changing and partly discongruent shapes. This is the historical problem with which socializing humanity in the Middle East has been faced for millennia: the raucous host of "others," with strange ideas and alien customs, visiting, working, conquering, settling, enticing with partnerships to fabulous cargoes, or arriving themselves as cargoes of stripped humanity, yet with invitation to fashion social relationships. The difficulties of sustaining some degree of order and stability in social life against such odds have been immense, and have called for drastic remedies. At one extreme are the countermeasures of conversion and assimilation, or isolation and "fanaticism." Thus, Wahabi fundamentalists have swept large parts of Arabia clean of all religious and most cultural variation, as they very nearly did for Sohar in the wars of 1800–13 (see Lorimer 1908–15). Similarily, the Ibadhi Imams of interior Oman maintained a complete ban on Hindus and Christians (see Thesiger 1959), and most other strangers, and so sustained an Ibadhi world where only town and bedouin, man and woman, and freeman and (local, ancient) slave were allowed as cultural variants. At the other extreme, perhaps, are social systems like that of Sohar: designed to articulate with a changing world and to accommodate an unspecified variety of persons and allow them to coreside and interact. In stark contrast to the social system that organized the cultural diversity of traditional India (see especially Marriott 1969), this is *not* done by welding them into an organic system of occupational castes, fixing them hierarchically by pervasive idioms of pollution and interactional constraints, and integrating them conceptually by a perpetual struggle of Sanscritic reinterpretation. There has been, I think, an implicit and unanalyzed tendency to cast Middle Eastern pluralism as some kind of variant of such an Indian ideal type. This would misrepresent the present case badly. Instead, Sohari society is based on a set of rules and institutions which enables particpants simply to allow each other to persist, and to enter into optative transactions and relations. The key parts of this structure, if so tangible an imagery may still be used, are the code of politeness, the ideal of self-regard through individual autonomy, the abdication of political control to a minimally interfering and innovating centralized state, and the depersonalization of market transactions—their disjunction both from other aspects of social relations and from the commitments of the person's own core identity.

Such a brief statement must necessarily generalize and abstract the social realities that I wish to refer to rather too much. For a fuller explication, I refer back to the analysis I have attempted in the preceding chapters, especially chapters 11–15. I would urge strongly for a reconsideration of other local variants of Middle Eastern complex societies in similar terms.

Having established this model of the enduring structure of the society in Sohar as a context for the mingling and coexistence of cultures, I shall now try to extract some valid generalizations about the dynamics of pluralism within it.

I have observed the fact of ordering of most cultural variation in a limited number of streams and traditions, each identified with a major recognized social identity within Sohar. What might I be able to specify of axiomatic conditions for the persistence of such traditions—which presumably must have been satisfied in the past, since the traditions have survived till the present—and what can I observe with regard to contemporary processes reproducing these traditions? Clearly the persistence of a cultural stream of this kind presupposes, on the one hand, the recruitment and replacement of personnel who will embrace the identity in the sense of practicing it and, on the other hand, that this personnel observes an orthodoxy in the cultural content which they embrace and practice so that "the culture" survives—not unaltered, but with sufficient replication to constitute a meaningful continuity. I have emphasized the need to acknowledge dynamism and change in every cultural tradition (and for us as observers to make a special effort in the case of minority cultures not to become concerned with the authentic antiquity of cultural traits; see p. 210). In practice, the critical measure is the extent to which disappearing traits are replenished, and not continually reduced. Unless cultural contrasts are replenished, all change will entail homogenization, a movement toward fewer and fewer differences between coexisting traditions, and so a steady reduction in their cultural salience. This change, of course, need not reduce the *organizational* salience of the contrasting identities: they may become transformed into memberships in drastically opposed but culturally similar interest groups, parties, or sects. The feature of *cultural* pluralism, in other words, presumes processes both of recruitment/embracement and of transmission/replenishment.

I shall note the operative processes whereby such contrastive replenishment may take place. It is more difficult to operationalize, and thus defend, the imagery of "traits" and "distinctive traits" that I fall back on to express how the stuff of these cultural traditions, and the extent of their differences, might be somehow describable and measurable. I have discussed some of these difficulties in chapter 16 and in my analysis of change in bedouin culture in chapter 19. Whereas a qualitative description along these lines seems feasible, I do not envisage any quantification, resurrecting trait lists or developing other quantitative procedures. For one thing, the multiplicity of levels and structures that is embraced in the description clearly invalidates such counting. Nor am I able to identify key structures of contrast: from the various glimpses of actual courses of change there do not seem to be distinctive features of higher order, which are somehow (logically) necessary to maintain contrast between streams; of the features I identify, I have no way of saying that one may go, whereas another must remain in the event of change.

I have noted, but can only speculate on, the peculiar character of the bases, or rather lack of bases, for these coexisting cultural traditions in their material circumstances (p. 163ff.) Whereas most anthropological analyses somehow link cultural traditions to particular ecologic and economic circumstances, the differences between cultural traditions in Sohar cannot be so linked, since there is occupational diversity and mobility within the personnel that perpetuate most traditions— indeed, every person is also "the carrier" of several cultures, by virtue of his or her repertoire of identities. It would be very interesting if one were able to characterize the "kinds" of differences that obtain between the cultures that coexist under these conditions, and the (presumably other and greater) kinds of differences that obtain in plural situations where the ecologic and economic bases of coexisting traditions are distinct. But I have not been able to identify any particular configuration of differences in the Sohar material (see pp. 91 ff.)

Returning to the preconditions of persistence for cultural traditions, the processes of recruitment and transmission are generally linked with family reproduction, and household socialization of children. This actualizes the issue of endogamy with respect to each of the relevant identity categories. I have described a considerable range of practice in this respect, from very high among bedouin and within the religious divisions to considerably less in the case of ethnic groups. Quite plausibly, Soharis link this lower frequency of endogamy with trends toward assimilation and loss of distinctive culture traits between ethnic groups. It might be tempting to see the processes behind recruitment and transmission as uniquely tied to the family mode of reproduction and argue that endogamy is the significant structural prerequisite, and its contemporary relaxation the cause of current trends toward the reduction of pluralism. But I have no sound evidence for postulating changes in the rates of endogamy to explain the apparent contemporary trend toward greater homogeneity. What is more interesting, the presence of men's and women's cultures alerts us to the existence of other modes of enrollment in an identity and the practice of a cultural stream than that of being born into a household that is homogeneous with respect to identity and culture. Are there special qualities or processes of recruitment to gender that facilitate the adoption and practice of *one* of the gender cultures in a context where *both* are ubiquitously practiced, even within the household? Or is it similarly possible for children of an ethnically mixed marriage to grow up as participants in different ethnic culture streams? Quite clearly, categorical endogamy is neither the only nor the necessary prerequisite, and childhood/household socialization is not the only process, whereby cultural embracement is determined. But I would need better and other data on *xanith* (transsexuals), and on mixed households of various kinds, to be able to identify significant variables.

The striking feature of Sohari cultural pluralism, however, is how the contents of traditions are in a position to affect each other, not only by their confrontation and enactment in cross-cultural encounters and relationship—when members of two distinct traditions meet—but also by the accommodation that is necessary *within* the person, by virtue of their ubiquitous association as multiple identities of single persons. For example, "practicing Arab culture" must entail activities that are possible to pursue whether you are Sunni or Shiah, man or woman or *xanith*, townsman or bedouin (while yet remaining impossible if you are Ajam or Baluch, but otherwise occupant of the same additional identities). The concept of "role congruence" seems too weak to handle this as a problem in the dynamics of cultural traditions. I have sought to show how such identities coalesce in whole persons, who manage themselves and their affairs in terms of an integrated concept of self—quite consciously and explicitly in the case of many men—and by relatively unitary standards and priorities across these identities. This is where the overall structure of Sohari society impinges directly on the person, and thereby sets parameters within which all the component traditions must be reproduced. It is also here that I am able to provide the most convincing analysis of some of the conditions of persistence, and sources and processes of change.

The analysis requires the acknowledgment that Sohar cannot be adequately depicted by a simple rule-following model of social organization: with Ali, we must accept as our premise for understanding that "each person must be responsible for himself " (p. 182). Thus, I have argued, even (as on p. 122) where an explicit, ideologically sanctioned rule agrees with a prevalent practice, that the factors that determine the practice may be others than the explicit rule. In this sense, life is ever problematic to Soharis, and their behavior is ever being shaped by them, in terms of priorities and embraced values, not merely as a perpetuation of precedence, custom, or the practice of others. What I am stressing is that we cannot assume that a Sohari will act in a certain way simply because he was born a Baluch, or an Arab, and that is what a person with that identity is expected to do, or because he was inculcated a set of customs. Not only is transmission precarious, but youths should be free to live a life suited for *their* times. Also, action may require a searching or even agonizing personal evaluation whether a certain identity is imperative, one that must be intensely embraced, or whether a person has the option to leave the entailments of that identity latent, or even repudiate them. Likewise, the person will have difficulties in adopting a simple orthodoxy regarding the received cultural particulars of an embraced tradition: are these particular views or practices enlightened, will their practice reflect favorably on his integrity, are they as fashionable, elegant, admirable today as they were/were not some years ago, etc.? In other words, identities and cultural traditions, to be reproduced, must be constantly reaffirmed and embraced, and to be so they must appear congenial and honorable in terms of each relevant actor's self-image.

It is here that I can identify certain new ideas and criteria of excellence with profound implications for the reproduction of plural cultural traditions. One is the ideal of Omani unity, of equality and collective welfare within a centralized state. The other is the vision of progress, indeed of swift change toward enlightment, modernization, and welfare. The first would be threatened or negated by the practice of communal divisions and dissensions, and by the old-fashioned and discredited inequities of slavery and religious intolerance. In the case of the second, a person may fear that he is resisting it by almost any and every form of traditionalism or orthodoxy, any unwillingness to embrace change and innovation. In the heady atmosphere of sudden and apparently swiftly growing private and public wealth and rapid modernization, the value of old-fashioned virtues of any kind may appear questionable: the task is to shape new and better lives.

The effects of the embracement of such values may best be highlighted by reconstructing what may reasonably be assumed to have been their traditional counterparts—less compelling, perhaps, yet deeply constitutive of guidelines for honest and honorable behavior. The person would have found his basic anchoring in his kin, people, and congregation—in embraced values that could most clearly be affirmed through *group rivalry* for excellence, the elaboration of ethnic and communal emblems, the cultivation of distinctness in terms of the identities occupied by the person. Remember also the "world system" of which the cosmopolitan aspects of such a style of presentation were parts within living memory: the highly pluralistic and communal world of British India, colonial Africa, imperial Iran, and Ottoman Turkey. As to the second of the new ideals mentioned above, how could one, in this world, better show one's strength, courage, and personal integrity than by practicing one's own traditions with orthodoxy and elegance, being true to one's own identities in a motley crowd of different others?

For persons deeply involved in shaping themselves and their own behavior, in excelling in a perpetual tournament of elegance and good manners, the parameters for practicing and reaffirming participation in locally contrastive cultural traditions will thus have been very radically altered by the change in these two value parameters. The replacement of the one set by the other also generates the extraordinary, and intuitively so implausible, conjunction that one experiences in Sohar and elsewhere in Oman: of extremely traditional, confident, and elegant life forms and a headlong and sometimes even vulgar bustle of modernization; of great local diversity yet striking value consensus on a total disregard for exquisite and highly appealing local cultural manifestations. There is thus no particular evidence, or explanatory need, for the usual appeal to economic change and a supposed invasion of world markets and commerce as a primary factor in producing such a transformation. Most aspects of these institutions were long present in Sohar and the structure of society and person was such as to insulate other aspects of life rather well from the effects of economic perturbation (see chapter 14).*

In terms of the passing reference made to the concept "symbolic violence" (p. 242), I might note how a similar relationship obtains between local Sohari forms of consciousness and international influence. The two basic value changes that are transforming the whole pattern of cultural pluralism in Sohar are exogenously caused—they do not arise from local cognitive developments or experiences. This is not to say that there are no traditional values that are congenial to the new value premises. Soharis' respect for others, their reluctance to exercise dominance, their respect for universal law, and their emphasis on graceful social relations provide excellent bases for participation in

---

*This is no prediction, however, regarding the future consequences of an increasing economic growth into the development of "consumerism," and the changes such opportunities may have on life style, interaction patterns, and cultural ideas.

a modern welfare state. But the new interpretation of citizenship and statehood reflects directly the rhetoric of Western ideology and United Nations institutional premises; the key event in its adoption was no doubt the present Sultan's takeover in 1970, strongly supported by big power and oil development interests. Sohari concepts of progress, individual betterment, and the good life have likewise been recast under the massive influence of modern, external ideology and mass communication, and one may question the extent to which they capture adequately the qualities of local values, experiences, and strivings. Yet by the force of their articulation, and the global force of the interests and groups that promote them, they will inevitably serve increasingly to guide the thoughts and efforts of Soharis, and I would expect them to be questioned by Soharis only if the discrepancy between the vision that they provide and the life that eventuates becomes quite glaring.

Finally, the question may be asked how a system of such intricacy and historical tenacity as Sohari pluralism can change and threaten to dissolve so easily and swiftly. The answer I would give derives from the analysis of Sohari society that I have developed. I must emphasize again that Sohari social structure is *not* one of culturally distinct groups articulating in a conceptual or functional whole: it consists of a set of values and ideas on how to handle interpersonal relations and how to strive to construct your own person and behavior. There is no reason to think that these ideas are not tenacious and will not persist: it is their particular consequence in an intricate pattern of cultural pluralism that is undergoing change. A cultural pluralism based on *tolerance*—such as has eventuated in Sohar—does not insist on the perpetuation of differences, it merely allows them; and a praxis of *tact* accommodates such differences as exist by underplaying them and ignoring them in interaction, not by enshrining them in interpersonal ritual. Thus, how the cultural traditions of Sohar will reproduce themselves, change, disappear, or be replenished will depend on the judgment of Sohari actors as to how their practice can permit or facilitate a person's performance in the perpetual tournament of good manners. I cannot suppress the hope that the standards which Soharis will use in the future to judge the goodness of their manners will be such as to allow them to cultivate their diversity and be true to identities with deep roots in their community.

References

Anderson, J. W. 1982. Social structure and the veil. *Anthropos* 77: 397–420.

Barth, F. 1959. *Political leadership among Swat Pathans*. London School of Economics, Monographs on Social Anthropology no. 19. London: Athlone Press.

————— . 1960. The system of social stratification in Swat, North Pakistan. In *Aspects of caste in South India, Ceylon, and North-west Pakistan*, ed. E. R. Leach, pp. 113–46. Cambridge: Cambridge Univ. Press. (Reprinted in Barth 1981.)

————— . 1964. *Models of social organization*. Royal Anthropological Institute, Occasional Papers no. 23. London: Royal Anthropological Institute (reprinted in Barth 1981.)

————— . 1978a. Factors of production, economic circulation, and inequality in Inner Arabia. In *Research in economic anthropology*, ed. G. Dalton, Vol. 1, pp. 53–72. Greenwich, Conn.: JAI Press

————— . 1981. *Process and form in social life*. London: Routledge & Kegan Paul.

————— . ed. 1969. *Ethnic groups and boundaries*. Oslo: Universitetsforlaget, and Boston: Little, Brown.

————— . 1978b. *Scale and social organization*. Oslo: Universitetsforlaget, and New York: Columbia Univ. Press.

Berger, P. L., and Kellner, H. 1964. Marriage and the construction of reality. *Diogenes* 46:1–24.

Bott, E. 1951. *Family and social network*. London: Tavistock.

Bourdieu, P. and Passeron, J.-C. 1977. *Reproduction in education, society, and culture*, trans. R. Nice. London: Sage Publications.

Brown, K. 1976. *People of Salé: Tradition and change in a Moroccan city, 1830–1930*. Manchester: Manchester Univ. Press.

Buckingham, J. S. 1830. *Travels in Assyria . . .* London: Henry Colburn.

Coon, C. S. 1951. *Caravan: The story of the Middle East*. New York: Henry Holt & Co.

Cordes, R. and Scholtz, F. 1980. *Bedouins, wealth, and change*. Tokyo: United Nations Univ.

Fieness, R. 1977. *Where soldiers fear to tread*. London: Hodder & Stoughton.

Firth, R. 1951. *Elements of social organization*. London: Watts.

Geertz, C. 1973. *The interpretation of cultures*. New York: Basic Books.

Geertz, C.; Geertz, H.; and Rosen, L. 1979. *Meaning and order in Moroccan society*. Cambridge: Cambridge Univ. Press.

Grünebaum, G. E. von. 1964. Islam: Experience of the holy concept of Islam. *Diogenes* 48:81–104.

Hannerz, U. 1980. *Exploring the city.* New York: Columbia Univ. Press.

Hopwood, D. ed. 1972. *The Arabian peninsula: Society and politics.* London: Allen & Unwin.

Keesing, R. M. 1974. Theories of culture. In *Annual review of anthropology,* ed. B. J. Siegel, Vol 3, pp. 73–98. Palo Alto Calif.: Annual Reviews.

Kelly, J. B. 1968. *Britain and the Persian Gulf, 1795–1880.* Oxford: Clarendon Press.

————. 1972. A prevalence of furies: Tribes, politics, and religion in Oman and Trucial Oman. In *The Arabian peninsula,* ed. D. Hopwood, pp. 107–41. London: Allen & Unwin.

Kelly, R. C. 1977. *Etoro social structure.* Ann Arbor, Mich.: Univ. of Michigan Press.

Landen, R. G. 1967. *Oman since 1856.* Princeton, N. J.: Princeton Univ. Press.

Lapidus, I. 1973. The evolution of Muslim urban society. *Comparative Studies in Society and History* 15:21–50.

Lorimer, J. G. 1908–15. *Gazetteer of the Persian Gulf, Oman, and Central Arabia.* 3 vols. Calcutta, India: Superintendent of Government Printing.

Marriott, M. 1959. Changing channels of cultural transmission in an indigenous civilization. In *Intermediate societies, social mobility, and communication.* ed. V. F. Ray, pp. 66–74. Seattle: American Ethnological Society.

————. 1969. Little communities in an indigenous civilization. In *Village India,* ed. Marriott, pp. 171–222. Chicago: Univ. of Chicago Press.

Miles, S. B. 1919. *The countries and tribes of the Persian Gulf.* London: Harrison & Sons.

Mintz, S. W. and Price, R. 1976. *An anthropological approach to the Afro-American past: A Caribbean perspective.* Philadelphia: Institute for the Study of Human Issues.

Nadel, S. F. 1957. *The theory of social structure.* London: Cohen & West.

Oman. 1972. Muscat: Department of Information.

Philips, W. 1971. *Unknown Oman.* Beirut: Librairie du Leban.

Pitt-Rivers, J. A. 1965. *Honour and social status.* London: Weidenfeld & Nicholson.

Radcliffe-Brown, A. R. 1952. *Structure and function in primitive society.* London: Cohen & West.

Redfield, R. 1956. *Peasant society and culture.* Chicago: Univ. of Chicago Press.

————. 1962. *Human nature and the study of society.* Chicago: Univ. of Chicago Press.

Singer, M. 1968. Culture *In International encyclopedia of the social sciences,* ed. David L. Sills, Vol. 3, pp. 527–42. New York: Free Press.

Smiley, D. 1975. *Arabian Assignment.* London: Leo Cooper.

Snow, C. P. 1969. *Two cultures—and a second look.* Cambridge: Cambridge Univ. Press.

Statistical year book, Sultanate of Oman. 1975. Muscat: National Statistical Department.

Thesiger, W. P. 1959. *Arabian sands.* London: Longmans Green & Co.

Thomas, B. 1929. Among some unknown tribes of South Arabia.   *Journal of the Royal Anthropoligical Institute* 59:97–112.

————— . 1931. A journey into the Rub al Khali. *Geographical Journal* 77:360–81, 78:209–42.

————— . 1932. Anthropological observations in South Arabia. *Journal of the Royal Anthropological Institute* 62:83–103.

Wikan, U. 1977. Man becomes woman: Transsexualism in Oman as a key to gender roles. *Man* (new series) 2, no. 2, pp. 304–19.

————— . 1978. The Omani *xanith*. *Man* (new series), correspondence, 13, nos. 3 and 4, pp. 473–5, 667–71.

————— . 1982. *Behind the veil in Arabia: Women in Oman*. Baltimore: Johns Hopkins Univ. Press.

Williamson, A. *Sohar and Omani seafaring in the Indian Ocean*. Muscat: Petroleum Development (Oman) Ltd.

Index

THE JOHNS HOPKINS UNIVERSITY PRESS

Sohar

This book was composed in Baskerville text type by
Brushwood Graphics from a design by Lisa S. Mirski.
It was printed on S. D. Warren's 50-lb. Sebago Egg-
shell Cream Offset paper and bound in Holliston
Roxite A by The Maple Press Company.